PR658. R55 MUL

WITHDRAWN
FROM STOCK
QMUL LIBRARY

Romance on the Early Modern Stage

Romance on the Early Modern Stage

English Expansion Before and After Shakespeare

Cyrus Mulready
State University of New York at New Paltz, USA

palgrave
macmillan

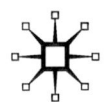

© Cyrus Mulready 2013

All rights reserved. No reproduction, copy or transmission of this publication may be made without written permission.

No portion of this publication may be reproduced, copied or transmitted save with written permission or in accordance with the provisions of the Copyright, Designs and Patents Act 1988, or under the terms of any licence permitting limited copying issued by the Copyright Licensing Agency, Saffron House, 6–10 Kirby Street, London EC1N 8TS.

Any person who does any unauthorized act in relation to this publication may be liable to criminal prosecution and civil claims for damages.

The author has asserted his right to be identified as the author of this work in accordance with the Copyright, Designs and Patents Act 1988.

First published 2013 by
PALGRAVE MACMILLAN

Palgrave Macmillan in the UK is an imprint of Macmillan Publishers Limited, registered in England, company number 785998, of Houndmills, Basingstoke, Hampshire RG21 6XS.

Palgrave Macmillan in the US is a division of St Martin's Press LLC, 175 Fifth Avenue, New York, NY 10010.

Palgrave Macmillan is the global academic imprint of the above companies and has companies and representatives throughout the world.

Palgrave® and Macmillan® are registered trademarks in the United States, the United Kingdom, Europe and other countries.

ISBN 978–1–137–32270–8

This book is printed on paper suitable for recycling and made from fully managed and sustained forest sources. Logging, pulping and manufacturing processes are expected to conform to the environmental regulations of the country of origin.

A catalogue record for this book is available from the British Library.

A catalog record for this book is available from the Library of Congress.

Typeset by MPS Limited, Chennai, India.

For Colleen

Contents

List of Illustrations	viii
Acknowledgements	ix
Introduction: Romance and the Globe	1
1 Romancing Shakespeare	33
2 "Asia of the one side, and Afric of the other": Sidney's Unities and the Staging of Romance	52
3 Imagined Empires: The Cultural Geography of Stage Romance	78
4 Chronicle History, Cosmopolitan Romance: *Henry V* and the Generic Boundaries of the Second Tetralogy	108
5 Containing Romance and Plotting Empire in *The Tempest* and *Pericles*	143
6 Milton's Imperial *Maske*: Staging Romance on the Border of Wales	172
Coda: Global Romance after Shakespeare	193
Appendix: Titles and Dates of Stage Romances	200
Notes	204
Bibliography	224
Index	243

List of Illustrations

0.1 Detail from Gerard Mercator's 1569 Wall Map, Sig. Kartenslg. AA 3–5; reproduced by permission of the University of Basel 4

0.2 Frontispiece to *Historia Mundi: or Mercator's Atlas* (1635); by permission of the Folger Shakespeare Library 8

2.1 Woodcut from *The Hystory of the two Valyaunte Brethren Valentyne and Orson*, London (nd), Sig. R4v (from the collection of the Beinecke Library, Yale University) 53

5.1 Map showing "A figure of Geography of the former age," Abraham Ortelius, *Theatrum Orbis Terrarum* (1590); reproduced by permission of the Huntington Library, San Marino, California 147

Acknowledgements

This book has been enabled by the encouragement and hard work of many teachers, friends, and colleagues over the years; it is a tremendous pleasure to thank them for their contributions. The project began with a singular observation about Philip Sidney and magical horses by the extraordinary Margreta de Grazia, who has aided me throughout with her characteristic poise, care, and generosity. The book has also been enriched by the expansive knowledge and support of Barbara Fuchs, a constant advocate and friend. Valerie Wayne took an early interest in the project and has continued to be a wonderful ally in its completion. I feel fortunate to have been a part of the thriving community of medieval and Renaissance scholars at the University of Pennsylvania, and their influence has become part of this study in large and small ways, especially Zack Lesser, Ania Loomba, Sean Keilen, Peter Stallybrass, and David Wallace. I also owe special thanks to Melissa Sanchez for her careful reading of an early draft of the manuscript. My classmates from Penn continue to be a source of great professional and personal support, especially Jane Degenhardt, Scott Krawczyk, Jared Richman, Kurt Schreyer, and Kathy Lou Schultz.

The English department at SUNY New Paltz has been an exceptionally nurturing environment for me and my work, thanks in large part to colleagues like Tom Olsen, Tom Festa, Dan Kempton, Mary Holland, and Stella Deen, all of whom read drafts of chapters and gave generously of their time and friendship. Nancy Johnson and Lou Roper read the full manuscript and provided timely advice and championing. Dean Jim Schiffer offered key support to the project, including the use of professional development funds for the images included in the book. The Provost's Office granted a pre-tenure leave award that allowed me to finish the manuscript, as well as a research award for work at the British Library. I also wish to thank the staff at the Sojourner Truth Library, who filled countless requests for books and materials. Finally, I am very grateful to my stellar research assistant, Nicole Hitner, who (among other feats) helped secure permission for the book's images, and to James Sherwood, who prepared the index.

Some good luck brought me to the team at Palgrave Macmillan, and I am very thankful for the keen eye and support of Felicity Plester, who first commissioned the manuscript. Ben Doyle has been a model editor, and I owe great thanks to Sophie Ainscough and Christine Ranft for patiently working through the many details of publication with me. I also wish to thank the publisher's anonymous reader, whose insightful recommendations helped give final shape to the book.

I owe much more than thanks to my amazing family: my daughter, Maureen, and my son, Desmond, particularly, who make this work worth doing. Without my wife and best friend, Colleen, there would be no book. Her support has been instrumental from the start, as she has freely given to this project more than can be enumerated. My feelings of gratitude to her are, likewise, boundless.

Earlier versions of sections of this book have appeared in Wiley-Blackwell's *Literature Compass* (6.1 (2009): 113–27) and in the essay collection *Staging Early Modern Romance: Prose Fiction, Dramatic Romance, and Shakespeare,* ed. Mary Ellen Lamb and Valerie Wayne (London: Routledge, 2009). I thank these publishers for their permission to reprint the materials here.

Introduction: Romance and the Globe

When Martin Frobisher and his crew set off in search of a northwest passage to China in 1576, they were outfitted with a host of charts, maps, globes, sea manuals, and other books and navigational equipment. These purchases included "a greate globe of metal in blanke in a case," "a great mappe universall of Mercator in prente," a "bible Englishe great volume," and, perhaps the most surprising item in the inventory, "Sir John Mandevylle (Englishe)" (Collinson ix–x).[1] The notoriously fantastical *Mandeville's Travels* (which Frobisher most likely read in any of its five English editions up to 1576) thus sat alongside material such as Gerard Mercator's landmark 1569 world map, a set of texts that seem to point in very different epistemological and even chronological directions.[2] Sir Walter Ralegh, too, had read his Mandeville; his description in *The Discovery of Guiana* of the "Ewaipanoma," "a nation of people whose heads appear not above their shoulders" receives verification from the book.[3] "Such a nation was written of by Mandeville, whose reports were holden for fables many years; and yet since the East Indies were discovered, we find his relations true of such things as heretofore were held incredible" (93). Territorial expansion had transformed old "fables" into new truths, a pattern of discovery that Ralegh himself hoped to replicate in his search for *El Dorado*, the city of gold.[4]

Perhaps even less known than these connections between English explorers and the fabulous tales of medieval romance is the existence of an early English commercial play based on the wonders found in *Mandeville's Travels*. From 1592 to 1593, Lord Strange's men put on eight performances of a play we know only as "Sir John Mandeville." It seems this was not a new play, based on the notations that preserve records of its performance in Henslowe's diary, and could have been a part of the company's repertory since as early as 1580. Since the play is lost, we can only speculate about its content—judging from the title pages of sixteenth-century editions of *The Travels of Sir John Mandeville* the presence of "meruailes of Inde" and representations of "other Lands and Countries" were likely among the play's selling points. Descriptions of fantastical creatures as those witnessed in Ralegh—people with hound heads, dragons, men who eat snakes and therefore speak with serpents' tongues—might also have found their way into the stage's spectacles.[5]

However much direct representations of wonders and foreign places drove the continuing interest in Mandeville's stories through the sixteenth century, another, perhaps more subtle feature of the text must have appealed to Frobisher, Ralegh, and Henslowe's audiences alike. In the closing of his narrative, quoted here from Thomas East's edition of 1581/82, Mandeville offers this alluring promise: "There are many other Countryes where I haue not yet beene nor seene, and therefore I cannot speake properly of them. Also in countries where I haue been are many meruailes that I speake not of . . . for I will say no more of meruailes that are there, so that other men that goo thether may find enough for to say, that I haue not told" (Sig. W2r). Here, the writer of *Mandeville's Travels* exploits a defining trope of the romance story. Building on the description of places real (Jerusalem, Rome, India) and imagined (Prester John's Kingdom), he ends with purposely withheld empirical truth, a marvelous "thither" that exists partly in the imagination yet also within the enticing reach of experience. Ralegh used the same rhetorical maneuver in telling the story of the Ewaipanoma, a group he never actually observed but whose existence he could verify based on the stories that Mandeville and others had reported. In that moment, Ralegh, the reader of romance, has turned romance writer, deploying the tropes of the form for an audience with an appetite for such stories.

These narrative and archival traces provide a glimpse of the historical intersections of drama, romance, and the materials of overseas expansion that are the topic of this book. I argue that romance, as it developed from its roots in medieval narrative into a stage genre, offered material and formal resources through which the English envisioned overseas commercial and imperial expansion. Such a reading only becomes possible, however, once dramatic romance is unmoored from its exclusive association with Shakespeare. Rather than a group of plays localized within a psychological narrative of the poet's life, I argue that the stage romance, as I will call it, was a thriving genre from the earliest days of the commercial theater in London. For audiences, the expansiveness and exoticism of romance in dramatic form bridged the world of fantasy and imagination with the more concrete realities of overseas trade and empire. Stage romances responded to the public's interest in these historical events, but also gave form to the audience's expanding geographic and cultural imaginings. This introduction will show the pressing need for an examination of stage romance in its global context, firstly by demonstrating what such a formal approach has to offer the continuing examination of England's place within a burgeoning global empire. Secondly, I move to the romance itself to show how its emergence as a stage genre coincided with and even informed the discourses of early English empire and its geographic imaginings. It is, finally, this enlarged understanding of romance that I will use to challenge the view of romance that has been limited to Shakespeare's "late plays" and to expand upon our knowledge of the stage's earliest representations of foreign worlds.

The imaginative geography of romance

It was not only in the realms of narrative and drama that romance provided the kind of imaginative provocations found in Mandeville. In cartography as well as in the theater the allurement of romance served as a powerful enticement to territorial and colonial involvement. This point is illustrated in another of the items found within Frobisher's inventory, Mercator's historic 1569 wall map.

Situated on the inventory alongside what could be one of the most popular works of medieval and early modern romance is the first printed map developed using the "Mercator projection," which Jerry Brotton asserts "was to revolutionize not only sixteenth-century geography, but ultimately the future development of modern western cartography" (*Trading Territories*, 166). The work of Brotton and others has made valuable contributions to our understanding of the influence of the "new geography" on various political and cultural spheres, particularly the early modern theater.[6] On the other hand, Mandeville figures prominently in accounts that highlight the Americas and other newly discovered territories as part of a "discourse of wonder," to use Stephen Greenblatt's influential formulation.[7] Thus, while one series of investigations orient themselves toward the scientific advances that have come to define the early modern, another sees in the corpus of travel narrative the vestiges of earlier traditions of travel writing and geographic imaginings. This distinction, represented in the difference between Mercator and Mandeville, looks strikingly less assured on closer inspection—even within the frame of Mercator's own map.

On the 1569 world map, Mercator includes an inset illustrating the Arctic regions, along with a narrative cartouche, in the lower left-hand

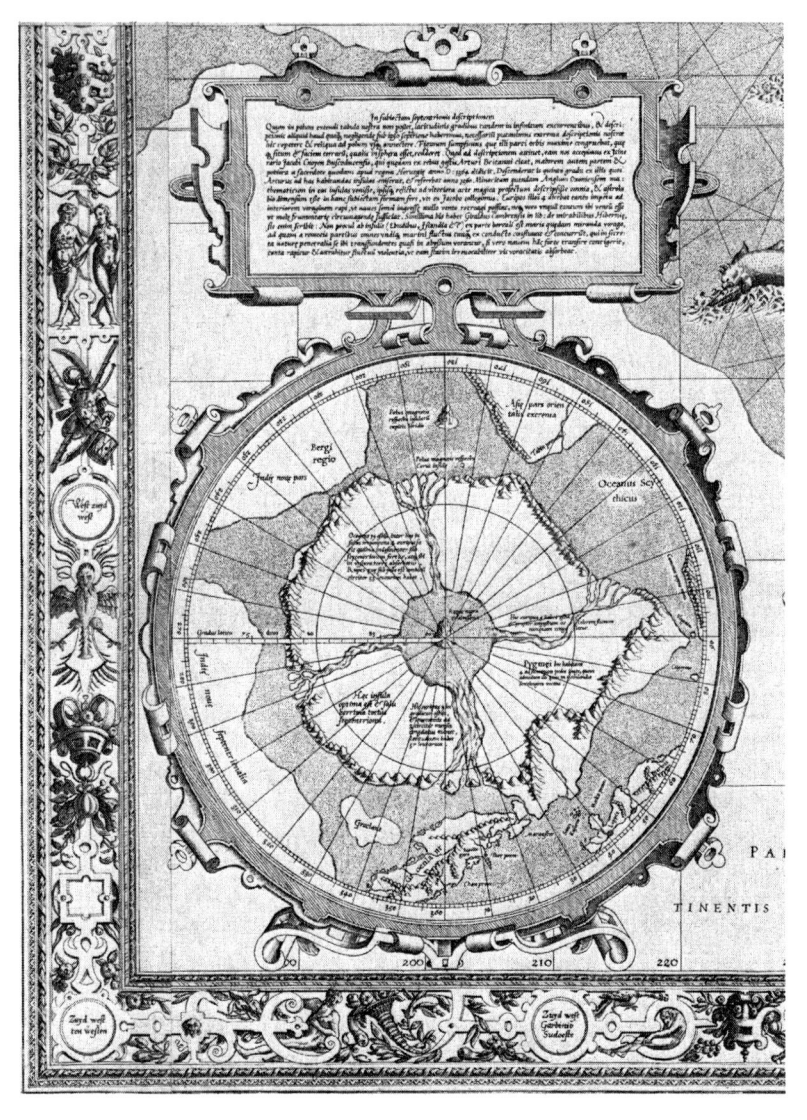

Figure 0.1 Detail from Gerard Mercator's 1569 Wall Map, Sig. Kartenslg. AA 3–5; reproduced by permission of the University of Basel

corner (see Figure 0.1). In it, he attributes his knowledge of this region to a book he calls *"Gestis Arthuri Britanni"* (*The Deeds of Arthur*) and a medieval Dutch traveler named Jacob Cnoyen. Mercator writes in the cartouche, "So far as the description goes, we have accepted that of Jacobus Cnoyen of Buscoducensis, who quotes some material from the *Gestis Arthuri Britanni*, but the greater and more persuasive part he takes from a certain priest at the Norwegian court in 1364" (MacMillan and Abeles 86).[8] According to Mercator, who appears to have been the only one to read these allegedly extant sources, Cnoyen reported that this priest, an unnamed Franciscan and "mathematician" from Oxford, attended the King of Norway in 1360. The friar told stories of the people and places he found while traveling through the islands in the frigid waters beyond the country's coasts.[9] The friar includes accounts of "Pygmies" and a whirlpool so powerful that if a ship came too near, "it would be snatched and pulled with such violent currents that it would immediately and irrevocably be sucked in by the force of the swallowing" (MacMillan and Abeles 87).

Sometime after reading this account on Mercator's map, John Dee, Queen Elizabeth's advisor, geographer, and the first person to use the formulation "British Empire," wrote to his friend Mercator to inquire further about the remarkable details of the story he included from Cnoyen in the cartouche. For Dee, it was not the descriptions of tiny men and women or ferocious whirlpools that gave the story its appeal, but rather the claim that these lands might have been inhabited by descendants of King Arthur's knights as late as 1360. This was because Dee's interest in the map were territorial: he founded a significant part of his argument for British dominion in the new world on a careful examination of documents relating to King Arthur's putative imperial conquests in the North Atlantic world. Dee collated numerous sources on Arthurian empire (including Mercator's cartouche) in the "Limits of the British Empire," a manuscript Dee first presented to Queen Elizabeth and her advisors in the late 1570s, around the time of Frobisher's first voyage and Humphrey Gilbert's preparations for establishing a colony in North America.

The purpose of Dee's treatise was to exhort the Queen to grant patents allowing for exploration and territorial possession in North America, and to legitimize those efforts by proving the legal basis for English expansion. He was persuading the Queen, in Dee's own words, that "this recovery & discovery enterprise ys speedely and carefully to be taken in hand" (MacMillan and Abeles 48). The key word here is "recovery," for it is Dee's argument that the lands, waters, and islands of North America were part of a *British* Empire established first by King Arthur himself.

Dee aggressively claimed that because of Arthur, Saint Brendan, and the Welsh prince Madoc, the Queen had title "to all the coastes and ilandes begining at or about *Terra Florida*, and so alongst or neere unto *Atlantis*, goinge northerly, and then to all the most northern ilandes great and small" (MacMillan and Abeles 43). For, if the British become aware of their historical legal rights to this territory, they will, Dee argues, "become marveilouslie emboldned and encouradged to spend their travailes, goodes, and lives (yf nede be) in the recovery, possession, and enioying of such your Majesties imperiall territoris, duly recoverable and to be possessed" (MacMillan and Abeles 91). Telling the empire-forming mythologies of Arthur, Dee believed, would inspire the recreation of that empire in his time.

In the "Limits of the British Empire," Dee does go to some lengths discussing the amazing story told by Mercator in the cartouche of his 1569 map. He includes a piece of private correspondence with Mercator, dated 1577, in which Mercator supplied further details about the Cnoyen narrative. Mercator opens his letter to Dee by saying that Cnoyen "travelled the world like Mandeville but described what he saw with better judgment" (Taylor 57).[10] Mercator also verifies that as late as the 1360s, descendants of Arthur had inhabited the lands in the Arctic. "But in A.D. 1364 eight of these people came to the King's Court in Norway ... the eight [were sprung from?] those who had penetrated the Northern Regions in the first ships" (Taylor 58). In a marginal note, Dee calculates the number of generations (about 25) that must have passed between Arthur and the men from his original "colonies." Dee also states in a marginal note that the details from the *Gestae Arturi* constituted "rare testimony of great importance to the Brytissh title to the Sep-trentional Regions Atlantis in particular" (Taylor 57). Dee believed that if the English crown could lay claim to having continuously inhabited the "Septrentional Lands" through the times of the Norman and Scandinavian invasions of the eleventh century, that would assure the rights of the English crown to that land in the sixteenth century.[11]

Richard Hakluyt, too, would include the text of Mercator's cartouche in both editions of his *Principal Navigations*, along with narratives from Geoffrey of Monmouth on Arthur's conquests. Also like Dee, Hakluyt corresponded with Mercator in an attempt to verify the report contained in the cartouche. In 1580, he received a letter from Mercator explaining that he no longer had the text of Cnoyen on hand: "The historie of the voyage of Jacobus Cnoyen Buschoducensis, throughout all Asia, Africa and the North, was lent me in time past by a friend of mine at Antwerp. After I had used it I restored it again: after many yeares I required it again of my friend but he had forgotten of whom he had borrowed it" (Qtd. in Taylor 61).[12] Both Dee and Hakluyt were apparently satisfied enough with the authority of Mercator to confirm the truth of Cnoyen's reports. They each use the story of Arthur's first "British Empire" as part of their narratives for establishing the legitimacy of a British Empire (Dee) and the voluminous history of English voyaging (Hakluyt).

What the stories of Mercator and Dee illustrate, partly, is the excitement that was generated in the sixteenth century by the very form of maps themselves. These early atlases and maps allowed for the meeting of a cross-section of cultural narratives. The frontispiece to Gerard Mercator's 1635 *Atlas* (see Figure 0.2), for instance, opens the collection of maps with an argument about the inseparability of history and geography. The title of the book is draped over the Atlas figure in the center of the page: "Historia Mundi or Mercators Atlas. Containing his Cosmographicall Descriptions of the Fabricke and Figure of the world. Lately rectified in diuers places, as also beautified and enlarged with new mapps and Tables . . . " The idea that the "history of the world" could be represented geographically is one of the recurring themes of the frontispiece and its accompanying prefatory materials. The importance of "history" to the collection is also illustrated by the figure of the historian on the left, who, with the geographer on the right, anchors the globe in the center. Atlas's globe is here blank, which both suggests that the volume itself offers a chance to fill in the gaps, but also asks for the creative imagination of the readership. "History and World Geography" the Latin inscription on the globe translates, "are the light of the age." With this Latin aphorism, the engraver of this frontispiece updates a Ciceronian commonplace, quoted in historical treatises throughout the period, which held history to be "the eye-witness of times, the light of truth, the life of memory, the messenger of antiquity . . . "[13] In the engraver's rephrasing of the quotation, history is augmented by geography, a concept that the verse on the facing page expounds:

> Grave *Hist'rie*, and renown'd *Geography*
> Keepe Centry here; their quickning flames doe flie
> And make a *Sunne*, whose more refulgent rayes
> Lighten the *World*, and glorifie our *Dayes*

The volume further elaborates this connection between history, geography, and time ("our Dayes") later in its address "To the Gentrie of Great Brittaine." The collection of Mercator's maps will allow the reader, this brief discourse says, to see an expanding world without

Figure 0.2 Frontispiece to *Historia Mundi: or Mercator's Atlas* (1635), by permission of the Folger Shakespeare Library

the danger and inconvenience of travel: "seeing personall travels in these tempestuous times, cannot be attempted with any safety, here you may in the quiet shade of your Studdies travel at home" (Sig. A3r). In another preface to the reader, the compilers similarly advertise that their volume can

> containe and represent the whole Globe of the Earth, with all the Countries, Kingdomes, Dominions, Woods, Mountaines, Valleys, Rivers, Lakes, People, Cities and innumerable Townes thereof, with the Seas flowing about it all which any one may here view on dry land, without endang'ring his body or goods, and in this travel his friends shall not be solicitous or take care for him in his absence, or earnestly desire his returne. (A4r)

The volume thus facilitates what it calls "eye-travell" (A4r), allowing the reader to take in the entire world in a sitting. Thomas Blundeville, a mathematician who wrote influential treatises on geometry and geography, expresses a similar idea: "Now if you would know what kingdomes, Regions, Cities, Mountaines, Fluds, Lakes, also what seas tegither with their Islands, Ports, Capes, Points, & baies doe belong to euerie one of the foresaid foure parts, then studie well these moderne Maps: and with your eie you shall beholde, not onely the whole world at one view, but also euery particular place contained therein. Which to describe at the ful, in writing would reuire a long time" (Thomas Blundeville, *A Briefe Description of Vniversal Mappes and Cardes* . . . 1589). The holder of map can grasp the "Fabricke and Figure of the World," as the phrase in Mercator puts it, a microcosm that draws together the four corners of the globe. Or, as it states audaciously in the poem glossing the atlas's frontispiece:

> By that faire *Europe* viewes the *Asian* shore,
> And wilde *Americk* courts the Sunburnt *Moore*:
> By this, th'extreme *Antipodes* doe meete,
> And Earths vast bulke is lodg'd within one *Sheete*.

Before even opening to the extensive material contained within, the reader holds the "vast bulke" of the world together "within one sheete."

The stage romance needed to solve the problems of representation created by these new discoveries; it shared the strategies of what I call "romance geography" exemplified in Dee and Mercator. Mercator begins the text in the 1569 cartouche by pointing to the problem of mapping zero degrees latitude in two dimensions: "As our map could not be extended up to the pole (since the degrees of latitude would reach to infinity) and as we think that a description of the arctic regions should not be omitted, I have thought it necessary to repeat here the end of our description and to add other things as to the polar region" (MacMillan and Abeles 86). The problem of representation here is cartographic, and in order to fill out the image of the northern regions, Mercator adds his narrative to verify the (fantastical) map featured in the cartouche. Mercator lends credence to the outrageous story of Cnoyen by giving it bearings. Romance, in these cases, allows for the blurring of empirical report with the fabulous and helps to solve the difficulties of representing the unknown. This is also the same appeal that the dramatist makes to the viewer of the stage romance, an idea expressed boldly in by St. George in *The Seven Champions of Christendom*: "Bravely resolv'd, at all the world we'le play, / But Christendome that is our tiring house, / The rest our stage" (D1$^{r\text{-}v}$).

My work thus develops from the interdisciplinary insights provided by "cultural geography," a field that has been early to recognize the common textualities of literature and cartography (among other kinds of geographical knowledge). And in pursuing the shared textuality of space in theater, fiction, and cartography, I hope to show how literary historical concepts like genre and romance can be used to broaden our understanding of these spaces. The "cultures of exploration," as the geographer Felix Driver contends, subsumed a "wide variety of practices at work in the production and consumption of voyages and travels" (8). These studies have argued that maps are not neutral expressions of space, but textual, even "rhetorical," as J. B. Harley argues, and therefore open to the tools of literary critical analysis ("Deconstructing" 153; "Maps" 53–4). Such interpretations have tended toward a top-down model, whereby mapmaker (or the government that sponsored them) imposes a meaning upon space that speaks to the authoritative concerns of that government.

While I acknowledge the insight of such readings, my interest in maps is on the readers of those texts and how they employed these representations of space. One of the key features of early modern maps, recognized by John Gillies, was not just the representational space, but the gaps and undescribed places that also appeared. Maps could open readers onto the kind of speculative imaginings articulated by Mandeville, a chance to reflect on those places yet to be found and explored. Readers of maps were able to project imaginatively into these places, experiencing a different kind of power structure than that implied by Harley.[14] Importantly, this could lead to a reader's engagement with the map that was beyond the control or intention of the mapmaker. This kind of "speculative geography," in other words, moved the power from the mapmaker to the reader and his or her suppositions about the places on the map. The mastery of space by individual readers spoke to a collective sense that space was not merely "out there," but also, in the case of maps and atlases, quite close at hand. These new geographic materials thus allowed what Gillies calls "imaginative possession," a sense of mastery over the foreign that was also generated in the theater (36). The poetics of this geography (building on Gillies's terminology) offers a window into the mutually reinforcing experiences provided in the theater, in the pages of romance, and in maps and geographical discourse.[15]

The forms of storytelling and representation found in romance materials shaped the geographic "spaces" found in these plays and stories (usually remote, foreign, or imaginary). Here I adapt the influential language of Michel de Certeau, who in *The Practice of Everyday Life* articulates a difference between objective, inert "places" and subjectively constructed and dynamic "spaces." This idea can be illustrated by returning to Walter Ralegh's beguiling reference to the Ewaipanoma, the Mandevillian characters with heads below their shoulders. At the moment Ralegh mentions the existence of these people, the *Caora* river, the location of their habitation, is transformed from a simple geographical place name into the space of romance. The embellishment Ralegh adds to the story makes the change more pronounced: "The son of *Topiawari* . . . told me that they were the most mighty men of all the land, and use bows, arrows, and clubs thrice as big as any of *Guiana* . . . " (92). Here the hyperbole of romance, in this suggestion of an otherwordly enemy, contributes to the multilayered characterization of Guiana Ralegh offers. With the tropes of romance, he opens a new possibility for understanding this space and the possibilities (as well as dangers) that it holds for his audience of readers at home. My reading of de Certeau thus returns me to the question of genre. De Certeau contends that stories provide the "labor" through which place can be transformed into space or spaces back into places (118). Furthermore, the way in which we think about geography is necessarily tied to the *kinds* of stories told about the places represented. De Certeau suggests that "it would be possible to construct a typology of all these stories in terms of identification of places and actualization of spaces"; one of the ways to define literary genre, in other words, is through an understanding of how distinct forms create and manage space.

Romance and the cosmopolitan stage

Alison Games has argued that the period was one in which the globe beckoned through "new commodities in the marketplace" as well as print: "foreign ventures in the steady stream of travel accounts, promotional literature, and histories that English printers produced for an interested market." (9). As such, stage romance proved to be a central genre for tapping into the demands and interests of the English, a people with an increasing desire to become more globally aware and "cosmopolitan," (to use Games's term). How did the theater help audiences think globally? What did that global thinking look like in the sixteenth century? What other cultural discourses did the theater borrow from in developing its global engagement?

European experience with foreign worlds was largely mediated by this range of cultural products and practices. As Andrew Hadfield has recently argued, travel was looked on in the period with significant skepticism ("Benefits" 101–2). Fiction, along with travel writing, cartography, ethnography, and other modes of discourse, allowed readers to gain knowledge of these foreign places; such discourses also promoted an imaginative engagement with territories abroad that became decisive in the growth of an overseas British Empire. Particularly in its expression as a stage genre and in the practices of live performance, romance helped establish early speculations of a global British Empire. From its ubiquitous origins in medieval culture, romance transported readers beyond the realms of everyday experience. Northrop Frye identified this facility as definitive of romance stories; in its capacity to mediate the here and now with imaginary or ideal other worlds, romance established itself as the major secular genre of the medieval and early modern world (186). The adventures of knights carried them across lands and seas and into worlds both known and unknown. But as Frye also articulates, the content of these stories was more amenable to "fiction" with its "sequential and precessional form," and thus "we know it better from fiction than from drama" (186). Through an examination of romance as a popular dramatic genre, *Romance on the Early Modern Stage* thus introduces a consideration of what happens in the movement from romance fiction to drama. I present a new reading of how English overseas exploration and economic expansion influenced theatrical practice. As a genre that represented fantasy, faraway voyages, and a logic of freedom of space, movement, and expansion, romance in its dramatic form both appealed to and shaped popular demand for plays that represented English interest in the expanding world.

What is the relationship between the productions of the early modern stage, long recognized among the defining artistic achievements of the sixteenth and seventeenth centuries in England, and the early expansionist and colonial activities of the period? This has been a central inquiry within dramatic scholarship since the earliest interventions of New Historicist criticism in the 1980s. Those studies placed drama as one among many voices in a polyvocal discourse that gave expression to structures of power and authority.[16] Scholars now mostly take as stated fact the key insight of this body of work: that drama cannot be isolated as an impenetrable cultural artifact separate from the social circumstances of its creation. Enmeshed in a field of social, cultural, and political expression, the stage necessarily operated within the ideological framework of its place and time. More recent studies of the influence of overseas encounters have subsequently shifted attention from "discourse" to material and economic concerns. These studies are exemplified in the rigorous Marxist critiques found in work by Walter Cohen and David Baker, for instance, who have sought to rectify the "collective underestimation of economics," in Cohen's words, that developed in the wake of New Historicism.[17] Derived (in part) from Immanuel Wallerstein's global systems theory, these studies call attention to the ways in which drama both participated in and represented the growing networks of overseas commerce that would come to define England's economy.[18] This economic scholarship has also intersected at times with an adjacent field of postcolonial critics who have explored the cultural and religious implications of English contact with the East. Particularly in the form of drama, these studies have established new ways of understanding England's encounters with and representations of the Islamic "other" throughout the early modern period.[19]

Even in light of this large and still-developing body of scholarship on England's cross-cultural contacts in the period, I believe there are key issues that have not been adequately addressed. I take seriously the admonitions raised in turn by Jeffrey Knapp and Walter Cohen about the nature of European expansion generally, and the English experience specifically. Cohen makes the point boldly: "oceanic imperialism did not capture the imagination of writers or playwrights and their presumed audiences in the way that other topics did" (3).[20] Today we risk placing too much emphasis on the limited representational examples of overseas European and English empire, with the consequence of our overvaluing this historical context. Nonetheless, Cohen's point is not to lessen the significance of European expansion but rather to call our attention to "the nonrepresentational impact of the New World at the level of literary form and conceptual innovation" (10). Likewise Knapp, in his seminal book *An Empire Nowhere*, begins by acknowledging the material limitations of English empire and colonialism in the sixteenth and seventeenth centuries. As a result, Knapp argues that the "poetical empire" imagined by English writers moved to worlds beyond. English literature of this period, Knapp contends, "imagines the more appropriate setting for England's immaterial value to be a literary no-place that helps the English reader see the limitations of a material investment in little England alone" (7). The material limitations of England determined the shape of its engagement with overseas territories and peoples, a point that I wish to explore in terms of literary "form" and the relationship between these generic definitions and geographic boundaries. The English came to a unique imagining of their colonial and expansionist future precisely because of their relatively circumscribed involvement in early imperial activities. In David Quint's analysis, romance was not the genre for the "victors," those who wrote the histories of conquest and expansion. Within the particular circumstances of English literature and drama, however, this heretofore non-imperial genre, with its stories of wandering knights in foreign lands, became an apt articulation of early English empire precisely because it carried its audiences beyond the material limitations of its geography and history. Romance, I will show, was a significant genre for the expression of England's peculiar history of expansion and imperialism exactly because its fictions were historically determined by its treatment of margins and limits.

English colonization and overseas trade, in its earliest period, remained largely the stuff of fantasy and speculation. As Jyotsna Singh has recently argued, "England's era of expansion was conceived imaginatively as much as it was given practical form via mercantile and financial ventures" (24).[21] But it would be a mistake to say that England was not already envisioning itself as an empire (having already established one in Ireland and Wales). "Imperialism encouraged an unprecedented and fateful sense of expansiveness," Cohen argues, "geographically, of course, but also imaginatively, culturally, psychologically, philosophically, cosmologically, and scientifically—a sense that the world was Europe's oyster" (6). Cohen accordingly concludes that we need to heighten our sense of the importance of "imperial nonrepresentation" (11)—of locating imperialism not only in direct representations of European engagement with other lands, but also in the impact of these discoveries "at the level of literary form and conceptual innovation" (10). Positioning this book within the recent project to build a more robust account of the "Global Renaissance," I aim to develop Cohen's suggestive point that the "literature of empire" must be interpreted through form as well as content.[22]

My interest in romance thus intersects with a question that has become central to the study of early English literature and culture: how did the insular "precolonial" world of the English create the conditions for a colonial and postcolonial world system? English drama was a significant imperial antecedent and catalyst because it helped to remap the spatial imagination of early modern England. The genre of romance was instrumental in transforming the representational capacities of the stage and in opening playwrights and audiences alike to a more expansive (and expansionist) method for viewing fictional space. And as a set of stories that embodied a native cultural history, it served to project an ideal vision of the past. Romance had also, from its very earliest inception, reached outwards toward the people and cultures at the rim of European and Western knowledge. The founding mythology of King Arthur, for instance, as told in Geoffrey of Monmouth's *Historia Regum Britanniae*, integrated reports from the Crusades and contacts with the East into its fictions. For this reason, romance stands as a rich example for what Barbara Fuchs has termed "imperium studies," an approach that examines both the internal mechanics of the forming nation state and the outward, colonial thrust of overseas expansion.[23]

Romance: genre, history, strategy

The term "romance" has achieved wide acceptance in Shakespeare studies today. Our collected works neatly separate the four plays, *Pericles, The Tempest, The Winter's Tale,* and *Cymbeline*, into a distinct unit; scholars and teachers frequently organize critical anthologies, conferences, symposia, and seminars under the rubric of "Shakespearean Romance"; and countless essays and monographs have sought the unifying logic of these plays, those characteristics that give coherence to their diversity. While these numerous scholarly and editorial endeavors have accurately identified a key term within early modern stagecraft, they have also limited the scope of study into romance and the early modern theater. Such a comfortable certainty about the topic of romance in early modern drama, as a result, hides gaps in our knowledge of the genre.

There is, however, a broader history for romance than has previously been recognized within dramatic scholarship. Critics have remarked that Shakespeare would not have used the term "romance" for his plays.[24] That fact says more about the evolution of dramatic terminology in the early modern theater than it does about romance itself. "Romance," perhaps because of its origins in the narrative tradition, never quite seemed an appropriate term, even as its stories suffused the drama. As romance traveled from the pages of prose and verse narratives to the commercial theater the relationship between audience and text also altered. This change in material form amounted to a challenge to tradition that concerned, even flummoxed, classically-oriented viewers like Philip Sidney. For Sidney, drama, as a representational art, could not contain the narrative eccentricities of romance without unacceptable violations to dramatic form. His reluctance to allow for romance's entrance on the stage is telling, and provides a moment of key insight for this study—in Sidney's rejection of romance as a dramatic genre, I read an important alteration in stagecraft and dramaturgy that was prompted by the social and economic conditions that surrounded the stage.

In fact, stage romance pressed beyond the classical paradigms of "comedy," "tragedy," or even tragicomedy, creating an instructive definitional problem.[25] As the dedicatory epistle to one of these plays, *The Seven Champions of Christendom* (1638), describes, plays adapted from romance were identified generically as "history," or story, acknowledging the plays' association with the wandering tales of romance: "The Nature of the *Worke*, being *History*; it consists of many parts, not walking in one direct path, of *Comedy*, or *Tragedy*, but having a larger field to trace . . . " (A3v–A4r). The spatial metaphors the author John Kirke uses reflect back on the materials of romance—ranging stories that required the action of the stage to move beyond the parameters of representation established by classical precedents. Kirke's play is very much a case in point. Founded on the long tradition of the "seven champions," St. George, St. David, St. Patrick, and other legendary figures from European history, also celebrated in a popular prose fiction by Richard Johnson, the play carries its audience on fantastical adventures through the world.[26]

Delving into the records of sixteenth- and seventeenth-century theatrical productions, book catalogues, and dramatic allusions produces the record of a thriving genre that moved between print and dramatic culture throughout the period. The generic kinship of the group of more than forty plays I have identified for this study (see Appendix) has, until recently, gone virtually unremarked.[27] The plays operated within a "horizon of expectations," in Hans Robert Jauss's important formulation, a series of motifs and generic parameters that playwrights adapted from the various streams of narrative tradition. Romances were, according to Helen Cooper, "a mass of stories available to everyone who could read English or hear it read to them . . . These were the stories that the

Elizabethans grew up with" (*English Romance* 7).[28] Thus the shape and origins of this cultural institution were known, without much reflection, to any sixteenth-century viewer who watched Guy grappling with the giant Colbrand, Sir John Mandeville in the court of Prester John, or Godfrey of Bouillon taking back the Holy Land.[29]

Considering romance as a theatrical genre raises a problem that has been little discussed in recent studies. While the content of stage romance was central in defining its make-up to early modern audiences, the arrival of romance into dramatic culture must also prompt us to approach genre from the perspective of form. Barbara Fuchs helpfully posits that romance be thought of as a "strategy," a concept that emphasizes what romance *does* as much as what it *is* (9). This model usefully explains how romance could move from the pages of narrative onto the stage. Once it arrived on the stage, romance had crossed what the period viewed as discrete generic boundaries: narrative and drama. Viewing romance as strategy raises the importance of the materiality of genre, a perspective that is overlooked when we focus exclusively on the motifs, plots, and characters of romance (or any genre).[30] As romance became incorporated into its new dramatic form, the expectations associated with its features were also subject to change. The relationship between the audience and action of the stage, for instance, changed, as readers became viewers. Playwrights also adapted the tools of the stage (props, verbal cues, narrative speeches) in order to make the romance workable as a dramatic genre. Indeed, it is in such "transitional moments" that Fredric Jameson identifies for romance "the ultimate condition of its figuration" (148). Romance was the inheritance of a Middle English corpus that presented exemplary heroism in men and beauty in women, feats of magic, travels into otherworldly places, imperial ambitions, mediations in historical material, religious conflicts, and amorous pursuits. Yet it also remained a dominant genre of the early print culture, as witnessed by the popular narratives of writers such as Robert Greene, Richard Johnson, and Thomas Lodge. As the stage made room for this popular content, it updated and molded the stories into a world with new commercial opportunities where promises of territorial expansion also led to changes in social relations.

If we do distinguish an early modern theatrical genre of romance it is within the well-known category of "Shakespearean Romance," a group conceived in the nineteenth century by Edward Dowden to set apart Shakespeare's final plays: *Pericles, The Tempest, Cymbeline,* and *The Winter's Tale*. As I will discuss in more detail in my first chapter, Dowden assigned the term "romance" to the final plays in Shakespeare's canon, those plays that marked the crescendo in Shakespeare's career. These "last plays," Dowden believed, showed an artistic and psychological progress beyond the tragedies, and marked a new achievement not only in the development of Shakespeare's work, but in English drama more broadly.[31] These were "spiritual" and "romantic" plays (*Mind and Art*, 368, 403), Dowden argued, because they revealed in Shakespeare's subject matter (familial reconciliation, forgiveness, reunification) a mellowing and maturity of the artistic mind. For Dowden, "romance" never, therefore, constituted a true *genre,* if we mean that term to indicate a nonauthorial field of cultural expression. At best, and following the critical paradigm modeled by Dowden, early stage romances become malformed attempts at an art Shakespeare would perfect at the end of his career. Rather than a "resource" (to use Rosalie Colie's influential concept) to be developed by other playwrights, Dowden's "romances" were a peculiar expression of Shakespeare's "mind and art."[32] The continued attention to Shakespeare's "late plays" as romances has therefore obscured the rich history of romance adapted to the stage in the sixteenth and seventeenth centuries.[33] As an innovation that effervesced from the singular motions of the artistic spirit, these "romances" had no history before, or beyond, Shakespeare.[34]

The writings of Francis Kirkman, a seventeenth-century book publisher and prolific reader of romances, open to us a different view of romance in the period. In separate publications, Kirkman offers a remarkably thorough record of the romance texts available to readers in the period. "I my self have been so great a Lover of Books of this Nature," Kirkman writes in his prefatory epistle to *Don Bellanis of Greece* (1673), "that I have long since read them all" (*Honour of Chivalry* A4r). What he presents in this epistle is a kind of reader's guide, a connoisseur's account of the genre of romance in English and translation from the past one hundred years. "I will set down some of my Observations," Kirkman promises, "to give thee some Order and Method that thou mayest proceed in" (*Honour of Chivalry* A4r). Of the more than forty titles he mentions, eight were also produced as plays earlier in the seventeenth century—plays like *Old Fortunatus* (printed 1600), *The Seven Wise Masters* (performed 1600, lost), *The Four Sons of Aymon, Valentine and Orson,* and the aforementioned *Seven Champions of Christendom.* Kirkman wrote elsewhere of the appeal these books held for him as a young reader, especially a copy of *Doctor Faustus* he borrowed from a schoolmate: "[it] also pleased me, especially when he travelled in the Air, saw all the world, and did what he listed" (*Unlucky Citizen* 10). Such a fantasy of global travel was central to the appeal for viewers of stage romance.

By the time of Kirkman, however, romance had again receded into a primarily textual realm. What pleased him (and the readers he as a publisher was trying to entice) was an experience that differed in important ways from the dramatic performances I will treat in this book. The immediacy of performance, of encountering bodies in space, transformed narrative romance into a powerful theatrical mode. Thomas Heywood's *Foure Prentises of London* opens, for instance, with the enticement of such a journey: "Had not yee rather, for nouelties sake: see Ierusalem yee neuer saw, then London that yee see howerly" (A4v). As the action of the play moves forward, the Chorus who speaks these lines appeals to (or incites) the audience's militant desires for conquest, "Grant them your wonted patience to proceed, / And their keene swords shall make the Pagans bleed" (C2r). As promised, the play delivers a hopeful vision of English dominion over the East. Through a series of chance adventures and heroic exploits, the loosely historical characters of Heywood's play claim victory in the Holy Land under the signs of the tradesmen they represent—the mercers, goldsmiths, grocers, and haberdashers that were likely members of their audience.

This example from the *Foure Prentises* captures an important insight of this study. The play begins immersed in the material conditions of early modern London: in the hierarchy of masters and apprentices, the movement from feudal estates to urban commercialism, and the celebration of trade organizations. But these economic conditions only tell us so much about the play and its immanent meanings to the early modern audience. Just as important are the geographic signals and inducements offered in the course of the play. As the apprentices of the title move outside of London, variously, to Ireland, the Mediterranean, and finally, Jerusalem, they forge new identities and allegiances that are only possible because of their shifts in geographic place. In leaving early modern London to travel in the circuits of the medieval Crusades, the characters find new "conquests" of foreign spaces possible. Geography was important to early modern theatrical audiences, in the words of Jean Howard, because it "connected to real-world developments: England's rapid commercial expansion into distant parts of the globe" among them (313). The practices of stage enactment created a kind of fluidity between experiences within the social realm of London and the imagining of other possibilities that were increasingly available to early modern audiences.

Recent critics (including Howard) have therefore turned to the question of literary form in what has been called the "New Formalism." For while New Historicism may have broken down the conceptual barriers between culture and history, it tended to do so by stripping away the features of cultural expression that have been the purview of literary criticism. More concerned with "discourses of power" than in the particular forms the expression of those discourses took, New Historicism has been subject to the critique that it underestimates the complex workings of literary forms. Stephen Cohen observes that it "never systematically or consistently engaged the complex issue of form," as he also demands that "the politics of theatricality must be augmented by a historicized theory of dramatic and theatrical forms" (2, 8).[35]

Historical formalism produces valuable insights to the literature of the past when it uncovers the inner workings of forms and genres as they were understood in their time. A broad tradition of critics dating back to Northrop Frye have argued for the centrality of romance within European culture, and its ability to engage a range of social and historical circumstances. Recent work on romance, including the authoritative account offered by Helen Cooper in *The English Romance in Time*, has done much to expand our understanding of the genre long identified with the ahistorical realms of fantasy.[36] While many of these studies of genre have touched upon dramatic romance in passing, the nuances of theatrical culture and the peculiarities of romance's move into performance have garnered less critical attention. Indeed, this foundational criticism has tended toward a smoothing over of differences between narrative and dramatic forms of romance, noting instead the mutability of romance as a genre in its ability to cross over traditional generic boundaries. In isolating romance as a dramatic genre during this period, then, *Romance on the Early Modern Stage* builds on this scholarship while staking out critical space for the study of romance as a genre of performance.

Romance, as it had been understood for hundreds of years before the sixteenth century, was a genre concocted for books and readers. The trials and triumphs of the famous Guy of Warwick, Amadis de Gaul, Saint George, or King Arthur unfolded in voluminous pages of prose or verse, a space and form suited for their ambling adventures and romantic conquests. Several Middle English examples cited under "romance" in the *Oxford English Dictionary* tellingly connect the genre with the act of reading: people in the court of *Havelok* engage in "romanz reding on the bok." The fifteenth-century *Troy Book* advises, "Iff he be ferd of any chaunce, Lete him sitte & rede romaunce." And the opening lines of the encyclopedic *Cursor Mundi* proclaims "Men yhernes [desire] rimes for to here, And romans red on maneres sere . . . " ("Romance," def. I.1.a).[37] In the sixteenth century, Roger Ascham witnessed sadly that few books in

English were read in "our forefathers tyme . . . savyng certaine bookes of Chevalrie . . . for pastime and pleasure" (27ʳ). But with the rise of a commercial theater in London in the 1570s, the textual monopoly on romance ended. By 1600, a theatergoer could find a host of popular romances in theater company repertories—plays ranging from the still familiar (*Guy of Warwick, Orlando Furioso*) to the now obscure (*Old Fortunatus, Clyomon and Clamydes, The Seven Wise Masters*). Romance had leapt out of books and onto the stage.[38]

Why did a genre so long associated with narrative move suddenly (and perhaps unexpectedly) into dramatic culture? This seemingly quiet generic shift was, in fact, profound. With the introduction of romance into the popular theater, drama took on a set of popular narrative materials that were not crafted originally for dramatic enactment.[39] A central element of this genre's draw was its promise of embodying familiar old stories, and the interaction between audiences and performance the theater allowed. George Puttenham, in *The Art of English Poesy*, followed Aristotle in defining plays, those "sundry forms of poesy dramatic reprehensive [representational]," as poetry "put in execution by the feat and dexterity of *man's body*" (124, my emphasis). Thus, romance as a genre on the early modern stage arrived, firstly, as a form of narrative expression requiring execution within physical time and space. Plays that drew on the stories of romance almost uniformly take "history" as their generic term in publication and in contemporary allusions. The nature of the drama as tied to story, or narrative, separated these plays from the dramatic forms of tragedy and comedy, not merely because of their rootedness in narrative (tragedy, for instance, often borrowed tales from well-known narratives) but because of the nature of romance itself as stories that moved freely through narrative space and time, ungoverned by the "laws of poesy" that Sidney mandated in his *Defense of Poesy*.

How action is to be staged within space and time seems at first a strictly dramaturgical or formal problem. For Aristotle, these constituted the defining set of formal characteristics for drama: there could be no coherent representation of action without attention to how it unfolded within time and space. But beyond the theater there were also changes in perceptions of time and space in a variety of fields, from mapmaking and historiography to agriculture. As recent scholarship has shown, the representation of time and space in early modern drama resonated with the formulations of burgeoning commercial, national, and political ideologies.[40] The shift in romance from a narrative form to a representational dramatic genre marks an important but unrecognized point in the history of this genre and early modern theatrical culture. This transformation represented more than an alteration within literary and dramatic tradition; romance on the early modern stage accompanied, heralded, and in some ways, helped shape England's exploration, colonization, and commercial global ventures in the period.

Indeed, stage romance had a particularly important place in this new global cultural marketplace. Plots that were once only imaginable in narrative could now be encountered in space and time. This alteration was comparable to the materialization of goods, maps, and travel stories that flooded London in the wake of new geographic discovery. Thriving commercial markets and reports from travelers abroad represented these experiences anew, and thus confirmed that the exotic places and products were not just the stuff of legend. What was previously the domain of fantasy (oftentimes originating in the pages of romances like *Mandeville's Travels*) became the commerce of everyday, inciting a cultural taste for fiction and drama that engaged these new worlds of experience. To adapt the metaphor employed in *The Seven Champions of Christendom*, stage romance was a "tiring house" for English conquest.

Following Fredric Jameson's influential orientation of the genre in the history of feudal disintegration and social and economic "dilemmas," subsequent criticism on romance has identified the intersections between romance and early modern legal culture, early contacts between Islam and Christianity, and New World exploration (Jameson 139).[41] These studies have encouraged us to see the transnational origins for romance, as well as its extension beyond the realm of English literary and theatrical culture. Genres have roots and significance far beyond the situations in which we find them, as Wai Chee Dimock has lately observed. She calls genres a part of a "world system, a diffusional process more or less coextensive with the history and geography of human beings on the planet" (1383). My interest in genre is thus both literary and historical, as I aim to combine local readings of romance as they were expressed in early modern dramatic culture with the global purview of a genre that had at its very origins a cross-cultural and global reach.

Even before the sixteenth century, the romance was recognized as a genre that reached beyond the traditions of classical literary history and form. The distinguishing expansiveness of their landscapes, plots, and characters historically situated romance as a genre vis-à-vis the epic, as its relation to classical narrative became one of the most hotly contested topics in Italian criticism. Theorists such as Castelvetro, Minturno, Giraldi Cinthio, and Guarini sought either to locate romance in the tripartite Aristotelian system of genre (epic, lyric, and drama), or dismiss it as a generic imposter. Writing of Ariosto, Minturno says, "I cannot affirm that his romances and those of the others contain the kind of poetry that Aristotle and Horace taught us" (Gilbert 277). Minturno explained the origins of "romance" as a genre that developed in the Romanized colonies outside of the political and geographic center of empire. Minturno called the name "romance" for a genre "strange," but speculated that it must have been formulated as such because areas of Spain and Provence used their language to tell of "actions and the loves of the knights more than any other subject" (Gilbert 277). These tales became known as "romance."

The romance was thus, like the language of its composition, a genre that stood outside of the tradition of classical learning and writing practiced by the Romans.[42] Though the attention to Shakespearean romance creates a limited, authorial approach to the question of genre, romance itself had always been implicated in international networks of commerce, meaning, and creation. A series of important postcolonial readings in medieval romance has, in recent years, shown how the genre provided cultural expression of empire, foreign travel, encounters with non-Europeans, and definitions of nation and identity.[43] It was perhaps because of its exoticism and origins beyond the classical world that romance provided an important outlet for writers and audiences interested in the changing world of global expansion. It became commonplace for writers in travel accounts and geographic treatises to note how far present-day discoveries had exceeded the achievements of the classical world. Richard Chancellor, the sixteenth-century Englishman who traveled to Moscovia in search of a passage to China, marveled at the achievements of his contemporaries, who had pressed beyond the boundaries of the ancient world. "Hercules and great Alexander," he commented, "trauayled only into India" (Anghiera 285). Chancellor imagined that the Europeans could "withowt comparyson farre excell all the noble factes that euer were doone by Iulius Cesar or any other of the Romane Emperours. Which thynge they myght easely brynge to passe by assignynge colonies to inhabite dyuers places of that hemispherie, in lyke maner as dyd the Romanes in prouinces newely subdued" (Anghiera 285).

Staging romance in Greene's *Orlando Furioso* and *Tom a Lincoln*

There is a similar evocation of promising new worlds through the language and stagecraft of romance in Robert Greene's adaptation of *Orlando Furioso*, staged by the Admiral's / Strange's company during the

1592/3 season along with the lost play of Mandeville. Edward Alleyn, the lead actor in the Admiral's Men (which had merged with Strange's Men in the early 1590s) would have likely played the role of Mandeville, just as he did of Orlando in Greene's *Orlando Furioso*. In the play's final speech, Orlando addresses the legendary "twelve peers" of France, who are gathered in Africa for the play's denouement.[44] Orlando tells his "friends of France" to "Frollicke, be merrie; we wil hasten home" (1431–2). He concludes the play with a rich description of the ships that will ferry them:

> Meane while weele richly rigge vp all our Fleete
> . . .
> Our sailes of sendall spread into the winde;
> Our ropes and tacklings all of finest silke,
> Fetcht from the natiue loomes of laboring wormes,
> The pride of Barbarie, and the glorious wealth
> That is transported by the Westerne bounds;
> Our stems cut out of gleming Iuorie;
> our planks and sides framde out of Cypresse wood. (1435–44)

Orlando further promises, "So rich shall be the rubbish of our barkes, / Tane here for ballas to the ports of France, / That Charles him selfe shall wonder at the sight" (1451–3). In this speech, Greene uses the nautical language of maritime trade ("rigge," "tacklings," "stems," "planks," "barkes," "ballas[t]," "ports"), leaving the audience in this final moment with a vision of Orlando as an opportunistic merchant or explorer preparing to return home to present his king with a bountiful yield. The fleet of ships that Orlando imagines returning him to France is itself an assemblage of rich foreign commodities (fine linen, silk, cypress wood, and ivory), further presenting Orlando and his "peers" in a mercantile vein distinct from their aristocratic origins. The version of the speech found in the Alleyn manuscript amplifies such a connection between Orlando and the global market, as he tells his men to "comaund" the wealth that is "with in the clime of Africa" as well as "what pleasures [be]longs the co[a]sts of mexico" (Collins 277).[45] Thus, for a play whose fictional world is set in the eighth century, the "Westerne bounds" of the New World loom large.

Sir John Harington's voluminous and learned English translation of the *Orlando Furioso* first appeared in 1591, and was available in bookstalls at the same time that this, Greene's version of the play, appeared on the London stage. But readers of Harington would not find this speech, nor would they see mention of Mexico, or an incitement of the audience's imagination to the riches and plunder of conquest. This alien language was the domain of the London stage, as Greene's adaptation was made to fit Ariosto's Italian narrative to the culture of English dramatic romance.

Tom a Lincoln, another of the romances remembered in Kirkman, also led its audiences through far away geographical spaces. The play shows romance fiction, here drawing inspiration from the annals of Arthurian legend, mixing with the global geography and language of overseas exploration and voyaging. Arthur's legend travels beyond England and even Europe, as Tom (his illegitimate son) and the Knights of the Round Table voyage to India and the Amazon inhabited Fairy Land (Sir Tristram worries that the women, "lyke Caniballs" might "thirst for bloud" (1277)). Upon arriving in Prester John's kingdom, Tom learns that the land has been ravaged by a "fiery dragon treple tonged, huge, / deformed, fearfull, vast, and terrible" (1842–3) who guards a golden tree that once belonged to Prester John. Tom successfully slays the dragon (bringing its head onto the stage), and Prester John rewards him with a monument that declares the accomplishment: "[T]hy self shall stand in marble pillar framed / and these thy acts in order shalbe named / A stranger knight vpon our shore dyd land / and slew a three tongued dragon by his hand" (2244–7). Tom repays the kindness of Prester John by stealing away with his daughter in the night and returning to England.

Both *Tom a Lincoln* and *Orlando Furioso* create a complicated temporality with their allusions to and adaptations of ancient mythology, medieval romance, and early modern trade and voyaging. Orlando boasts that his triumphant peers have outdone Jason and his Argonauts, paradigmatic foreign voyagers, and Tom mimics the exploits of romance heroes and the medieval traveler Sir John Mandeville, who also ventured to the kingdom of Prester John. Such an overlapping of fiction and fantasy, past and present can also be found in the travel materials of the period. Maximilianus Transilvanius, the first reporter of Magellan's circumnavigation, found the story of Jason to be the relevant classical antecedent for his voyage. He calls the Magellanic voyagers:

> Mariners doubtlesse more woorthy to bee celebrate with eternal memorie then they whiche in owlde tyme were cauled *Argonauti* that sayled with Iason to win the golden fleese in the region of *Cholehic* and the riuer of Phasis in the greate sea of *Pontus*. And the shyppe it selfe, more woorthye to bee placed amonge the starres then that

owlde Argo which departynge owt of Grecia, sayled to thende of that great sea. (Anghiera 262)

The story of the Argonauts prompts a boast for these sailors who have circumnavigated the globe. What they have done surpasses the classical example, exceeding the accomplishments of the ancients. The stories of Greene's *Orlando Furioso* and the anonymous *Tom a Lincoln* pose a paradox characteristic of romance, as they invoke a distant past through a genre that is definitively old-fashioned to engage with present concerns about travel, cross-cultural contact, and overseas expansion. These conflations of chivalric narratives and mercantile or colonialist ideology help define romance. As far back as Homer's *Odyssey*, romance was a strategy for representing worlds beyond, for bridging the imaginative with the real, and in its dramatic form, for *enacting* the fantastic possibilities opened by an expanding globe. Although they are not widely read or studied today, Greene's *Orlando Furioso* and *Tom a Lincoln* were part of a popular early modern dramatic genre that helped shape the way the stage took on the challenge of representing what was unknown in classical and medieval drama.

Tom a Lincoln also stands as a persuasive illustration of the effects that the traditional critical framing of the romances as Shakespeare's "late plays" has had on editorial and critical practices. *Tom a Lincoln* was discovered in 1973 in a manuscript found among the papers of Sir John Coke, King Charles I's Secretary of State.[46] The play, which lacks a title in the manuscript, adapts Richard Johnson's popular sixteenth- and seventeenth-century romance of the same title.[47] Given the paucity of extant examples of dramatic romances, the discovery of this play is of tremendous importance to those who study early English theater. Yet *Tom a Lincoln*, a focus of further study in my third chapter, has garnered almost no critical attention, even since the publication of G. R. Proudfoot's masterfully prepared and edited transcription of the play for the Malone Society. Such a lack of scholarly response suggests a need to generate critical categories that can integrate this play into our understanding of early modern drama.

But the ways in which early modern theatrical romance was a part of these larger cultural, literary, and historical forces has been obscured by the attention to narrative forms of romance and obeisance to a narrowly defined Shakespearean romance. It is not surprising, for instance, that Proudfoot, the editor of the Malone Society's transcription of *Tom a Lincoln*, is not interested in the engagement of the play with such global issues or with a broader archive of romance drama. For Proudfoot, the play is remarkable primarily for its connections with Shakespeare's late plays. Indeed, on the vexed question of assigning a date to the undated manuscript, Proudfoot assigns a *terminus a quo* based on "what appear to be allusions to *The Winter's Tale*, *The Tempest*, and perhaps *Cymbeline*" (xix).[48] The echoes of the play with Shakespeare's language, Proudfoot notes, may provide "striking testimony to the memorability of those [Shakespeare's] plays" (xxvii). But Proudfoot also moves to distinguish the play from Shakespeare, in language that is strikingly reminiscent of Dowden, by pointing to: "Shakespeare's intention and achievement in transmuting this generic pattern [of the "romantic play"] into plays of wide sympathy and deep feeling" (xxvii). Playing down the play's value on its own terms, Proudfoot's justification for including this edition in the Malone Society's reprints rests on the relevance to the study of Shakespearean drama (the series takes its name from Shakespeare's prolific eighteenth-century editor, Edmond Malone). *Tom a Lincoln* only achieves its generic bearings once Shakespeare's plays arrive to give the category authority, even dignity—"wide sympathy and deep feeling."

Plays that are so richly suggestive of the history of English exploration, plays like *Tom a Lincoln* and Greene's *Orlando Furioso*, will receive here a better account of their place in both theatrical and global history than a simple comparison to Shakespeare's "late plays" can allow. As Benedict Robinson has persuasively argued in his study of romance and Islam in early modern England, romance allows us "to explore the multiple relationships between a text, its immediate historical moment, and a literary and cultural history that extends all the way from the Crusades to the first phases of colonization" (*Islam* 2). Interpreting this "sedimented polytemporality" of genre, as Robinson calls it, shows how early modern authors dealt with the raw materials of the genre and its modulations through time, molding it to their contemporary world. When brought to the stage, romances provided audiences with a means of engaging with an imagined past as well as present fantasies of expansion, conquest, and economic ascendancy. Romance itself always carries with it the intriguing paradox of being an old genre, located in the conventional "long ago" that resonates not only with medieval European chivalric literature, but also a new one, whose overlapping and intertextual narrative style seems to prefigure future genres. Bringing this history into view, *Romance on the Early Modern Stage* disrupts the charged temporal division between early modernity and the Middle Ages, showing that instead of a sharp break between the two, genre and geography yields continuity as well as differences across these centuries.[49]

Overview

I seek to turn away from traditional considerations of romance in Shakespeare studies, as I show in my first chapter, "Romancing Shakespeare." In this chapter, I establish how the category of Shakespearean Romance emerged from the romantic "mind and art" criticism of Edward Dowden (1843–1913). Building on the eighteenth-century project of ranking Shakespeare's works in chronological order, Dowden was the first to align the four genres of the Shakespearean canon with four periods of Shakespeare's life. He was thus able to rationalize the canon by arguing for a progression in Shakespeare's plays that corresponded with the development of the playwright's "mind." Unable to find a satisfactory classification for Shakespeare's "late plays" in the original genres of the 1623 First Folio (Comedies, Histories, and Tragedies), Dowden grouped *The Tempest, The Winter's Tale, Cymbeline,* and *Pericles* under the Coleridgean term "romance" to indicate the transcendent quality of these plays—and of the playwright—in the waning days of his career, Shakespeare's "period of large, serene wisdom." I argue that the preservation of "Shakespearean Romance" carries with it a critical apparatus that implicitly endorses Dowden's psychological divisions—a romantic model that influences, and obscures, genre criticism to this day.

Chapter 2, "'Asia of the one side, and Afric of the other': Sidney's Unities and the Staging of Romance," centers on Philip Sidney's brief discourse in the *Defense of Poesy* on dramatic unity, in which he insists that playwrights observe the difference between "reporting" and "representing." I focus on his puzzling comment about dramatic representation: "I may speak (though I am here) of Peru, and in speech digress from that to the description of Calicut; but in action I cannot represent it without Pacolet's horse" (244). Here, in a strange juxtaposition, Sidney brings the expanding world of global exploration, discovery, and commerce into conversation with neoclassical dramatic theory. I connect Sidney's concerns with dramatic unity in the *Defense* to the advent of plays in the sixteenth century that attempted to translate narrative romance into dramatic action. Sidney's citation of Pacolet's horse, a figure drawn from the popular romance *Valentine and Orson*, reveals that his call to preserve dramatic unity came as a direct response to the popularity of the stage romance. In translating the elements of romance narrative (travel to foreign lands, feats of magic, fanciful creatures), dramatists stretched the representational capacity of the stage. In Sidney's citation of "Peru and Calicut," I argue, we see the extravagant geography of an expanding world affecting both the matter and the form of drama.

The remaining chapters of the book use this foundation to examine more canonical works in light of these earlier romances. Instead of treating these plays as predecessors to the inevitable rise of a Shakespearean form, I view the stage romance as an integrated part of the theatrical culture. In the third chapter, I develop the connection between geography and romance elucidated in Sidney's commentary through an analysis of a recently discovered seventeenth-century play, *Tom a Lincoln* (discussed above). I connect the play to sixteenth-century globes, maps, geographic treatises, and imperial prospectuses by Gerard Mercator, John Dee, and Richard Hakluyt. These materials offered a similar pleasure to that of stage romance as they presented the enticing possibility of viewing the wider world through imaginative exploration. Writers like Dee and Hakluyt also used romance to establish a precedent for English dominion over recently discovered territories. *Tom a Lincoln* enacts this expansive history, presenting King Arthur and his knights as the creators and overseers of a premodern British Empire. Taken together, the play and these geographical materials illustrate the mutually reinforcing set of reading and interpretive practices that arced between the theater, cartography, and the pages of romance. With this background, I reevaluate Shakespeare's *Merchant of Venice* within both theatrical and geographic contexts. The "speculative geography" that characterized both romance and writings from early modern geography and cartography inform my reading of Shakespeare's rendering of Venice and Belmont. I thus argue through a reading of these geographic materials that Shakespeare's play offers a complicated engagement with the imperial, economic, and literary contexts of romance.

I argue in Chapter 4 that Shakespeare's *Henry V*, with its invocations of the audience's imagination and martial aspirations, relies on a generic affiliation with romance as well as the history play to represent its imperial fantasies. Though originally published in the First Folio as a "history" and in quarto editions as "chronicle history," Shakespeare's *Henry V* is encoded with the language and dramatic strategies of popular stage romance. Considered in this way, *Henry V* marks a departure from the earlier installments in Shakespeare's second tetralogy, a series of plays constrained in plot and structure by their chronicle history source. Like Thomas Dekker's *Old Fortunatus* and Shakespeare's *Cymbeline, Henry V* extends beyond "this little world" of John of Gaunt's England, and uses the dramaturgical tools of stage romance, specifically in the theatrical device of the Chorus, to open its audience's imagination to empire and territorial extension. Whereas previous criticism has emphasized the play's importance in coalescing a language and politics of nation,

I show how the play moves beyond these boundaries as it reaches toward the cosmopolitan sense of British identity endorsed in romance.

While I would dispense with the notion of a "Shakespearean Romance," *The Tempest, Cymbeline, Pericles,* and *The Winter's Tale* will receive new critical treatment here in light of my lesser-known romances. Once Shakespeare's plays are posited in this tradition, we can view previously unexplored ways in which Shakespeare and other poets and playwrights engaged with the genre. In Chapter 5, "Containing Romance and Plotting Empire in *Pericles* and *The Tempest*," I contrast *The Tempest*, Shakespeare's most unified and compact play, to the ranging *Pericles*, arguably his most obvious contribution to the genre of stage romance. Though *The Tempest*'s integration of various travel accounts has been widely discussed for generations, the relevance of the play's attention to the unities has not been linked to its global outreach. Why is this play that is so evocative of worlds beyond England also so contained in its dramatic structure? I read *The Tempest* and *Pericles* as presenting differing responses to geographic shifts brought on by the expanding globe. The over-determined unity of *The Tempest* stands, I argue, as a solution to the problem of dramatizing romance: unifying a story of many places and many times. By comparing the treatment of time and space in the two plays, I show that the self-conscious unity of *The Tempest* positions the play as anti-romance, a response to this genre that is centrally occupied with issues of temporal and spatial representation. Through a reading of *The Tempest*'s treatment of time and space, I connect the formal with the historical, and show how the play contains romance in the controlled space of its island setting.

The final chapter, "Milton's Imperial *Maske*: Staging Romance on the Border of Wales," extends my generic analysis to the court masque and Milton's *Comus*. Later in his career, Milton wrote that as a young man he was stirred by "lofty Fables and Romances"; my chapter queries how he deploys stage romance in this masque. Unlike the dramatic space of the public theater, by its nature spare and representational, the masque relied on elaborate staging that attempted to integrate its surroundings (and ultimately the audience) into the spectacle. An occasional piece, Milton's *Maske* was designed for a specific moment and place, identified on the title page of the 1634 edition: "at Ludlow Castle, 1634: On Michaelmasse Night, before the Right Honorable, John Earle of Bridgewater." Despite this specificity, Milton's remote and "wild" space of Wales and the Marches invokes the same kind of expansionist landscape that we see in other romance drama. The *Maske* thus shows romance moving into another mode, one in which the drama is beholden to the political exigencies of the Ludlow Court.

Even in the masque form, however, romance still functions to move England beyond its geographical boundaries through representations of the exotic, unknown, and imaginary. This outward reach of the genre leads in to the book's Coda, "Global Romance after Shakespeare," where I revisit one of the early stage romances, *Valentine and Orson*, through a surprising reference to the story in a late seventeenth-century travel narrative. In the contact between an English sailor and a captured South American native, the romance of Valentine and his lost brother Orson, I find a genre fit for the imperial project of the eighteenth and nineteenth centuries, where it flourishes in children's literature, travel writing, and even contemporary genre fiction. It is the unrecognized history of dramatic enactment that this moment recalls, I argue, that makes this redaction, and those that follow, so important in the legacy of British imperialism and Shakespeare's current global reach.

Conclusion

I began with a discussion of *The Travels of Sir John Mandeville* and the way in which it inspired English imaginings of foreign places. There is a final material connection that binds "Guiana" and "Mandeville," new worlds and the stories of romance. Further suggestion of the lost play of Mandeville can be found in Sir John Harington's inventory of the roughly 130 play titles he held in his library. Included in his copious list are a number of plays that adapted romance sources to the stage through the early seventeenth century: Thomas Dekker's *Old Fortunatus*, the anonymous *Sir Giles Goosecap*, *The Dumb Knight*, and *Trial of Chivalry*. Harington organized his plays into bound collections, numbered "Tomes," that reveal no apparent alignment according to dramatic subgenre. Inserted in brackets between the plays listed in the fourth and fifth tome is a curious entry: "Note that Guiana ys sorted / wth Virginia and Maundev'."[50] Harington refers to this title "Maundevil & Virginia" a second time in the manuscript, including it in "A note of thinges sent to London" where he lists "Guiana / mandevil & Virginia." Why would Harington include mention of this separate volume in and among his play collection? W. W. Greg, who reproduced the "The Harington Collection" as an appendix for his *Bibliography of the English Printed Drama*, suspected that the Guiana entry was errant, with "no relation to the rest of the document" (1313). He inferred, instead, that the note related to Harington's books from another section of the library, perhaps his collection of travel accounts (1306, 1313).

There is another possibility, though, that Greg does not consider. While it may be impossible to prove that this manuscript provides evidence of lost plays about Guiana, Virginia, or Mandeville, through the course of this study I hope to demonstrate that there was, indeed, a relationship between these evocative names and the early modern stage. Moreover, Harington's catalogue suggests that romance, in its ability to cross over generic categories of narrative and enactment, could find its way into a diverse set of discourses in the period—from travel narratives located in Guiana and Virginia to plays that evoked these and other places. This gives a different picture of the neatly contained "romance" that was the invention of the nineteenth century, the genre that would come to be associated exclusively with Shakespeare's "mind and art." The sixteenth-century romance, both a part of the stage and emanating to places beyond the theater, was a more dynamic cultural resource, one not easily catalogued and contained within lists like Harington's.

In expanding the definition of romance and drama, *Romance on the Early Modern Stage* demonstrates the possibilities for reading form as a means to historically inflected criticism. Drawing on materials from early modern cartography, literary theory, historiography, travel writing, and racial theory, my chapters relate the transformations in dramatic form to the social and historical issues raised by England's expansion into new territories. The intersection of history and legend romance provided in performance was well suited to the imaginative space generated by England's involvement in transnational commerce, exploration, and colonization. For Shakespeare and English playwrights seeking to tap their audience's interest in these developments, the fictional resources of romance promoted performances that helped them, and us, to see with "imaginations more swift than thought," those faraway realms (*Tom a Lincoln* 205).

1
Romancing Shakespeare

Fredric Jameson's influential study of the romance genre, "Magical Narratives: On the Dialectical Use of Genre Criticism" (*The Political Unconscious*), opens with an epigraph from *The Winter's Tale*: "O, she's warm! / If this be magic, let it be an art / Lawful as eating" (5.3.109–11).[1] The speech belongs to Leontes, and it comes at the moment he embraces his revivified wife Hermione, whom both the king and audience had previously imagined dead. The magical return of Hermione bodies forth Jameson's argument that romance wends its way through literary history, dialectically altering its forms and modes as it reanimates in varying social circumstances. Such a narrative of romance's development would include "its brief moment on the stage in the twilight of Shakespearean spectacle before being revived in romanticism . . . " (136).[2] Jameson's choice of *The Winter's Tale* for his epigraph thus reveals the now definitive association between "Shakespeare" and "Romance" in our critical vocabulary. He never needs to elaborate on or contextualize this quotation. It is assumed that the reader knows that *The Winter's Tale* is romance—one of those plays from "the twilight of Shakespearean spectacle."

The wistful tone of his phrase clashes with Jameson's overarching and foundational project to "invent a new, historically reflexive, way of using categories, such as those of genre" (107). Jameson is not alone in leaving the category of "romance" in Shakespeare unquestioned. Helen Cooper, in *The English Romance in Time*, her magisterial study of the romance genre in English literature, sets even more emphasis on Shakespeare's "last plays," marking "the death of Shakespeare" in her subtitle as the very endpoint of the romance tradition. She calls Shakespeare's "own last plays . . . almost the final works to profit from the power of those endlessly transforming traditions" (23). Even in these most probing historical examinations of the genre, dramatic romances remain where they have been since the late nineteenth century, encompassed by Shakespeare's poetic life story.

This chapter explores the foundations of that critical terminology and its continued influence on dramatic study today. As several scholars have acknowledged, Edward Dowden was the first to apply the term "romance" to the last plays of Shakespeare. But Dowden's contribution to our understanding of genre and the Shakespearean canon extends beyond merely giving a new name to these plays. His project was more probing, and significantly amplified, as I will argue, the Romantic Shakespeare criticism heralded earlier in the century by Coleridge and others. It is this broader project, with all of its attendant problems and controversies, which influences and obscures Shakespearean genre criticism to this day. Shakespeare's "romances," as they were originally conceived, constituted a restrictive category, a unique expression of a singular artistic mind. Intended only to pattern Shakespeare's internal genius, this view of genre was fundamentally ahistorical.

Uncovering this story of the dramatic romance's origins in psychological and philosophical romantic criticism will serve to properly contextualize the emergence of the category. But I will also use the recognition of Dowden's romances as a point of contrast to the proliferative versions of "romance" that circulated before the nineteenth century. Dowden's conception of "romance" severed the meaning of the word from its earlier signification: the erring narratives, exotic locales, foreign conquests, and alinear developments that characterized the genre for centuries. Thus, instead of abandoning the term, I seek in the course of this chapter to restore the meanings that it held before Dowden. Rather than an innovation in Shakespeare, this understanding of romance connects the Renaissance stage to a rich cultural history that has been lost.

The "late plays": Edward Dowden's generic chronology and the "Romances"

We take it for granted today that Shakespeare had a "career," a story that allows us to map the development of his plays alongside his progress from Stratford to London and back: from rough-and-tumble "early comedies" like *Comedy of Errors* to the "maturity" expressed in *The Tempest* or *The Winter's Tale*.[3] Along with the enduring vogue of Shakespearean biography, this narrative is represented and preserved in the way that we structure the canon. In their *Textual Companion* to the Oxford Shakespeare (1987), Stanley Wells and Gary Taylor explain their reasons for organizing the plays according to putative dates of composition: "If one does not know the order of composition of an author's works, one cannot form any notion of his artistic development; if one has no notion of his artistic development, it becomes fatally easy to acquire the notion that (artistically) he did not develop, but instead sprang, like Athena, full-grown from the forehead of the nearest available muse"(36). Though Wells and Taylor marshal their logic in the cause of ostensibly twentieth-century critical concerns (subverting the conception of Shakespearean genius), their language is strikingly similar to that of Dowden. "The most fruitful method of studying the works of Shakspere [sic]," Dowden wrote in his Shakespeare *Primer*, "is that which views them in the chronological order of their production. We thus learn something about their origin, their connection one with another, and their relation to the mind of their creator, as that mind passed from its early promise to its rich maturity and fulfillment" (32). It is a testament to the quiet but enduring influence of Dowden that the *Norton* and the *Riverside Shakespeare*, standard texts in the American classroom, continue to observe Dowden's four genres of the Shakespearean canon.[4]

But, as Barbara Mowat has also argued, it was not always the case that the "Romances," "late plays," or "last plays" were so self-evidently aligned (129–30). The First Folio included only three of these plays, and grouped them within its "Catalogue's" tripartite structure: *The Winter's Tale* and *The Tempest* with the comedies, and *Cymbeline* with the tragedies. Until its publication in the second issue of the Third Folio (1664), *Pericles* circulated only in quarto editions.[5] Later in the seventeenth century, dramatic chronicler Gerard Langbaine offered an even more variegated characterization for the plays in this group in his 1691 *Account of the English Dramatick Poets*. *The Tempest* remains a comedy, and *Cymbeline* a tragedy (though Langbaine notes its partial source in Boccaccio). But *Pericles* is a "History," and *The Winter's Tale* a "Tragicomedy" (455–66). When Dowden began his project of realigning the Shakespearean canon, he had almost no critical precedent for separating out these particular plays into a separate, rational category.

In his *Shakspere: A Critical Study of His Mind and Art* (1875), Dowden crafted an understanding of Shakespeare's plays that relied on two key and related principles: first, that Shakespeare's "organic" development as a "human" could be traced through the growth of his "art," and second, that an artistic career has a trajectory, a teleology, that can help explain both the artist and his artifacts.[6] "In such a study as this,"

Dowden wrote, "we endeavour to pass through the creation of the artist to the mind of the creator" (3). He further explains:

> The essential prerequisite of such a study was a scheme of the chronological succession of Shakspere's plays which could be accepted as trustworthy in the main. But for such a study it is fortunately not necessary that we should in every case determine how play followed play. It would be for many reasons be important and interesting to ascertain the date at which each work of Shakspere came into existence; but as a fact this has not been accomplished, and we may safely say that it never will be accomplished. (*Mind and Art* 378)

Mowat has usefully shown the influence of the chronologies created by his contemporaries in the New Shakespeare Society's metrical analysis projects—the process by which they sought to construct a definitive chronology for the plays based on the internal evidence provided by alterations in rhyme and meter (130). But Dowden strikes a note of ambivalence in this passage about the assuredness of these labors. He insists upon the importance in finding the succession "not of Shakspere's plays, but of Shakspere's chief visions of truth, his most intense moments of inspiration, his greater discoveries about human life" (*Mind and Art* 378). The only complete chronology, he argues, is the one that marks both biographical and psychological development:

> We do not now place "A Midsummer Night's Dream" and "The Tempest" side by side as Shakespere's plays of fairyland. We know that a long interval of time lies between the two, and that they resemble one another in superficial or accidental circumstances, they must differ to the whole extent of the difference between the youthful Shakspere, and the mature, experienced, fully-developed man. (*Mind and Art* 7)

It is significant that Dowden groups his plays based on psychological categories rather than "accidental" or arbitrary taxonomies (Comedies, or even "plays of fairyland"). The plays had to be assigned to categories that *coincided* with the periods of Shakespeare's life, but also reflected on the development of the artist's mind.

Although he never cites him in these passages on chronology and genre, Dowden carried on a method of generic classification practiced by Samuel Taylor Coleridge earlier in the century. Dowden praised Coleridge for ushering in "a new era in the criticism of Shakespeare . . . the criticism of genius, of reverence, and of love" (*Shakspere*, 163) Dowden also admired Coleridge because he "conceived of Shakespeare's work as a whole; he observed the fruit as it hung in living beauty on the tree" (*Introduction*, 102). Like Dowden, Coleridge questioned the ordering of Shakespeare's works on the "external" evidence of independent historical analysis. Coleridge thus challenged the models of editors such as Edmond Malone, and privileged instead, as one reporter of his lectures put it, "a psychological, rather than a historical mode of reasoning" (2:67). Coleridge attempted several different schemas and progressions for Shakespeare's plays, each of which somehow mapped the playwright's psychological growth.[7] In his *Literary Remains*, for instance, he separates out *Troilus and Cressida*, *Cymbeline*, *Merchant of Venice*, *Much Ado About Nothing*, and *Taming of the Shrew* into the third period or "class" in Shakespeare's progression, commenting that they represent "a greater energy—not merely of poetry, but—of all the world of thought, yet still with some of the growing pains, and the awkwardness of growth" (1:212).[8]

In Dowden's reckoning of Shakespeare's life, the lusty young poet, newly arrived in London, wrote frolicsome early comedies; in the second period, as Shakespeare "was gaining a sure grasp of the positive facts of life," he wrote the histories and "the brightest and loveliest comedies"; the middle-aged Shakespeare turned to more reflective and serious tragedies; the older Shakespeare, "in his period of large, serene wisdom" capped his career with "spiritual" and "romantic" plays that culminated with his farewell to the stage, *The Tempest* (*Mind and Art* 362, 68, 403). Dowden inserted this last category, the "Romances," to solve a generic problem created by the chronological organization of the Shakespearean canon. The first edition of Shakespeare's plays, printed in 1623 under the title *Mr. William Shakespeares Comedies, Histories, and Tragedies*, was not, as the title suggests, ordered by date of composition, or even performance, as was Ben Jonson's 1616 *Works*. If one intended to honor the three genres of the first collected edition of Shakespeare's works, one had to accept that the Shakespearean career ended with a seeming hodge-podge of genres: two collaborative plays not included in the First Folio (*Pericles* and *The Two Noble Kinsmen*), two plays drawn from the annals of British history, a "tragedy" (*Cymbeline*) and another collaborative "history" (*Henry VIII*) and two "comedies" (*The Winter's Tale* and *The Tempest*). Such a conclusion was unacceptable for Dowden, who saw an essentially harmonious generic progression through Shakespeare's career up to *Pericles*—from comedy to history and tragedy.

It would seem particularly difficult for Dowden to explain why *The Tempest*, which he saw as the culmination of the Shakespearean canon, appeared first in the collection under the section of "Comedies," and *Cymbeline*, the final play in the Folio collection, was gathered in 1623 with the "Tragedies." Undaunted in his efforts to create a rational narrative for the canon, Dowden saw the First Folio's arrangement as "remarkable": romances were the alpha and omega of the collection, underlining his notion that these plays deserved special attention (*Mind and Art* 42). "The circumstance may have been a piece of accident; but if so, it was a lucky accident, which suggests that our first and our last impression of Shakspere shall be that of Shakspere in his period of large, serene wisdom, and that in the light of the clear and solemn vision of his closing years all his writings shall be read" (*Mind and Art* 403). Thus, from their original conception in Dowden, the Romances helped dissolve the divisions of the 1623 collection (or even give that organization a new logic) and brought together a group of plays that, instead of indicating a confused close to the canon, could signal Shakespeare's "maturity" at the end of his career. Dowden managed to paint a picture of an artistic career that mirrored the rich spiritual life of the author. From its very inception, Dowden's study of Shakespearean genre was a biographical project, and the romances provided the psycho-generic lynchpin that allowed the development of the canon to coincide with Shakespeare's life story.

Romance as period term: Coleridge and the "romantic drama or dramatic Romances" of Shakespeare

Beyond the biographical interest that these "late plays" held for Dowden, his choice of the term "Romances" for the last four plays of the canon also derived from the nineteenth-century reframing of Shakespeare as a poet of a "romantic" era. Coleridge called *The Tempest* "a specimen of the romantic drama," which he further described as "a drama, the interests of which are independent of all historical facts and associations, and arise from their fitness to that faculty of our nature, the imagination ... which owns no allegiance to time and place."[9] For Coleridge, all of Shakespearean drama was "romantic," as his assessment of Shakespeare's plays as "romantic" had less to do with genre than with his interest in creating Shakespeare as the prime mover of a literary historical epoch. "We must find a new word," Coleridge insisted, "for the plays of Shakespeare" (1:175). Shakespeare was romantic, for Coleridge, because he was not bound to the strictures of classical drama—the unities and rules of decorum that the eighteenth century ascribed to Greek and Latin theory. He argues, "the deviation from the simple forms and unities of the ancient stage is an essential principle and, of course, an appropriate excellence of the romantic" (1:175). Hans Ulrich Gumbrecht identifies this periodizing move with a broader tendency in the early nineteenth century. "By designating their own time as 'romantic' with a specific history stretching back to the literary genre of chivalric romances, the poets of the early nineteenth century instituted the Middle Ages . . . as the beginning and high point of a Christian period that was completely different from antiquity and at the end of which the romantics found themselves" (90). Shakespeare's departure from the codes and practices of ancient drama marked, for Coleridge, an essential division between the classical past and a romantic era that stretched to his present time.

Dowden thus inherited "romance" and "romantic" predominantly as terms associated with a period or movement, rather than a genre. In fact, the great contribution of Dowden was to marry the Coleridgean idea of Shakespeare as the central literary-historical figure in the development of a romantic English canon with the more precise project of tracing a development in genres in his canon. As I have shown, Coleridge had also set up some rudimentary systems of "epochs" by which he organized the canon, but he described all of Shakespearean drama as "romantic," not just a subset of it.[10] Coleridge saw only that Shakespeare's status as a "romantic" developed in opposition to the classical and rational. As Jonathan Bate has argued, Shakespeare's perceived resistance to the neo-classical precepts of Aristotle made him "the cardinal precedent for their own artistic principles and practice" (2). Thus, to establish a system of genres within the Shakespearean canon was a problematic endeavor for Coleridge, Dowden, or anyone interested in preserving the romantic notion of Shakespeare's genius. Dowden's solution was to create a narrative arc for Shakespeare that revealed, through these genres, the development of a great romantic mind.

Coleridge's treatment of Shakespearean drama is notable for its disavowal of history ("all historical facts and associations") as a contributor to the formation of genre. The romantic, Coleridge contends, is definitively ahistorical: it "owns no allegiance to time and place."[11] When Dowden later codified the Shakespearean canon into his four species, he, too, was unconcerned with either history or how the term "romance" may have been used in its early modern context. If anything, for Dowden, the "romances" of Shakespeare represent a progression beyond medieval or early modern romance. This is clear in his little-known essay on "Elizabethan Romance," where he refers to the genre as "a dead literature of pleasure." In comparing the Shakespearean "romances," with Elizabethan narrative romance, Dowden contends:

> Prince Hamlet and Othello, Imogen and Juliet, are with us in the close of the nineteenth century as truly as they were with the frequenters of the Globe or Blackfriars three hundred years ago. Caliban and Ariel, Prospero and Miranda are creatures of an enchanted world over which time owns no sway . . . It is not so with the romances of the Elizabethan age . . . not one of these romances, in the true sense of the word, lives; they are prey for the moth and worm. (*Essays* 351–2)

Dowden clearly sees the narrative romances of the sixteenth century (he cites narratives by Sidney, Greene, and Lodge, for instance) as less sophisticated and developed than the drama that so captivates him. The plays of Shakespeare are not only of a different genre, but achieve a timeless eminence. While the narrative romance remains steadfastly in its time, and subject to the decay of passing days, Shakespeare's plays are outside of history and time, and as a result, part of their own, separate history—one that carries forward into Dowden's age.[12]

This insistence on the timelessness of Shakespeare, in part, develops from the twin projects of chronologically ordering the canon and coordinating genres with literary life stages. Although Dowden saw the creation of a Shakespearean timeline as potentially facilitating questions of the plays' historicity, the logic of chronology does the exact opposite.[13] Margreta de Grazia makes this point, arguing:

> Because that creative process possessed its own inherent purpose and design, it no longer needed to depend on the outside world of history for its significance. Self-referential and self-perpetuating, it "gradually expanded itself," spontaneously unfurling over the years. The organization of the plays along a temporal spectrum provided the mechanism for releasing them from the history that had supplied the very co-ordinates by which that spectrum had been constructed in the first place. (*Shakespeare Verbatim*, 150)

The legacy of Dowden into the twentieth century was to seal off the romances not only from their own historical context, but from the canon as well. As "Shakespearean Romance" came to be its own category, it produced a critical apparatus that implicitly relied on the psychological divisions of Dowden's generic premises.

The "romance brain": Dowden through the twenty-first century

Following the influence of Dowden through the twentieth century, we can see several earnest efforts to infuse Dowden's "romances" with varying degrees of theoretical, historical, and even lexical meaning.[14] E. C. Pettet (*Shakespeare and the Romance Tradition* (1949) and Howard Felperin (*Shakespearean Romance* (1972)) each attempt to connect the late plays of Shakespeare to broader medieval and early modern romance traditions. For, in the wake of Dowden's criticism, it becomes difficult to formulate a discussion of "romance" and "Shakespeare" without some invocation of Dowden's four-part structuring of the canon, or his notions of the unique thematic interconnections between these plays. Recent essay collections organized around the topic of "Shakespeare's Romances," or "Last Plays" find inherent thematic unities, or shared sources in these plays. In her introduction to *Shakespeare's Romances* (2003) Alison Thorne identifies

> a striking family resemblance owing to their mutual reliance on a set of readily identifiable thematic motifs and structural devices: the loss and recovery of royal children; flawed rulers who, after enduring many years of hardship, find redemption through the restitution of their families; miraculous twists of fate, reunions and resurrections of characters presumed dead engineered by some divine agency, providential force or mage-like figure. (Thorne 1)

While Thorne finds typical patterns of "thematic motifs" within these last plays, Russ McDonald identifies a set of stylistic characteristics that bring coherence to the last plays. Operating with a set of "microscopic" details (syllables, line breaks, diction, verse), McDonald articulates a principal of separation based on peculiar elements of style. Though he warns against prioritizing these plays, as Dowden did, for their maturity, the category of romance remains both tied to Shakespeare's lateness and a singular product, now with a definitive style. And for McDonald, this insight about style provides an opening to "the new kind of story to which Shakespeare was contemporaneously attracted" (37).

Dowden's category has also found new support in the computational linguistic analysis of Michael Witmore and Jonathan Hope, who use their data to conclude that "on a truly pervasive linguistic level, the late plays seem to do what many audiences and readers have experienced them doing on the page: they make way for inner life and revelation through memory and recognition; they pivot theatrical and readerly attention on the movements of mind engaged in thought" (151). It is not surprising that Witmore and Hope's final conclusions echo the "mind" based criteria of Dowden's original genre, for their experiment is premised upon his divisions. Separating the plays into the three First Folio genres and the "late plays" included in the collection, they sought "factors . . . that differentiated the genres from each other" (143). Though the product of a complicated statistical parsing of the First Folio's language as linguistic data, this method follows the same pattern of generic classification inaugurated by Dowden. The "late plays" are first separated as a separate, *a priori* category. Only then can the details that justify such an alignment surface. Witmore and Hope implicitly admit the potential flaws to this methodology in a footnote: "The experiment showed us that with enough observations . . . a statistical portrait of a genre can be created out of almost anything; the trick is knowing what to make of what you count—being able to connect a quantity of something counted to an activity that is meaningful" (141 n. 16). Any set of details can be employed to argue for the coherence of a genre, whether they be linguistic features or motifs. As has been the case since Dowden's original framing of the Shakespearean canon, critics who look for evidence of the playwright's mind and art are bound to find it, even in the results of a decidedly contemporary experiment.[15]

Even those critics who tacitly question Dowden's arrangement and category of romance find it indispensable. Stephen Greenblatt, for instance, in *Shakespearean Negotiations* (1988) at once allows that there is "no exclusive, categorical force behind these generic distinctions" but also calls them "useful markers of different areas of circulation, different types of negotiation," including the romances, which demonstrate "an acquisition of salutary anxiety through the experience of a threatening plentitude" (20). And Barbara Mowat, who has offered one of the most compelling and complete accounts of the spotted history of the term, still endorses the utility of retaining the category, although with a slightly altered name: "Shakespearean Tragicomic Romances" (143). She argues, "When we place his plays within this particular genre, we are rewarded first by a clearer recognition of the kind of romance story that his 'romances' dramatize" (136).

Another current of post-Dowden genre criticism has sought to give historical context to the romances, and thus do for them what Dowden would not—orient them toward history rather than psychology. Frances Yates links the development of Shakespearean Romance with the political vicissitudes of James I's reign and his designs on succession, "It is this real situation which was at the back of Shakespeare's mind in the Last Plays, and his deep concern for the issues of his times was behind the poetry which flowed from his genius in these last years" (13). Some critics also continue to reproduce the psychological readings of Dowden through the treatment of a developing canon.[16] Simon Palfrey mirrors the political concerns of Yates, but with an intensified sense of Shakespeare's mental state during this late period:

> There is a movement away from verisimilitude, into a kind of exploratory mode of discourse which is at base level responsible to Shakespeare's "generic task." And this task, conceived of in figurative terms, is one of replacing a more traditional genre's pre-Copernican "meta-*body*" with a proleptically modern generic *brain*: a seat of stimulus, response, organization, complementarily crossed and individual, single and multi-tracked, centrifugal and centripetal . . . (viii, author's emphasis)

In a resounding echo of Dowden's criticism, Palfrey calls this forward marching and innovative state Shakespeare's "romance brain," that quality of the plays that helps to define Shakespeare's modernity.

Yet all of these approaches beg the question of the genre's very origins. And as much as these efforts aim to orient Dowden's romances toward more contemporary concerns, the underlying assumptions of the "mind and art" criticism remain intact: a new and idiosyncratic category is needed in order to name the alteration of the playwright and his plays at the end of his career. Furthermore, by revisiting themes that were only roughly manifest earlier in his career, Shakespeare brings his career to a tidy ending, allowing us to see his work as a "whole," as Coleridge would have it. This was a "new" category for Dowden, after all, one that succeeded in updating Shakespeare and bringing him into the nineteenth century.

By perpetuating the separation of these plays, even those who question the psychological foundations of Dowden's classification system close off new possibilities for situating Shakespeare's plays in relation to other generic genealogies. As Barbara Fuchs has argued, the category of "Shakespearean Romance" has "the unfortunate consequence of obscuring the many genres with a claim to being considered English renaissance romances" (*Romance*, 93–4). Aligned with a supposed new turn in Shakespeare's career, the plays have an existence separated from the rest of London's dramatic culture. The hermetically sealed generic world of the Shakespearean Romance allows for only its own reproduction and perpetuation. The creation of the "Shakespearean Romance" has assured that no other playwright had access to the genre; Shakespeare was alone in formulating as well as realizing "dramatic romance" as we know it today.

Locating early modern dramatic romance

The answer to the challenges presented by the persistence of Dowden's schema, however, is not to adopt a broader skepticism toward genre criticism. The Oxford editors' choice to arrange the plays chronologically is radically dismissive of genre, in part as a corrective to the dubious schemes of critics such as Dowden. Consequently, historicist criticism has largely written (or edited) away genre from dramatic criticism. In rejecting the generic grouping of plays, Stanley Wells and Gary Taylor claim that the entire history of Shakespearean genre criticism was corrupted by the false pretenses of the First Folio's artificial construction of the genres. The book's tripartite "catalogue," these editors argue, "suggests the author's allegiance to strict distinctions of genre which the plays themselves disregard, and this palpable discrepancy between form (of the Folio) and content (of Shakespeare's actual plays) surely contributed to the subsequent fruitless centuries-long critical preoccupation with decorums of genre" (Wells and Taylor 38). It is, of course, evident that the organizing principle governing the assembly of the 1623 Folio was different from that of Dowden and the Oxford editors. But it is not so clear that the Folio's "Catalogue" was aberrant in its organization by genre. Francis Meres employed a similar logic as the compilers of the 1623 Folio for classifying the plays in his catalogue from *Palladis Tamia: Wit's Treasury* (1598):

> As *Plautus* and *Seneca* are accounted the best for Comedy and Tragedy among the Latins: so *Shakespeare* among the English is the most excellent in both kinds for the stage; for Comedy, witness his *Gentlemen of Verona*, his *Errors*, his *Love's Labor's Lost*, his *Love's Labor's Won*, his *Midsummer Night's Dream*, & his *Merchant of Venice*: for Tragedy his *Richard II*, *Richard III*, *Henry IV*, *King John*, *Titus Andronicus* and his *Romeo and Juliet*. (282)

Instead of using his plays as the key to unlocking his biography or the "artist's mind," the compilers of the Folio were, rather, intent on making the book into a monument to Shakespeare. Their organization of the plays by genre worked well within this project. They either grouped plays under familiar classical rubrics ("Tragedies" and "Comedies"), or elevated the unclassical members of the canon (the English "Histories," a category unknown to Meres) by placing them in between the accepted genres. Whatever their motivations, the result was decidedly achronological. Unlike Ben Jonson's 1616 *Works*, which assigned the order of the plays based on their date of first performance, the 1623 Folio foregrounded the generic status of the plays. Meres's taxonomy suggests that in the long history of generic categorization it was Jonson's collection, in fact, that was more the oddity. Further, unlike the chronologies of Coleridge and Dowden, there is no suggestion by Jonson in the 1616 *Works* that his plays developed, progressed, or could tell us anything about the status of the artist's mind.

While I want to recall this sixteenth- and seventeenth-century practice of arranging plays and poetry generically, the absence of the term "romance" from the First Folio or, more broadly, its diminished use as a generic term in the period does not indicate that it was insignificant (or even non-existent) as a dramatic kind. Jean Howard makes an important point about the study of Shakespearean genres in light of the First Folio's divisions: "One of the consequences of the later textual materialization of the Shakespeare canon into the three categories of comedy, tragedy, and history is that such a materialization tends to occlude the way in which particular Shakespearian plays may have been in conversation with other genres or sub-genres during their performative lives" ("Shakespeare and Genre," 304). Howard's analysis of the city comedy in her essay and elsewhere illustrates how dramatic sub-genres can materialize into a recognizable tradition.[17] These genres often originate outside the Shakespearean canon, as Shakespeare adapted and engaged with the popular genres of the day. As Stephen Orgel reminds us, "Shakespeare thought of genres not as sets of rules but as sets of expectations and possibilities. Comedy and tragedy were not forms: they were shared assumptions" ("Shakespeare and the Kinds of Drama," 158). These "shared assumptions," it is important to add, also share a history and are part of their historical and social moment. That is, genres, by their very nature, both exist in history and have a history.[18]

The genre criticism proposed by Howard and Orgel, then, is in direct opposition to that of Coleridge and Dowden. Instead of beginning with Shakespeare and the characteristics of his plays, we must first move beyond his plays, even outside of the playing world, to find how history helps shape the categories of art and drama. Such approaches to the genre of romance can be found in recent work by Valerie Wayne and

Lori Humphrey Newcomb, both of whom argue for the fundamental interconnectedness of *Cymbeline* and *Pericles,* respectively. Wayne, for instance, finds that *Cymbeline,* far from being a singular expression of Shakespeare, is enmeshed in a centuries-long tradition of wager stories that crosses many languages and cultural origins.[19] Newcomb undermines the logic by which we attribute *Pericles* exclusively to Shakespeare, showing the play to be a product of various strands of the romance tradition ("Sources of Romance"). A great deal of critical ground in early modern studies is lost by giving over the term "romance" to an isolated group of Shakespearean plays. Indeed, as many will recognize, the broader use of the term romance in the period is notoriously, even definitively, evasive.[20]

To begin, as it would have been used in the period, the term "romance" was widely understood to refer to a fictional *narrative* form. Gerard Langbaine, the previously mentioned seventeenth-century chronicler of English theater history, copiously noted this distinction between romance narrative and the plays that were based on romances. His *Account of the English Dramatick Poets* (1691) was among the earliest and most extensive records of English dramatic history. In his 1691 edition, Langbaine expanded considerably on his earlier *New Catalogue of English Plays*, and in the preface advertises that on the subject of dramas "which are founded on Romances or Forreign Plays, I have much enlarg'd my *Remarks*" ("The Preface"). He can do so, Langbaine further explains, "having employ'd a great part (if not too much) of my Time in reading Plays and Novels, in several Languages; by which means I have discovered many more Thefts than those in the former Catalogue" ("The Preface"). What Langbaine means by "romance" is a fictional narrative, probably borrowed from a foreign tradition. He notes throughout his catalogue the many places where playwrights draw their plots from such "romances." Langbaine writes, "I have shew'd whether they were founded on History, or Romance, and cited the Authors that treat on the Subject of each Dramma [sic], that the Reader, by comparing them, might be able to judge the better of the Poets abilities, and his skill in Scenical Performances" (162). Thus, when Langbaine writes of "dramatick romance," he refers to plays that are based, in part or whole, on narratives ranging from *Don Quixote* and "the *Grand Cyrus*" to Sidney's *Arcadia*.

Prior to Langbaine, in 1637, the English translation of Corneille's play, *Le Cid* (it, too, based on a romance narrative), is advertised by the translator, Joseph Rutter, as being "like a romance." Further investigation of Rutter's translation raises more questions about the category

"Romance" on the early modern stage than it answers, for Rutter also refers to the play as "a true history," and the title page of the play calls *Le Cid* a "Tragicomedy." I find it instructive that at this point Rutter and his publisher take Corneille, today considered the progenitor of French neoclassicism, and describe his play in quite unclassical terms: "true history," "Romance," "tragicomedy," a constellation of words revealing the problems of categorization that romance created. Indeed, one of the reasons we do not see "romance" used as a generic term more widely in the period is that its place in the system of genres (particularly dramatic genres) could not yet be imagined. English writers and printers often relied on the term "history" as a catch-all for both plays and narratives that we might today call romance.

Such definitional problems (which continue today) point to what is for me the second defining feature of romance in the period: it was viewed as a genre that stood outside of the classical system established by Aristotle and further refined in the sixteenth century by his commentators and redactors. One of these writers, the Italian Antonio Minturno, described the origins of the term "romance" as a genre that developed in the Romanized colonies outside of the political and geographic center of empire.

> But certainly the word [Romance] is strange, and in the Spanish as well as in the Provencal I believe it refers to the vulgar tongue. In Spain and in Provence because of the Roman colonies Latin was generally diffused to such an extent that men spoke there in a Romanized fashion (for the Romans occupied both regions, and barbarous nations dwelt there). Since the Roman language persisting in those lands, though for the most part contaminated and destroyed, was nevertheless more regular and more graceful than the Gothic and the Alanic, their native tongues, they applied themselves to learning and retaining it, and called it Romance and wrote in it. Therefore, because they dealt in that language with the actions and the loves of the knights more than with any other subject, the compositions made on that theme were called romances. (Gilbert 277)

The romance was thus, like the language of its composition, a "contaminated" genre, and one that superseded the tradition of classical learning and writing practiced by the Romans. Writing of Ariosto, Minturno says, "I cannot affirm that his romances and those of the others contain the kind of poetry that Aristotle and Horace taught us" (Gilbert 277). Many genealogies of romance continue to emphasize its roots in the non-classical. Geraldine Heng argues in *Empire of Magic* that medieval romance took the form that we recognize today in Geoffrey of Monmouth's *History of the Kings of Britain*. Significantly for Heng, Geoffrey's narrative developed out of European contact with the Levant during the First Crusade. At its origins, medieval romance gives "cultural authority" to the crusaders and provided the model for "the story of medieval Europe's history of overseas empire-making" (6). Paradoxically, Heng argues, medieval romance did so while appropriating its materials from the East. The Levantine colonies, Heng observes, "furnish Arthurian romance with narrative *materia* in the form of ideas, plots, characters, constructs, affects, landscapes, and memory" (6).[21] From its origins, romance was a genre that summoned fantasies of far removed places, and these places also provided the genre with its narrative and formal raw materials.

The usefulness of such a broad based approach to early modern romance in studying Shakespeare is that it can open questions about moments from the entire canon, including Dowden's "last plays": how is Shakespeare utilizing various understandings of "history," including romance, in his "History Plays"? How do the restrictions of dramatic enactment required by the stage alter the origins of romance, a predominantly narrative form? In what ways was Shakespeare responding to other dramatic adaptations of romance? And how are the terms "romance" and "romantic" to be understood in their early modern, pre-Romantic, context?

While the magically revived Hermione and the appearance of an actor in a bear suit stand as the central expressions of the romance tradition for Fredric Jameson and Helen Cooper, respectively, I would choose another moment from Shakespeare's *Winter's Tale* as the crucial connection to a romance tradition: the appearance of Time as a Chorus.[22] In the midst of the action, as the plot turns from Sicily to Bohemia, and moves forward sixteen years, Shakespeare brings out aged time to facilitate temporal and spatial movement. The action of *The Winter's Tale*, adapted from Robert Greene's *Pandosto*, requires such leaps in story and scene, as well as the invocation of Bohemia's sea-coast, Shakespeare's infamous chorographic misappropriation. John Pitcher, third series editor of the Arden Shakespeare *Winter's Tale*, calls Time's role in the play reminiscent of pageants and street performances, "audiences at the Globe would have seen Shakespeare's Time as a kind of pageant figure, with his out-of-date manners and stale old story . . . " (81). But Shakespeare was adapting a theatrical tradition that was likely better known to his audiences, the Chorus or narrator regularly employed by playwrights adapting romance. "Time as a Chorus" had been used at least twice previous to Shakespeare, first in *Guy of Warwick*, the dramatization of a popular romance, and later in *Tom a Lincoln,* a play roughly contemporary to *The Winter's Tale.* The intervention of the Chorus in these plays is both instrumental, insofar as the stories required the mediation of narrative, but also marks an important innovation in stage romance.

What seems at first, then, like a device merely to serve the plot, the hand required to turn the hourglass, connects intertextually and dramaturgically to the geographic disruptions found in other plays derived from romance. The Chorus of *The Winter's Tale* commands his audience to view the expanding stage as a pliant creation of its imagination. The transference from Sicily to Bohemia happens through an appeal to the audience's imaginative powers, as does the passage of sixteen years. This geographic feat, like the famous imagined seacoast of land-locked Bohemia, is a product of what I will call the imaginative geography of stage romance, the genre's ability to render space and time as compliant to the mutual will of dramatist and audience. Florizel's fib to Leontes in Act Five that Perdita hails from Libya might just be a laugh line, as Pitcher claims, but within the London theatrical world, it is also a recognizable generic trope. Like Tom or Guy, who find themselves welcomed in the faraway Holy Land or Prester John's kingdom, the fantasy of *The Winter's Tale* projects its audience into exotic locations. These locations, too, are at the very points of economic and geographic interest and fascination: the Mediterranean and Eastern Trade routes. Even the Muscovite family from which Hermione traces her lineage signifies in Shakespeare's world a potential trading outpost, a land of economic possibility. Time, more than a device, is the structural expression of the stage romance's chief characteristic—the ability to move its audiences with ease into far away realms, to translate fantasies of abroad into enactment at home.

Conclusion: rationalizing romance

Adhering to the psychologically-ordered taxonomies handed down from the nineteenth century makes us lose sight of how dynamic and textured generic categories such as romance actually were in their time. The romance, in particular, with its alinear plots, capacious literary and cultural origins, and global geographic imaginings, was a genre that defied the neat developmental arrangement Dowden proposed. Before Dowden, Hegel had in fact rejected the romance as a metaphor for the development of history and Spirit on the very grounds that it failed to capture what he saw to be the rationality of that process.

> The facts within that history [of philosophy] are not adventures and contain no more romance than does the history of the world. They are not a mere collection of chance events, of expeditions of wandering knights, each going about fighting, struggling purposelessly, leaving no results to show for all his efforts. Nor is it so that one thing has been thought out here, another there, at will; in the activity of thinking mind there is real connection, and what there takes place is rational. It is with this belief in the spirit of the world that we must proceed to history . . . (226–7)

For Hegel, "romance," previously synonymous with "history" in the generic descriptions of the sixteenth and seventeenth centuries, becomes the antithesis of the teleological bent of his reformed historical narrative. We can recognize the Hegelian underpinnings of Dowden's criticism in his essay on "Elizabethan Romance." Writing on the *Arcadia*, Dowden says bluntly that the modern reader cannot access the mind that found pleasure in Sidney's romance. "If we find ourselves unable to perceive the grounds of its popularity [the *Arcadia*], this can only be because we are unable to enter into the mind of a former age; and to admit this is to acknowledge an incapacity for the historical criticism of literature" ("Elizabethan Romance," 353). Dowden's comment exposes the profound depths of his dismissal. Romance (before Shakespeare) belongs to a different epoch, "the mind of a former age," one that the reader of the nineteenth or twentieth centuries has eclipsed. No amount of "historical criticism" could recapture this literature, and even if we could, it is not clear to Dowden why we should desire such a return to this "dead literature of pleasure." Shakespeare had revivified it. For Dowden, the achievement of Shakespeare was in casting off the unskilled indeterminacies of the genre.[23] Thomas Lodge's *Rosalynde*, for instance, "does not live by virtue of any inherent vitality; it lives because it was once read by Shakespeare, and because he found in it material for the most charming of idyllic comedies" (352).

Perhaps the greatest irony of Dowden's adoption of "romance" for Shakespeare's final period is its contrariness to the kind of romance Hegel imagines above. Dowden, moreover, gives the genre primacy in his division of the periods. He had another telling name for Shakespeare's last period; Dowden called it "On the heights," the relatively short time in which his dramatic art had reached its greatest achievement (*Shakspere*, 48).[24]

Locating "romance" in the mind of the most singular artist, Shakespeare, allowed Dowden to endow the romance with a kind of critical stability, transforming the designation into something proper to a modern genre—one that could effectively connect Shakespeare to the present age.[25] He thus carried romance out of the realm of irrationality and merely "chance events" and gave it bearings, coherence, and even eminence. Dowden was able to convert the most un-Hegelian of genres, with its extravagance, contingency, and aimlessness, into Shakespearean Romance, a category entirely befitting the poet's rational mind.

The motivation behind the Shakespearean Romance was to demonstrate the poet's immanence to modernity, not his location within a dead dramatic tradition. Dowden's position served him well, as the term romance would shake off its deep associations with randomness by the twentieth century. Dowden channeled this idea of the romantic into Shakespeare, using it to bespeak a logical close to his career. In the process, he transformed the meaning of romance. The genre's "mellow" disposition, tied as it is to the idea of Shakespeare's waning career, covers over the more uneven and turbulent nature of the genre in its expression through the period. In the remaining chapters of the book, I will look to re-establish another set of principles by which we can understand the early romance, focusing on geography, history, dramatic strategies, and the more extensive cultural and literary history from which the genre grew. Rather than replace Dowden's "Shakespearean Romance," I hope that this account will situate his category in its proper history, one that is separate from the traditions of the early London stage.

2
"Asia of the one side, and Afric of the other": Sidney's Unities and the Staging of Romance

At a crucial moment in his *Defense of Poesy*, Philip Sidney summons a magical horse. He does so in response to the question: "How then shall we set forth a story which containeth both many places and many times?" Sidney offers: "Again, many things may be told which cannot be showed, if they know the difference betwixt reporting and representing. As, for example, I may speak (though I am here) of Peru, and in speech digress from that to the description of Calicut; but in action I cannot represent it without Pacolet's horse" (244).

Editors of Sidney's treatise have long noted that "Pacolet's horse" alludes to a figure from the French romance *Valentin et Orson*.[1] In the story (quoted here from Thomas Watson's sixteenth-century English translation), a dwarfish enchanter named Pacolet fashions a magical wooden horse that allows him to travel throughout the world: "Euery tyme that he mounted upon the horse for to goo somwhere, he torned the pynne [turned the pin] towarde the place that he wolde go to, and anone he founde him in the place without harme or daunger, for the hors was of suche facyon that he wente throughe the ayre more faster than ony burde coude flee . . . " (*Hystory* N4r). In the scene depicted in Figure 2.1 two characters are flying over a castle on the back of Pacolet's magic horse to the wonder of the onlookers below.

Sidney's invocation of this flying wooden horse comes on the heels of his complaint that the English stage is "faulty both in place and time": it disregards the unities associated with Aristotle. But his response also indicates the extent to which the world had changed since the time Sophocles wrote his tragedies, Terence his comedies, and Aristotle his *Poetics*. In a strange juxtaposition, Sidney brings the expanding world of global exploration, discovery, and commerce into conversation with neoclassical dramatic theory. The figure that he derisively suggests

Figure 2.1 Woodcut from *The Hystory of the two Valyaunte Brethren Valentyne and Orson*, London (nd), Sig. R4v (From the collection of the Beinecke Library, Yale University)

can bridge this gap, that can "represent" such fanciful globetrotting "in action," is Pacolet's horse. It is surprising, and clearly ironic, that Sidney, a theorist who rigorously defended classical drama and the stage's "excelling parts of poesy" (246), would mobilize a character closely linked to romance. Why, then, would he invoke romance in his discussion of the unities? And why is Sidney, the author of *The Arcadia*, so dismissive of romance on the stage?

This chapter connects Sidney's concern with dramatic unity in the *Defense* to the advent of stage romance. Its claim is that Sidney's call to preserve dramatic unity came as a direct response to the popularity of the stage romance, a genre whose influence I trace to the earliest years of the commercial theater in England. The ease with which Sidney dismisses the question of representing "many places and many times" belies both the practical and theoretical problems stage romances created. In translating the elements of romance narrative (travel to foreign lands, feats of magic, fanciful creatures), dramatists stretched the representational capacity of the stage. The stage romance was troubling for Sidney because of the violations in representation that the genre required. With Sidney's citation of "Peru and Calicut," we also see the extravagant geography of an expanding world affecting both the matter and the form of the stage. This geographic expansiveness, a defining characteristic of the genre, was prompted by the popular tastes that demanded the staging of romance. Sidney's call for dramatic unity, I will argue, ultimately proved hopeless against the mounting demand for plays that gave audiences representations of an expanded world.

The stage romance was a *problem* for Sidney: one that was exacerbated by the geographic expansiveness of the genre and prompted by the popular tastes that demanded its representation on the stage. By first situating Sidney's criticism in the context of the Italian theorists who influenced his arguments, I analyze how Sidney brought the unities into English dramatic discourse. I demonstrate that Sidney's call to preserve dramatic unity grew as a response to the early popularity of dramatic romance. This chapter establishes an alternative genealogy for the genre of "romance" in early modern drama: one that begins not with Shakespeare's mind, but with the group of plays from the sixteenth century that I call stage romances. While these early dramatic romances drew harsh critiques in England, calls for dramatic unity ultimately proved hopeless against the mounting demand for plays that gave audiences representations of an expanded world. I conclude this chapter with an analysis of Thomas Heywood's *Foure Prentises of London* and Thomas Dekker's *Old Fortunatus*, two plays that demonstrate stage romance's explicit resistance to neoclassical unity and show us the appeal that this genre had for its audiences.

"This play matter": the early stage romance

Despite its limited treatment of the subject, Sidney's *Defense* remains one of the most cited documents in early English theatrical history and theory.[2] One would be hard pressed to find a treatment of English Renaissance attitudes about genre, dramatic decorum, and unity that does not somehow allude to Sidney. But we also hold on to the notion that Sidney's condemnation of English drama was, as T. S. Eliot put it, among the "lost causes" of Elizabethan criticism.[3] So there remain gaps in our understanding of Sidney's dramatic criticism and particularly his concerns with unity and genre. While we remember his rejection of "mongrel tragi-comedy"[4] and commentary on the infelicity of mixing "hornpipes and funerals," we have lost sight of the relevance of the *Defense* to early modern dramatic culture in these now well-worn phrases of Sidney's treatise.[5]

We might take Sidney's citation of *Valentine and Orson* as a mere turn of his estimable wit: because of the popularity of this romance and numerous allusions in French, "Pacolet's horse" became "a proverbial equivalent for extraordinary speed" (Dickson 218). Only rarely have critics considered that Sidney was, in fact, a knowledgeable critic of his contemporary dramatic world. His passing reference to *Valentine and Orson*, a tremendously popular romance in the sixteenth century, gives us some glimpse of that engagement. Sidney's discourse on drama generally provides descriptions of specific plots, characters, and scenes. It is not surprising, then, that the records of early English stage performances show that Sidney's allusions should be taken quite literally: the story of *Valentine and Orson* was indeed adapted for performance several times before the close of the sixteenth century. The Stationers' Register shows that "An enterlude of Valentyne and Orsson, plaid by hir maiesties Players" was licensed to Thomas Gosson and Raffe Hancock in May 1595, and Henslowe records in his diary that he paid five pounds to Anthony Munday and Richard Hathawaye for "a Boocke called vallentyne & orsen," in 1598. Finally, in 1600, "A famous history called Valentine and Orsson played by her maiesties Players" was licensed to William White. Printed versions of these plays are lost and we have no record of their performance beyond these entries (Dickson 287–8).

The sixteenth-century performance history of the story of *Valentine and Orson* also dates to before the opening of the commercial theater in London. At coronation festivities in Cheapside for King Edward VI in 1547, an observer reported that: "Before the Entry of the aforesaid Conduit stood two Persons resembling Valentine and wild Urson, the one cloathed with Mosse and Ive Leaves, having in his Hand a great Clubb of Yew Tree for his Weapon, the other armed as a Knight, and they pronounced their Speeches" (Dickson 314). *Valentine and Orson* tells the story of two brothers separated at birth: Valentine, who is raised at court to be a nobleman and chivalrous knight, and Orson, who is snatched away by a wild animal and carried to the woods where he is raised by a bear. Later in the story, Valentine encounters his lost brother and civilizes him with kind and gentle discourse. They become fast friends, Orson is baptized, and the two spend their days battling the Saracens and pursuing knightly adventures. In the 1547 scene described above, the two actors seem to be representing the moment in the story when savage Orson, clothed in moss and ivy, clashes with the civilized

Valentine. Perhaps the "speeches" they "pronounced" showed how the urbane Valentine was able to lead his lost brother out of the wilderness. The record of this pageant suggests that *Valentine and Orson* was not merely a popular story, but one that, in the practices of sixteenth-century drama, lent itself to dramatic performance.

After Edward's coronation and throughout the century, this romance and others flourished both in print and in performance. Other examples of plays drawn from the annals of romance narrative filled the repertoires of English theater companies: stories taken from the cycles of Arthurian legend were typical (*The Life (and death) of Arthur, King of England, The Misfortunes of Arthur, Uter Pendragon*), as were plays that shared titles with other popular romances (*Guy, Earl of Warwick, Huon of Bordeaux,* and *Orlando Furioso*). Bibliographers of drama in the nineteenth and twentieth centuries compiled lists of these titles that have remained largely unrecognized. In the Appendix I have compiled a table that gives the titles and dates, when known, for these plays, as well as the origins of the stories. Many plays from the 1570s and 1580s were adapted directly from romance. Most of these early plays have been lost, but accounts from the Court's Revels office preserve the titles of twenty-seven plays that were most likely dramatic romances, including: *Cloridon and Radiamanta* (1572), *The Red Knight* (1576), *The Historie of the Solitarie Knight* (1577), *The Irisshe Knyght* (1577), and *The Knight of the Burning Rock*.[6] The last of these, according to records from the Office of the Revels, required the construction of an elaborate, three-dimensional stage "rock" and stage effects that included smoke, an elevating chair, and spirits rising from the stage.[7]

Was *Valentine and Orson* (and Sidney's magical horse) among these early plays performed for the court or the public? Although we have no record of a staged production before 1595, a document from the Revels Office suggests the possibility that *Valentine and Orson* was a part of the court's entertainments in the early 1580s. According to a list of payments made by the Office between 1581 and 1582, Elizabeth's court produced some "v [five] Playes twoe Maskes & one fightinge at Barriers with diuerse Devises" (Feuillerat Table II). Along with payments made to mercers, weavers, and other "artificers," the report includes wages paid to one John Rose for constructing "a Mount with a Castle vpon the toppe of it a Dragon & a Artificiall Tree" and "a artificiall Lyon & a horse made of wood." While we have no record of the plays these set pieces and stage properties were a part of, and a wooden horse could serve many purposes, the document gives some idea of the kinds of plays and performances that entertained the court audience.

Beyond these documents of early performances, we find responses to dramatic romance in other critics of the stage. Stephen Gosson and George Whetstone both specifically cite the stage romance in their critiques. In *Playes Confuted in Five Actions* (1583), Gosson complains that popular prose and verse romances, such as "the Aethiopian historie, Amadis of Fraunce, the Rounde table" have been "throughly ransackt, to furnish the Playe houses in London" (D5v). In a preface to his 1578 play *Promos and Cassandra*, George Whetstone describes characteristic English drama in terms similar to Sidney. He maintains that the English playwright of his day,

> is most vaine, indiscreete, and out of order: he fyrst groundes his worke, on impossibilities: then in three howers ronnes he throwe the worlde: marryes, gets Children, makes Children men, men to conquer kingdomes, murder Monsters, and bringeth Gods from Heauen, and fetcheth Diuels from Hel. (A2v)

Gosson offers some indication of narratives that fueled theatrical plots, while Whetstone serves as another neoclassically-minded writer who was, even before Sidney, discouraged by the lack of "order" in the English theater.

By the 1610s the dramatic romance had developed into one of the staple genres of the thriving commercial theater in England. When Thomas Heywood's *Foure Prentises of London, With the Conquest of Jerusalem*, popular on stage in the 1590s, first appeared in print in 1615, its author prefaced it with a revealing apology. "It comes short of that accuratenesse both in Plot and Stile that these more Censorious dayes with greater curiosity acquire [require], I must thus excuse. That as *Playes* were then some fifteene or sixteene yeares agoe it was in the fashion" (A2r–v). Although apologetic in his rhetoric, Heywood is also disdainful of his current "more Censorious" time, as might be indicated by his use of "curiosity." It can mean simply "care or attention to detail," but according to the OED the word also connotes "care or attention carried to an excess or unduly bestowed upon matters of inferior moment" (Def. I.4). In this sense of the word, a comment in William Cornwallis's 1600 essays is remarkably close to Heywood's passage above: "We of these latter times full of a nice curiosity, mislike the performances of our fore-fathers" (P6r). For Heywood, the playgoers of this later time are more concerned with verisimilitude or "accurateness" in "plot and stile" (they are more Sidneian) than those who first watched his play some years ago. A version of the *Foure Prentises* appeared on stage as early as

1594 when both Henslowe and the Stationers' Register document a play (now lost) featuring the central character in Heywood's *Foure Prentises*: "Godfrey of Bulloigne, with the Conquest of Jerusalem." *The Knight of the Burning Pestle* (1609), Francis Beaumont's send-up of *The Foure Prentises* (and other plays "in the fashion"), shows us that, although "short" of current dramatic standards, by 1615 the stage romance was well enough established as a theatrical genre to be the subject of rich parody. Furthermore, Heywood, Whetstone, and Gosson all allude to the indecorousness of these plays and their lack of unity, suggesting that these formal transgressions became a hallmark of the genre.

Likewise, Ben Jonson, perhaps one of the "Censorious" Heywood alludes to, wryly describes plays like the *Foure Prentises* in his *Magnetic Lady* (1632): "a child could be born, in a play, and grow up to a man i'the first scene, before he went off the stage: and then after to come forth a squire, and be made a knight: and that knight to travel between the Acts, and do wonders i'the Holy Land, or elsewhere; kill paynims [pagans], wild boars, dun cows, and other monsters" (Chorus I.15–21).[8] For Jonson, the English stage had progressed no further from the outrageous spectacles Sidney catalogued some fifty years before this play. And once again, Jonson's denunciation of the stage invokes the romance plot for the way that it violates classical representational boundaries. Not only does the plot of the romance require the play to ignore the unities, it also gives the playwright liberty to employ spectacular devices (animals, characters in foreign dress, "monsters") that distort the play's verisimilitude. Though these plays have remained obscure in the study and production history of English drama, they were popular or "fashionable" (to use Heywood's term) well into the seventeenth century, perhaps for the very reasons that Jonson and others found them so loathsome.

Two of the earliest stage romances that do still exist in print give us a picture of what other plays of this kind may have been like: *Clyomon and Clamydes* (1583) and *Common Conditions* (1576).[9] The anonymous *Historie of the two valiant Knights, Syr Clyomon . . . And Clamydes* was first published in 1599. The only other information about its first performances is also on the title page, which informs the reader that the play has "bene sundry times Acted by her Maiesties Players," suggesting a performance history that predated its publication.[10] The play is based on a fourteenth-century French romance, *Perceforest*, which itself derives from the Alexander cycle of medieval romance. The action of the play begins in Northern Europe when the wandering knight Clyomon (the prince of Denmark) dupes Clamydes (the prince of "Swavia") out of his title and inheritance. To avenge this dishonor, Clamydes challenges Clyomon to a duel at the court of Alexander. The two knights travel separately to the court in Macedonia, where they are to face off in the king's annual tournament. Along the way, various dangers waylay each knight: a conniving enchanter, a "Forrest of Marvels," "The Isle of Strange Marshes," and a deadly serpent. The stage performance of *Clyomon and Clamydes* thus would have translated to the stage all of the elements of romance narratives: errant knights, heroic battles, magical spectacles, strange lands and people, and an episodic plot.

The structuring device of the play's action is the journey to Alexander's court in Greece. The play emphasizes this motif of travel with the repetition of words such as "wandring" and "native" that highlight the sense of dislocation inherent to romance. In the play's opening lines, the weary Clamydes steps onto a new land from the ocean. The alliteration in the first line both draws attention to the character's dislocation and also harkens back to alliterative medieval versification, marking the play from the start as part of an older tradition:

> As to the wearie wandring wights, whom waltring waves environ
> No greater joy of joyes may be, then when from out the Ocean
> They may behold the Altitude of Billowes to abate,
> For to observe the Longitude of Seas in former rate:
> And having then the latitude of Sea-roome for to passe,
> Their joy is greater through the the griefe, then erst before it was. (1.1–6)

Clamydes' remarks on the joys of passing from sea to land in these opening lines ironically predict continual motion for the characters in the play between land and sea, stasis and travel. Stage directions tell us that both of the title characters are "booted," a sign that they are travelers and a visual cue to the audience that the scene of the play cannot be static. Alan Dessen and Leslie Thompson note that "to enter booted is to imply a recently completed journey or one about to be undertaken and by extension to suggest weariness or haste" (35). But this continual fluctuation of the romance plot also causes the characters to lament their waywardness. After being captured and imprisoned by the enchanter, Bryan Sance Foy, Clamydes laments, "Ah fatall hap, where am I wretch, in what distressed cace, / Bereft of Tyre, head and sheeld, not knowing in what place / My body is, ah heavenly gods, was ere such strangenes seene?" (10.872–4). Clamydes's complaint reminds us of the problem of enactment Sidney feared would plague drama that so frequently changes geographic scenes: "the player, when he cometh in, must ever begin on telling where he is, or else the tale will not be conceived." Members of the audience might find themselves asking similar questions about the staging of the play, "where am I," "was ere such strangenes seene?" (243).[11]

An earlier dramatic romance, *Common Conditions* (entered into the Stationers' Register in 1576), shares with *Clyomon and Clamydes* these frequent shifts in geography. The play portrays the fate of the nobleman Galiarbus, who with his two children has been banished from court by the king of Arabia. The three are separated in Arabia and travel to Phrygia and Thrace. The play opens with Galiarbus's daughter, Clarisa, his son, Sedmond, and their servant wandering in a wood, "forced . . . to trace from native soil" (296).[12] While in the woods, the sister and brother are separated and Sedmond, Galiarbus's son, declares: "For now I will betake myself, a wandering knight to be, / Into some strange and foreign land, their comely guise to see" (476–7). In the previous scene, the lost Clarisa and her trickster servant, the eponymous Conditions, had decided to leave Arabia, as well: "For seeing wee are so ny the sea that wee may pas in one day / Cleane ouer the sea to Phrygia" (440–1). Years before Shakespeare's *Pericles*, a play that also covers the geography of the eastern Mediterranean and Aegean Sea, the play's scenes move from land to sea and from country to country, touching Arabia, Thrace, and Phrygia. Even from this brief discussion, we can see that Gosson could have had plays such as *Clyomon and Clamydes* and *Common Conditions* in mind when he wrote "Sometime you shall see nothing but the aduentures of an amorous knight, passing from countrie to countrie for the loue of his lady, encotring many a terible monster made of broune paper . . . " to which he adds "What learne you by that?" (*Playes Confuted in Fiue Actions*, C6r).

In the context of the dramatic tradition I have outlined here, Sidney's objections to the stage deserve new consideration.[13] Although moral apprehensions stoke Gosson's rejection of stage spectacle, Sidney's worries are ostensibly artistic or formal. And unlike Gosson, who is skeptical that any good can come from the English stage, Sidney holds drama in high regard. A central premise of the *Defense* is that poetry (in all of its forms) is superior to historiography or philosophy in teaching virtue. On this count, Sidney even admits that the romance *Amadis of Gaul*, though it "wanteth much of a perfect poesy" (227), may teach something to the right audience. Why, then, did Sidney believe these dramatic adaptations of romance to be so deficient? We know from the records of performances from the period that Sidney faced new genres that did not adhere to the classical doctrine of Aristotle, but also a public that wanted to see plays, like *Common Conditions* or, later, *The Foure Prentises of London*, that translated "Asia and Affric" into their plots. In turning to romance, the theater capitalized on precisely those features of English drama that Sidney saw as faulty: lack of unity, mixing of genres, representation of outlandish events and "gross absurdities."

"Very defectuous in the circumstances": Sidney's unities

Embedded in Sidney's discourse is an implicit definition of stage romance as it relates to the classical tradition. The first of Sidney's three objections to the English stage is that it does not follow the model for dramatic practice laid down by Aristotle in the *Poetics*.[14] As a result, Sidney writes, plays of his time produce "gross absurdities" (244). He contends "Our Tragedies and Comedies" observe "rules neither of honest civility nor skilful poetry" (243). So, while Sidney admires Thomas Sackville and Thomas Norton's *Gorboduc* (1561) for "climbing to the height of Seneca's style" and being "full of noble morality," he also calls it "in truth very defectuous in the circumstances . . . For it is faulty both in place and time, the two necessary companions of all corporal actions," and therefore it "might not remain as an exact model of all tragedies" (243). Sidney elaborates on the appropriate "circumstances" for drama by turning to Aristotle: "For where the stage should always represent but one place, and the uttermost time presupposed in it should be, both by Aristotle's precept and common reason, but one day, there is [in *Gorboduc*] both many days, and many places, inartificially imagined" (243).[15]

Sidney's annoyance with plays that are "inartificially imagined," conceived without skill or art, recalls both Aristotle and Horace, who believed the poet should artfully construct the plot to meet the demands of the form, not piece the story together incrementally or episodically. Episodic plots, Aristotle says flatly, "are composed by bad poets on their own accounts" (Gilbert 82). The notion that poetry should be unified originates, of course, with Aristotle, who said in the *Poetics* that poetry in all its forms should provide "one imitation of one thing." In this comment, Aristotle is specifically addressing plot, which he says "being an imitation of an action, should be concerned with one thing and that a whole, and that the parts of the action should be so put together that if one part is shifted or taken away the whole is deranged and disjoined" (Gilbert 81). Aristotle's commentary on the unity of plot or action (in chapter eight of the *Poetics*) laid the foundation for later theorists to deduce the tripartite rules of unity (action, place, and time). Horace echoes Aristotle in *The Art of Poetry* when he writes that the skilled poet does not begin "the

Trojan war from the twin eggs [*ab ovo*]: he ever hurries to the crisis and carries the listener into the midst of the story as though it were already known; what he despairs of illuminating with his touch he omits; and so employs fiction, so blends false with true, that beginning, middle, and end all strike the same note" (Gilbert 132–3). In both Aristotle and Horace, we see that the labor of the poet involves arranging and compressing, as necessary, the story so as to avoid the disfigurement of plot that Aristotle fears. Sidney therefore criticizes playwrights who do not know that "tragedy is tied to the laws of poesy, not history; not bound to follow the story, but having liberty either to feign a quite new matter or to frame the history to the most tragical conveniency" (244). Playwrights who reject the laws of poetry are, in Sidney's judgment, closer to the historian who slavishly ties himself to the chronicling of history than to the poet who works imaginatively.

Sidney's argument, however, is not grounded entirely on an appeal to the authority of the ancients. He is equally troubled that the "defectuous circumstances" in these plays, their violations of time and place, cannot accommodate "corporal actions" and therefore confound the senses of the audience. For Sidney, the movements of the actors' bodies must coincide with what the audience experiences. The act of translating plot into physical representation thus requires that time and space be limited. In Sidney's account, this is rarely the case with English drama, in which even "common reason" reveals gross shortcomings. His satirical rendering of a stage plot highlights, for him, the deficiency of typical English dramatic plots: "for ordinary it is that two young princes fall in love; after many traverses, she is got with child, delivered of a fair boy; he is lost, groweth a man, falls in love, and is ready to get another child; and all this in two hours' space: which, how absurd it is in sense, even sense may imagine, and art hath taught, and all ancient examples justified" (243). Sidney wittily intends both dominant meanings of "sense": the physical senses ("how absurd it is in sense") and cognitive ("even sense may imagine"). As he does throughout this section on drama, Sidney reminds the reader that drama is an enacted form, and in order for it to be properly mimetic, it must attend to "corporal actions" in ways that other forms of poetry do not. One can see the problems with English drama on this count when he broadens his indictment to include plays beyond *Gorboduc*, this time detailing violations in representing "place": "But if it be so in *Gorboduc*, how much more in all the rest, where you shall have Asia of the one side, and Afric of the other, and so many other under kingdoms, that the player, when he cometh in, must ever begin with telling where he is, or else the tale will not be conceived?" (243).

He goes on to describe once again the kinds of dramatic spectacle one might see on the English stage: in the same play the stage will stand for "a garden," a rock for a shipwreck, a cave from which a "hideous monster with fire and smoke" emerges, and finally, a battlefield on which "two armies fly in, represented with four swords and bucklers" (243). Such action violates the stricture that the stage should "but represent one place," but it also taxes the viewer's credulity when "four swords and bucklers" must stand synecdochically for "two armies." With this, Sidney concludes his *argumentum ad absurdum* against drama by emphasizing the discrepancy between the signifying performance and the signified reality. As playwrights attempt more ambitious representations, the "corporal actions" of the actors fall increasingly short of rendering them on stage.

Sidney's concern that the audience's "senses" not be offended by implausible representations in dramatic action recalls the Italian critics to whom he no doubt turned (and sometimes cites) in formulating his arguments.[16] In his 1571 translation and commentary on the *Poetics*, Lodovico Castelvetro elaborates on Aristotle's differentiation between epic and drama to develop his own neo-Aristotelian theory of unity. Aristotle drew a bold line between the proper representative capacities of drama and narrative. He regarded epic as the genre for telling stories (unified around one heroic figure) that unfurled over large expanses of time and territory. In contrast, tragedy and comedy, because of the restraints inherent in peformance, could not represent actions concurrently. In the *Poetics*, Aristotle had laid the broad parameters for these generic distinctions: "the epic has a capacity wholly peculiar to itself," Aristotle contends "because the nature of tragedy does not admit of the imitation of many parts of an action that occur at the same time, but only of the one part imitated on the stage by the actors" (Gilbert 105). Conversely, the epic can incorporate events that occur simultaneously, "weaving . . . dissimilar episodes into the action" a characteristic that Aristotle says gives epic "magnificence of effect" (Gilbert 105).

Because it is a form not bound to the strictures of enactment, epic (for Aristotle the most noble narrative form) is the proper genre for telling episodic stories that unfold across "many places and many times." By "nature" tragedy cannot engage in the same kind of imitation. For Aristotle this is one great shortcoming of tragedy: it lacks variety, "for uniformity quickly satiates an audience and makes tragedies fail on the stage" (Gilbert 105). Castelvetro differentiates between the properties of drama and narrative:

> It is further different in that the dramatic is less ample, in respect to places, than the narrative, for the dramatic method cannot represent

places very far apart, while the narrative method joins together places that are widely separated. It is also different in that the dramatic method is less ample with respect to time, for the narrative method joins together diverse times, something the dramatic method cannot do. (Gilbert 309)

Like Sidney, Castelvetro is concerned to distinguish between narrative and "dramatic method." Castelvetro's emphasis on "method" is important—*how* should one tell a story that encompasses many places and times? Throughout his commentary, Castelvetro reiterates what is, for him, the stark contrast between the narrative and dramatic method: "the narrative is able to relate in a few hours many things that happened in many hours, and to relate in many hours a few things that happened in a few hours. But the dramatic method, which spends as many hours in representing things as was taken by the actions themselves, is able to do none of these things" (310). Castelvetro concludes that drama should achieve its power through unified representation of action, "thence it comes about that tragedy and comedy . . . cannot last longer than the time allowed by the convenience of the audience, nor represent more things than those which came about in the space of time that the comedies and the tragedies themselves require" (Gilbert 310). Castelvetro anticipates Sidney's emphasis on the role of the audience's "senses." It is simply "not possible," Castelvetro contends, "to make the audience suppose that several days and nights have passed when they have the evidence of their senses that only a few hours have gone by" (310). Similarly, J. C. Scaliger wrote in 1561, "Since the whole play is represented on the stage in six or eight hours, it is not in accordance with the exact appearance of truth that within that brief space of time a tempest should arise and a shipwreck occur, out of sight of land" (Qtd. in Spingarn 96). Such drama lacks "the exact appearance of truth" and like Sidney, for whom both "sense" (physical and mental) and classical authority dictate the rules of dramatic unity, Scaliger worries that the audience's belief will be pressed beyond its limits by the physical impossibilities of drama that represents action over "many places and many times." The physical limitations that govern the body in dramatic space simply do not allow for these sorts of stories and representations.

Sidney thus reflects the arguments of Castelvetro and the other Italian neoclassicists when he suggests that the dramatist adopt the classical dramatic convention of the reporter, or *"Nuntius,"* whom he says the playwright should use to report action that cannot be acted on stage (244). Castelvetro also says that the dramatist can range beyond the boundaries of the play's action through the use of a messenger. But Castelvetro admits that even this practice is not entirely suitable to drama, "because when a messenger or a prophet is introduced, one passes into the field of the epic, and into the narrative method" (Gilbert 355). Castelvetro reminds us of the fundamental generic distinction between drama and narrative in ancient theory. When Sidney later comments on the mixing of tragedy and comedy, he alludes to what must have been a much less radical mixing of genres. The greatest concern Sidney had with romance's infiltration of dramatic genre, I contend, was its breakdown of the distinction between "reporting" and "representing."

"Asia of the one side, and Afric of the other": the extravagance of stage romance

An interesting counterpart to Sidney's *Defense* is the preface to John Lyly's 1592 play *Midas*. In it, Lyly apologizes for the mixedness of his play and English drama as a whole:

> Trafficke and trauell hath wouen the nature of all Nations into ours, and made this land like Arras, full of deuise, which was Broade-cloth, full of workemanshippe. Time hath confounded our mindes, our mindes the matter, but all commeth to this passe, that what heretofore hath beene serued in seuerall dishes for a feaste, is now minced in a charger for a Gallimaufrey. If wee present a mingle-mangle, our fault is to be excused, because the whole worlde is become an Hodgepodge. (A2r–v)

The metaphors Lyly uses here are strong: England has become like a rich but exotic tapestry fabricated from all the nations of the world. According to the OED, arras cloth often depicted "figures and scenes" (Def. 1.). That is, like a play or painting, they were representational. Lyly contrasts the "device" of the tapestry with the "workmanshippe" of broadcloth (according to the OED, a "plain-wove" black cloth). The metaphors here contrast the foreign (arras derives its name from a town in Artois) with the domestic, the exotic with the plain. Equally relevant to this discussion, these are also metaphors of unity with variety. Arras is unlike monochrome broad cloth because it contains designs and often images. Arras requires "device," a complicated conceit, while broadcloth is simple. He also picks up this contrast of unity and variety with his food metaphors. What Lyly calls a "feast" is a meal served in separate dishes, recalling perhaps the Aristotelian demand that the parts of poetry work together and complement one another, that they should not be mashed together in a "Hodge-podge." What is most remarkable about this apology is that Lyly attributes the changes in dramatic form to the advent of "traffic" (commerce) and travel. The opening of England's borders to the rest of the world, it seems, necessitates fundamental changes to dramatic practice. While Lyly asks his reader to excuse these flaws, he also seems to accept them as part of the reality of both his contemporary theatrical culture and the expanding horizons of England.

Like Lyly, Sidney responded to the dramatic practice of his time when he urged a stricter adaptation of dramatic rules. Though derived from Aristotle's ancient poetics, the theory of unity was as much a product of the sixteenth century as it was of the ancient world. A proliferation of new genres, especially the romance, and a corresponding liberty in the technique, mode, and style of drama and narrative inspired Sidney and Lyly to champion a more conservative poetics. Lyly further contextualizes for us Sidney's allusions to the exotic geographies of Africa, Asia, Peru, and Calicut (a city in the South Indian kingdom of Vijaynagar, one of the sixteenth century's great centers of trade). These geographic allusions point to the desire among playwrights and poets in the period to turn to romance as a means of "representing" the "many places and many times" of an expanding world—to align dramatic practice with the historical changes of which they (and their audiences) were becoming increasingly aware.

Sidney's allusion to romance in this discussion of dramatic unity merits further inquiry for its geographic emphasis: "As, for example, I may speak (though I am here) of Peru, and in speech digress from that to the description of Calicut, but in action I cannot represent it without Pacolet's horse" (244). At one level, Calicut and Peru simply represent to Sidney and his reader opposite ends of the map: the most remote eastern and western geographic points that one can conjure. Both places were familiar to Europeans by the late sixteenth century. In *A Treatyse of the Newe India* (1553), Richard Eden includes an extensive description of Calicut, a city he introduces with the heading "the most famous market towne of India" (16). Eden's descriptions highlight the region's bountiful and exotic commodities. Eden also describes Peru in his 1555 translation of Peter Martyr's *Decades of the Newe World* as the "rychest lande in golde, syluer, perles, precious stones, and spyces, that euer was founde yet to this day" (343).[17] What is remarkable about Sidney's invocation of Peru and Calicut is their very specificity. Sidney chose two geographic areas that, though they had only recently entered into European awareness, had already become important sources of trade, income (particularly for the Spanish and Portuguese), and fiction.

The reference to Pacolet's horse is important because, like many creatures and devices in romances, it presents its reader with a fantasy of unproblematic global travel.[18] According to the story, Pacolet was "full of greate wytte and understondynge, the which at the scole of telletee [Toledo] had lerned so muche of the arte of Nygromancye that above al other he was perfyte" (*Hystory* N4r). Pacolet uses his knowledge of magic to build his horse "by enchauntemente." The description of the horse also notes that "in the heade there was artyfycyelly a pynne that was in suche wyse set, that euery tyme that he mounted upon the horse for to goo somwhere, he torned the pynne towarde the place that he wolde go to, and anone he founde him in the place without harme or daunger" (*Hystory* N4r). Pacolet's horse is contrasted throughout the story to more conventional means of travel, particularly ships (which are featured in several woodcuts in the English edition). Rather than the weeks or months it would take a voyager by land or sea to reach his destination, the horse provides a fantasy of almost instant transport to exotic realms. The magical flying creature, in an era of expanding global exploration and commerce, is the fantastical version of the many merchant ships that reached out to the corners of the world. The "artyfycyelly" placed "pynne" in the horse's head, which the narrator mentions each time a character mounts the horse for a journey, suggests the compass's needle or pin, making the connection between the wooden horse and sea travel even more apparent. Sidney seems keenly aware of this connection, as Pacolet's horse for him bridges the seemingly unimaginable gap between Peru and Calicut.

"Your thoughts to help poore Art": Heywood, Dekker, and the problem of romance

In its adaptation of romance, the theater engaged a genre with a long critical history on the continent. During the sixteenth century, debates in Italy raged over the question of whether romance was a form known to the ancients or a modern innovation. There is a strong connection, for instance, between the language that Castelvetro uses in discussing dramatic unity and the discourse on generic difference between epic and romance in earlier Italian criticism on romance. In *L'Arte Poetica* (1564) Antonio Minturno denies romance a place among the ancient genres because of its lack of unity. He describes the difference between epic (which he classifies more generally under the title "heroic poem") and romance:

> The heroic poem ... sets out to imitate a memorable action carried to its conclusion by one illustrious person. The romance ... has its object in a crowd of knights and ladies and of affairs of war and peace ... he is to treat as many deeds by him and by the others as he thinks sufficient for the glory of those he is disposed to praise ... and he takes for description diverse and contrasted lands and the various things that happened in them during all the time occupied by the fabulous story of the matter he sets out to sing. (Gilbert 278)

The important differentiating characteristic of romance for Minturno is that it presents a variety of events, characters, and actions. Rather than follow the Aristotelian mandate that poetry be "one imitation of one thing," romances, according to Minturno, "bind together many things in one bundle," and because of its diversity in plot and matter, the romance strays from the classical examples set by Homer and Virgil (Gilbert 278). Minturno and, one might argue, Castelvetro, are responding to the praise that Italian writers such as Giovambattista Giraldi Cinthio gave to the famous Italian romances of the fifteenth and sixteenth centuries (particularly Boiardo's *Orlando Innamorato* and Ariosto's *Orlando Furioso*). In *On the Composition of Romances* (1549), Giraldi argues that it is the variety inherent in romance narratives that gives them their appeal: "diversity of actions carries with it the variety that is the spice of delight and so allows the writer a large field to use episodes, that is, pleasing digressions" (23). Unlike Minturno, who chastens romance writers for their disinterest in unified action, Giraldi commends the romances because they are compositions native to his contemporary world. Giraldi further contends that the modern Italian poet should not be held to the standards of Aristotle:

> Indeed these works [the romances] are not to be put at all under such laws and rules, but ought to be left with the boundaries set by those who among us have given authority and reputation to this form of poetry. Just as the Greeks and Latins have drawn the art of their writing from their poets, so we also ought to draw from our poets and hold ourselves to that form which the better poets of the romances have given us. (Gilbert 40–1)

Giraldi's claim stands in stark contrast to Minturno, Castelvetro, and Sidney, as he valorizes contemporary poetic practice and calls others to "hold ourselves to that form" rather than reject the romance. He instead asserts the value of romance as a peculiarly modern form.

The tradition of Italian theory illustrates the problematic status of romance inherited by Sidney. In their different ways, Giraldi, Castelvetro, and others register, just as Sidney does, the loosening categories of genre that characterize the sixteenth century. But for Sidney, the problems with romance are furthered by their adaptation into drama. As the two plays to which I now turn, Thomas Heywood's *Foure Prentises of London* and Thomas Dekker's *Old Fortunuatus* will demonstrate, Sidney's call to follow the rules of "honest civility and skillful poetry" were explicitly ignored by dramatists who turned to the genre best suited to incorporate stories of travel, trade, and experiences beyond the borders of the ancient world. Indeed, the brash challenge these plays raise to the dictates of Sidney (and neoclassical theory) was integral to the formulation of a stage romance.

Thomas Heywood's *Foure Prentises* boldly embraces the inherent disunity and "gross absurdities" of the romance plot. Heywood's *Foure Prentises* adapts its story from the First Crusade and thus takes the structure of a quest narrative. The play portrays four noble French brothers who have been banished to England where they must take up apprenticeships with four of the major city trades (grocers, goldsmiths, mercers and haberdashers). But their toils do not last long as the four take up arms and travel through Europe to defeat the Saracen and Persian guardians of Jerusalem. It is a story at once deeply rooted in medieval chivalric romance and in popular English drama of the late sixteenth century, when plays with Turks, Persians, Moors, and other exotic foreigners were common.[19] The play takes up many of the characteristic elements of other dramatic romances from the period. Early in the play, a shipwreck scatters the brothers (and their sister) across various areas in Europe (Ireland, France, and Italy). The prologue to *The Foure Prentises* gives us some insight to the particular appeal that stage romances had to their audiences. In it, Heywood brings out not a single speaker, the convention for dramatic prologues, but three separate actors "in blacke clokes, at three doores": one to excuse "the name of the play," one the "errours in the Play," and the last "the Author that made the play" (A4r). The prologue, as I will explore more carefully was an important dramatic strategy employed in stage romance. Heywood's turn to three prologues, though, is unconventional even for stage romance. The first speaker playfully marks the "superfluity" of the *Foure Prentises*: "O superfluous, and more then I ever heard of! three Prologues to one play!" While the prologues advertise that they will offer the typical apologies of the play (for the author, the errors, the title, etc.) what they offer instead is a bold justification of the play's excesses:

> *Prologue 1*: . . . Now what haue you to speake concerning the errours in the Play?
> *Prologue 2*: We acknowledge none . . . but if these cleere-sighted Gentlemen, with the eyes of their iudgements, looking exactly into vs, find any imperfections which are hid from our selues, our request is, you would rather looke ouer them, then through them, not with a troubled eye, that makes one obiect to seeme two, but with a fauourable eye, which hath power in it selfe to make many to seeme none at all. (A4v)

What is striking about this passage in the prologue is its attention to the language of unity and multiplicity. The play that follows, the prologue proclaims, may be filled with imperfections, but the audience has in it the power to bring the various strands of the plot together into a coherent story. The audience is also asked to "see" the places the play stages: "Had not yee rather, for nouelties sake, see *Ierusalem* yee neuer saw, then *London* that yee see howerly?" (A4v). The closing lines of this prologue thus reaffirm the viewer's power over the representation of the play: "Our Author submits his labours to you, as the authors of all the content he hath within this circumference" (A4v).

This act of giving over power to the audience, rhetorical though it may be, marks a shift away from Sidney, who wondered how an audience could possibly favor a dramatic spectacle that put such a burden on them. In another context of the *Defense*, Sidney says that it is incorrect to assume a credulous audience. The poet, Sidney writes (in a wonderful anticipation of Shakespeare's Prospero), "never maketh any circles about your imagination, to conjure you to believe for true what he writes" (235). Sidney is skeptical that an audience can be lured so deep into the dramatic spectacle that they believe they are transported to another place. "What child is there," Sidney ponders, "that, coming to a play, and seeing *Thebes* written in great letters upon an old door, doth believe that it is Thebes?" (235). But as we will see later in *Old Fortunatus* (and also in Shakespeare's *Henry V*, as I argue in Chapter 4), stage romances often do "conjure" the audience to assist in making the stage into another place. For Sidney, such drama violates the rules of mimesis, but also the common sense of its audience. But the invocation of the audience here and elsewhere is rhetorically empowering—Heywood's chorus does not ask his audience to "believe" the illusion, he invites them to be "authors" in creating the variety in plot and geography that the play calls for.

Indeed, it is notable that part of Beaumont's parody in *The Knight of the Burning Pestle* relies on the Citizen and his Wife dictating the terms of the plot and location of the play to the performers on the stage:

> WIFE: George let Rafe travel over great hills, and let him be very weary, and come to the King of Cracovia's house, covered with black velvet, and there let the king's daughter stand in her window all in beaten gold, combing her golden locks with a comb of ivory, and let her spy Rafe, and fall in love with him, and come down to him, and carry him into her father's house, and then let Rafe talk with her.
> CITIZEN: Well said, Nell, it shall be so.—Boy, let's ha't done quickly.
> BOY: Sir, if you will imagine all this to be done already, you shall hear them talk together. (4.33–42)

The Citizen and his wife get their knowledge of these kinds of productions from stories such as "Sir Dagonet" (4.48) and, of course, *The Foure Prentises of London*. In Beaumont's revealing parody, their knowledge of these and other narrative and dramatic romances alluded to throughout the play shape their expectations of what stories the stage should adapt. Additionally, in this scene and elsewhere, they have particular ideas of how those plays should be performed, enacted, staged, all the way down to the details of the kind of stage props the play needs, from a house covered in "black velvet" to a "comb of ivory."

Beaumont's parody also integrates the comic potential of a narrative and fictional source, a romance, being enacted on the stage. After crossing over into the play within a play, Rafe first enters, as the stage direction tells us, reading from a book: *Palmerin of England*, a sequel to the popular sixteenth-century *Palmerin* romances. While Rafe's attempts to write, or perform, his way into that story draw laughter from the audience, other plays in the tradition of stage romance cite their origins as books with less irony. *Old Fortunatus*, Thomas Dekker's late sixteenth-century play, opens with the title character lost in the woods, a typical romance predicament, and from the outset, Dekker's play refers to its status as a romance tale. Fortunatus jokes, "Shortly there will creepe out in print some filthie booke of the olde hoarie wandring Knight, meaning me: would I were that booke, for then I should be sure to creepe out from hence" (1.1.35–7). In this opening scene, the viewer is dually reminded of the play's continuity with the romance tradition: both the play's location in the forest and Fortunatus's self-definition as a romance "wandring Knight" serve to locate it in this dramatic tradition. Dekker also plays on the story's connection to the narrative romance tradition in calling attention to the play's origins as a "booke." Later in the play, after Fortunatus dies, his sons discover that their father has, indeed, left them a book that records his travels. One son will "sit and read what storie my father has written here" (2.2.327–8) and later, the other promises a "new Addition" to his father's story: "Ile treade after my Fathers steps; ile goe measure the world" (2.2.368–71). These two moments in the play present a tension between the story as "history" or narrative and its roots as enactment. But unlike Sidney, who thought one couldn't have it both ways, Dekker wryly references the play as narrative. It is not merely that the play is drawn from narrative or that it is citing its source; the play enacts that which the neo-Aristotelians claimed inartistic, or, to use Sidney's word, "inartificial": crafting a narrative history into dramatic enactment. Fortunatus climbs out of an old book and onto the stage.

As I have already suggested, the "Trafficke and trauail" of the English had a transformative effect on stage representation. The representational capacity of the stage and the pressures that romance put on that capacity find compelling expression in *Old Fortunatus*. In the prologue, the play establishes an association between geographic space and representational space:

> And for this smal Circumference must stand,
> For the imagind Sur-face of much land,
> Of many kingdomes, and since many a mile,
> Should here be measurd out: our muse intreats,
> Your thoughts to helpe poore Art, and to allow,
> That I may serue as Chorus to her scenes (Prologue 14–19)

Dekker's prologue asks the viewer to visualize the space of the stage as a kind of map, onto which he can project "many kingdomes." Likewise, Dekker prioritizes the viewer's involvement in creating the world of the play, "Your gracious eye, Giues life to *Fortunatus* historie" (23–4). The combination of narrative and dramatic enactment that romance demands, far from damaging the production (as Sidney would have it) "gives life" to the story of Fortunatus or Godfrey and his brothers.

And thus, in the same prologue, Dekker sees fit to flout the specific dictates of dramatic poetry laid out by Sidney. The muse of the play, the prologue tells the viewer, "begs your pardon, for sheele send me foorth, / Not when the lawes of Poesy doe call, / But as the storie needes" (20–2). By utilizing the classical device of the dramatic chorus, Dekker seems to be putting himself in the theatrical tradition that Sidney calls on the English theater to adopt. But this shift from "the lawes of poesy" (identical to Sidney's phrase) to "as the storie needes" signals an important departure from the way that Sidney and other neoclassical writers imagined the chorus to function. During the course of the play, the chorus will not merely narrate those moments that defy representation, as Sidney would have it. Rather, the Chorus serves the "storie." By announcing this, Dekker directly refutes Sidney's dictate that the dramatist is beholden to the "laws of poesy" and therefore "not bound to follow the story" (244). Further, the Chorus positions the "small circumference" of the stage and its actors as only a part of the action—it calls on the audience to complete its illusion ("your thoughts to helpe poore art"), specifically the many geographic shifts that the play requires. In Dekker's play, the action does indeed demand frequent intervention from the Chorus: characters travel from Turkey to Babylon, from Cyprus to England. Thus, Dekker overtly moves away from the neoclassical tradition of the unities in creating a story about the vagaries of global travel and commerce.

The German romance *Fortunatus* is precisely the kind of narrative that Sidney and others would have objected to converting into a stage production. If the playwright were to remain close to the original story, he could not dramatize it without spectacular violations of dramatic unity. Dekker's source for *Old Fortunatus* was an anonymous German romance taken from the same *Volksbuch* tradition as Marlowe's *Doctor Faustus*. The 1509 Augsburg edition of the German *Fortunatus* includes several woodcut illustrations, including one that depicts Fortunatus's son flying through the air past the battlements of a castle with the aid of a magic "wishing cap." After its first publication in 1509, *Fortunatus* was reprinted at least thirty times and in nine languages by the end of the sixteenth century, and several more times (including three English translations) in the seventeenth century. The story begins with the Cypriotic burgher Fortunatus experiencing hard times after falling into debt. Destitute, he encounters the goddess Fortune, who offers him a choice of gifts: "Reichtumb [riches], Stercke [strength] Gesundthait [health], und Schöne [beauty]." Fortunatus chooses riches, and Fortune grants him a magic purse that produces infinite stores of gold. Fortunatus takes the purse and travels the world, lavishing gifts on the courts of emperors and kings from India to England. In his travels, he dupes the Sultan of Alexandria into giving him a magic felt hat that, like Pacolet's wooden horse, allows its wearer to travel anywhere with a mere command. After returning home with the "wishing cap," Fortunatus dies and leaves his hat and purse to his two sons, Ampedo and Andelocia. The final part of the story narrates the sons' adventures in the court of England, the destruction of Fortune's gifts, and the sons' deaths.

As early as 1596, a play called *Fortunatus* appeared in London's playhouses.[20] In 1599, Henslowe commissioned Thomas Dekker to write a new version of the play for performance at court. The title page of *The Pleasant Comedie of Old Fortunatus* (1600) advertises that it was "plaied before the Queenes Maiestie this Christmas."[21] Dekker picks up the German narrative at Fortunatus's lowliest moment: lost in the woods and starving. Fortunatus chooses Fortune's gift of endless wealth, and the play shows him in his travels through the world.

The moral of the play is succinctly drawn up in the final scene, with Virtue proclaiming: "England shall ne're be poore, if England striue, / Rather by vertue, then by wealth to thriue" (5.2.259–60). Following a drama that presents its audience with a fantasy of global travel and commerce, one in which Fortunatus and his sons deck themselves with the worldly trappings of exotic foreign goods (tobacco, gold, silks, spices, fine clothing), the exchanges between Virtue and Vice / Fortune clearly allegorize debates about the propriety and morality of overseas commerce, trade, and expansion. Dekker's *Old Fortunatus* does not fit the pattern of any one genre. The play is advertised in the 1600 edition as a "pleasant comedie," a term we might best understand broadly as meaning simply "play."[22] In fact, the play incorporates generic elements from masque, Marlovian tragedy, fable, and romance. The play has two levels of action: a comic masque sub-plot of Virtue and Vice and the main romance plot involving the adventures of Fortunatus and his sons. Like Marlowe's *Doctor Faustus*, *Old Fortunatus* is a fable with a clear-cut moral: Fortunatus, given the choice between wisdom and riches (allegorized in the play in the characters of Virtue and Vice) selects riches, a choice that leads him and his sons to perdition. While the structure of the play is true to its medieval origins, the play provides its own contemporary concerns and perspectives on the development of global trade. The romance elements of the play (the magical purse and wishing cap, digressive travels around the world, amorous competition, and the main characters' chivalric aspirations) stand in contrast to the Virtue and Vice morality play. Nonetheless, the play's presentations of unencumbered travel and the commercial fantasies bound up in Fortunatus's magical purse outweigh the expected harsh moral judgments of Virtue.

Fortunatus and his sons force the stage to encompass "Asia" and "Affric," to use Sidney's phrase. After receiving the purse, Fortunatus proclaims: "Ile trauell to the Turkish Emperour: / And then ile reuell it with Prester Iohn, / Or banquet with great Cham of Tartarie, / And trie what frolicke Court the Souldan keepes" (1.2.197–9). And when Fortunatus steals the Sultan's wishing cap, he brags, "Your father hath the whole world in this compass, I am all felicitie, vp to the brimmes. In a minute am I come from Babylon, I haue beene this halfe howre in Famagosta [in Cyprus]" (2.2.123–5). The Chorus seems aware of the disorientation the audience might experience as a result of these shifts in geography, and act two opens with an account of Fortunatus's wanderings:

> Your quicke imaginations we must charme,
> To turne that world: and (turn'd) againe to part it
> Into large kingdomes, and within one moment,
> To carrie Fortunatus on the wings
> Of actiue thought, many a thousand miles. (2.1.5–9)

The Chorus asks the audience to imagine that "you haue saild with him vpon the seas, / And leapt with him vpon the Asian shores" (11–12), that it has "feasted with him in the Tartars palace, And all the Courts of each Barbarian king." Dekker's choice of words is again strikingly close to Sidney, who denied that playwrights "maketh any circles about your imagination." Here, the Chorus hopes to "charme" the audience's "quicke imaginations." It is in these moments that the play's moralizing force begins to fracture. The members of the audience are supposed to imagine themselves moving alongside Fortunatus in his travels and reveling in the excesses of his adventures, but are also, by the end of the play, expected to acknowledge and decry the characters' errant ways.

In addition to Fortunatus' travels, the play continually cites the exotic newly discovered places in the world. Fortunatus calls his purse, "a leather mint, admirable: an Indian mine in a Lambs skinne, miraculous" (333–5). Later, upon inheriting the purse, Andelocia tells his brother "here's all India in my hand" to which Fortunatus adds, "Inherite you (my sonnes) that golden land" (2.2.292–6). The purse thus works as a commercial or even colonial fantasy, as it allows the holder to have possession of not only the riches of India (or East India) but the "land" itself. Fortunatus's cap serves as a fantasy of easy overseas travel.

> In these two hands doe I gripe all the world.
> This leather purse, and this bald woolen Hat

>   Make me a Monarch: here's my Crowne and Scepter.
>   In progresse will I now goe through the world,
>   Ile cracke your shoulders, boyes, with bags of gold (2.2.218–22)

But it is at this very moment that Fortunatus's fantasies come to an end, as the goddess Fortune intervenes and ends his life. She is called the "true center of this wide circumference" as she establishes in her first speech, declaring that she has power over the "globe" and all the powerful people in it. *Old Fortunatus* offers to its audience an imaginary sphere of representation where characters can travel to foreign realms with a thought, gold is magically produced, and common people mingle with kings, gods and goddesses. The reliance on the spectator's "gracious eye" to give "life to Fortunatus historie" points us to the imaginary elements of romance, a genre closely associated with the marvelous. With its convergence of travel, commerce, fantasy, and drama, we see in *Old Fortunatus* the expression of a genre that could incorporate the world that surrounded the stage. Unlike Sidney, who limited the playwright's ability to represent newly discovered lands, Dekker and others sought ways to integrate the novelties of the world and explore the limits of stage representation. John Gillies rightly argues that "Sidney castigated the popular stage for its addiction to geographically expansive actions that it could not possibly hope to rationalize. For Sidney, the poverty of Elizabethan techniques of stage illusion—the sheer spatial givenness (and boundedness) of the stage—meant that the drama could have little legitimate business with geography" (Introduction 20). But, as *Old Fortunatus* shows us, no rationalization was necessary for the stage as it attempted to expand the boundaries of its representation. The bare stage became a potent space for "conjuring" both "many places and many times" in the geographically expanded imaginations of playgoers.

In addition to its shifts in geography and magical elements, this kind of engagement with the processes of stage representation and the forms of drama is characteristic of *Old Fortunatus* as a stage romance. The Prologue offers further evidence of the significance and pervasiveness the genre had in sixteenth-century theatrical culture. We see in Sidney's criticism and the dramatic performances of the time an attempt to accommodate this genre that was not part of the ancient generic taxonomy. Plays such as *Old Fortunatus* and *The Foure Prentises of London* also show that playwrights were as actively engaged by questions of representation and genre as the critics.

The stark contrast between neoclassical theory and early modern dramatic practice illustrates for us an important insight to the formation of new genres in the period. In the *Defense*, Sidney attempts to uphold generic categories, to preserve the difference between epic and tragedy, narrative and enactment, or even historiography and poetry. He argues vehemently for the preservation of Aristotelian and neo-Aristotelian rules in dramatic poetry and the genres that those rules support. But he also admits the power of the poet, who distinguishes himself with his ability to fashion new matter and "forms": "Only the poet . . . doth grow in effect another nature, in making things either better than nature bringeth forth, or, quite anew, forms such as never were in nature" (216). What Sidney advocates (particularly in dramatic poetry) is restraint in exercising these abilities. The poet should feign a situation to the most "tragical conveniency," that is, use his art to create a story that is believable enough to both delight and edify, for Sidney the two ends of all poetry. When he says that actors should "report" rather than "represent" that which cannot be framed within the time and space of the stage (Peru and Calicut), Sidney does not reject outright the attempt to represent exotic geography in drama, but he does require that dramatists use the proper classical conventions.

Sidney himself believed in the promise of colonial expansion; Richard Hakluyt dedicated his 1582 *Diverse Voyages touching the Discoverie of America* to Sidney, noting his "accustomed fauour towarde these godly and hounourable discoueries" (⁂4r).[23] Although Sidney's poetics did not allow for the enactment of fantastical expansion, his own interests indicate what seems to be a contradictory fascination with the global. Perhaps in Sidney we see the vestiges of a different mode of expansion tied to aristocratic grants and titular rights. Sidney resisted the more popular impulses of the drama, and the brazen representational strategies of stage romance may have appeared to him as outlandish as the upstart commercial sphere that was emerging around him. For rather than "report" events, dramatists turned to popular romance as a solution to the problem of telling stories that take place in both many places and over many times (as Sidney suggests with his citation of "Pacolet's horse"). As Sidney and Lyly both sensed, England's expanded horizons were exercising pressure on the matter of the theater in particular plays, but also on dramatic practice and the very categories of dramatic representation itself.

3
Imagined Empires: The Cultural Geography of Stage Romance

As the allusions to Peru and Calicut hinted in the previous chapter, the theatrical meanings of foreign geography frequently overlapped with economic interests in the sixteenth century. Sidney chooses two places associated with bullion and mercantile exchange, respectively, and the power of these references stems from their economic associations as well as their geographic eccentricity. The London stage was far more accommodating to the changes in global economics than was Sidney, in part because, as several scholars have noted in recent years, the theaters were situated at the nexus of an increasingly aware global society.[1] In the years that followed Sidney's writing of the *Defense,* and as the English became more intertwined in transnational networks of traffic and travel, the geographies of the stage continued to proliferate. In the present chapter, I will extend the trajectory of the book's argument by looking more specifically at how the spatial imaginings of the stage aligned with various geographic discourses in the period. I connect these discourses back to romance to show how even within more "scientific" undertakings romance continued to influence conceptions of geography. Through readings of geographic treatises, travel narratives, and imperial prospectuses, I will examine ways in which early modern England staged speculative engagements with its increasingly expanding world.

This alignment of discourses will present romance as a uniting resource for various strands of intellectual and creative thought, as well as the practical economic concerns of the early modern theater. As audiences sought stories that represented the prospects of an expanding geographic world, playwrights turned to romance. But the stage was a limiting resource for a genre that was known for its excesses. As Sidney noted, drama was incapable of giving a realistic representation of travel from Peru to Calicut. But the writers of these romances took that limitation and developed it into an enabling creative characteristic. The way in which the stage could bridge the gaps created in romance was through the invocation of the audience's imagination. This use of the imagination played a definitive role in the establishment of dramatic romance as an imperial genre. Rather than simply giving the story, it immersed audiences in fantasies of worlds created through the language of the plays and the spectacles on stage. Romance both enabled these representations and empowered theatrical audiences.

Whereas critics such as John Gillies and Jerry Brotton have explored how chorographic thinking and advances in map making were connected to an intellectual and scientific tradition in early modern Europe, I argue here that the literary and cultural legacies of romance were also determinate in geographical thinking. The geography of romance, teasingly indeterminate and yet suggestive of real world spaces, enabled a kind of spatial thinking that we also see present in early modern maps.[2] This romance geography, as I will call it, opened an imaginative expansionism that permeated early modern imperial culture. It was this fantasy of foreign and remote places that enticed theatrical audiences to the representations that they would find in *Old Fortunatus, The Foure Prentises of London*, as well as other popular plays of the period. In this chapter I thus prioritize an "imaginative geography," the term Edward Said coined in *Orientalism* to explain how centuries of European poetry, historiography, geography, and other discourse created the very idea of the East. Developed from Gaston Bachelard's analysis of "the poetics of space," Said argued that history and geography, as representations of time and space, are important subjects of cultural interpretation. In Said's reading, the Western tradition created a complex of chorographic descriptions and spatial constructs about the East that were as influential as the material geography heralded by the new discoveries of the Renaissance. "We need not decide here whether this kind of imaginative geography," Said comments, "infuses history and geography, or whether in some way overrides them. Let us just say for the time being that it is there as something *more* than what appears to be merely positive knowledge" (55, author's emphasis). Expounding upon Said's tentative formulation, the contemporary cultural geographer Derek Gregory notes "there is an important sense in which all geographies are imaginative: even the most formal, geometric lattices of spatial science are at once abstractions and *cultural constructions* . . . " (*Dictionary*, 373, my emphasis).

My goal here is to show how romance contributed to these "cultural constructions," both within the realms of geographic representation and on the stage. Informed by new discoveries and a range of cultural resources (including stories of romance) writers in the sixteenth and seventeenth centuries could tap into the news of geographic discoveries to market their fictions. Drama, as Julie Sanders helpfully articulates, "was one of the key means by which early modern English society strove to make sense of space . . . " (9).[3] Taking this perspective, recent critics have issued a number of important studies of specific places: London markets, public greens, brothels, households, and alehouses, to name only a few.[4] This body of research is premised upon the fruitful intersection of geography, performance, and sociology provided by the study of "cultural geography." I build on this scholarship by pursuing the connections between dramatic genre and a more global geography and thus follow a question first posed by Jean Howard: "do particular dramatic genres construct distinctive and discrete imagined geographies, and what does it mean, historically, if they do?" ("Shakespeare, Geography" 304).[5]

Romance, a literature defined by its imaginative geography, supplied the cultural idiom for this moment of British Empire not yet realized. It was the genre that had, since its medieval origins, provided readers with representations of foreign worlds that were dangerous but also easily traversed; it engaged its reader, all the while, in the pleasures of these places, removed as they were in the safe distance of reading. Romance was thus a part of a crucial cultural argument in sixteenth- and seventeenth-century England about the place of the British nation within a broader global framework. This is a case that has been made successfully within medieval studies by scholars such as Michelle Warren and Geraldine Heng, but has not been recognized fully into early modern dramatic studies.[6] Within a society shifting away from land-based economies and domestic commerce, romance staked out a more cosmopolitan view of space, one that was highly integrated and acknowledged the British within international networks of meaning. This idea also found expression in a little-known stage romance, *Tom a Lincoln* (discussed briefly in the introduction) which will serve as an example in this chapter of the intensified application of romance to questions of politics, empire, and, most importantly, the shaping of English attitudes and ideas about these enterprises.

The visual and verbal rhetoric of romance and geographic discourse alike cohere around a set of similar strategies: a promise that the reader or viewer could experience the broader world, that travel through the world was possible through the turning of the imagination, conceptual mastery could lead to real dominion, and perhaps most importantly, that the kinds of imaginative feats promised in geography and romance were active pleasures, activities that were edifying but also entertaining. These rhetorical principles, once deciphered, will help to explain the popular interest that romance on the early modern stage held for its viewers, and how these pleasures could be translated into the work that would be required in building an empire founded upon these imaginative conquests.

In this chapter, I thus explore two separate but related intersections of geography and romance in the sixteenth and seventeenth centuries. First, in globes, maps, and the pages of geographic treatises, I find a "rhetoric of presence" that disposes readers to cartography in a way similar to romance—I interpret in them what J. B. Harley calls a "literature of maps" as well as a mapping of literature and drama ("Maps, Knowledge" 53). Promising an opportunity to visualize and interpret geographic representations of the world, the materials of early modern mapmaking encouraged readers to imagine themselves as actively engaged with the geographic representations offered in maps. Secondly, I show how writers like John Dee and Richard Hakluyt used romance and maps together to provide a historical precedent for English dominion over newly discovered territories. *Tom a Lincoln*, a recently discovered seventeenth-century play based on pseudo-Arthurian material, enacts this expansive history, presenting King Arthur and his knights as the creators and overseers of a premodern British Empire. Moreover, the ideological work of the play, its alignment of medieval romance with contemporary views of British Empire, shows in dramatic form the discourse I observe in other forms in the period. Finally, I turn to Shakespeare's *Merchant of Venice* to demonstrate how a reading of stage romance and its geographical engagements might be used to intervene in some key critical questions about a play that has been well-established in current generic paradigms. Taken together, these plays and geographical materials illustrate a mutually reinforcing set of reading and interpretive practices that arced between the theater, cartography, and the pages of romance.

Speculative geography

Marlowe's Faustus, giddy with newfound power after meeting Mephistopheles, promptly conjures a fantasy of territorial domination:

> By [Mephistopheles] I'll be a great emperor of the world
> And make a bridge through the moving air
> To pass the ocean with a band of men;

> I'll join the hills that bind the Afric shore
> And make that land continent to Spain,
> And both contributory to my crown.
> . . .
> I'll live in speculation of this art
> Till Mephistopheles return again. (1.3.104–16)

Faustus's imagination bodies forth a world without limitations, one in which the hedging shores of Europe and Africa evaporate. In the passage, it seems initially that Mephistopheles's black magic opens the possibility for unencumbered travel, an enchantment similar to the wishing cap of Fortunatus or the wooden horse of Pacolet. But it is Faustus's "speculation of this art" that is actually at work here, his own cogitations on the power of Mephistopheles. Indeed, the extent of the devil's ability lags far behind Faustus's ambition throughout the play. While he sees moving continents and coronets in his mind, in reality his power yields only a series of crass pranks and parlor tricks.

Faustus's fantasy returns us to a time in which knowledge of the globe and overseas expansion was becoming available to a wide range of London's citizens. Behind this passage is also the dramatic tradition of representing travel and spatial maneuvering that Marlowe surely knew. In the course of the play, Faustus uses Mephistopheles to traverse the world, as did Fortunatus (whose story comes from the same German *Volksbuch* tradition as *Doctor Faustus*). A seventeenth-century reader of *Doctor Faustus* mentions this as the most memorable feature of the text: "[it] also pleased me, especially when he travelled in the Air, saw all the world, and did what he listed" (Kirkman, *Unlucky Citizen* 10). Faustus imagines both a feat of geography (combining separated territories) and a political coup ("I'll be a great emperor of the world").

A decisive quality in English imperial discourse and practice was also the ability to "see" an empire that is not there, markets that exist only in potential, unclaimed land that can bear fruit, even territories that were once claimed by the English but then lost. This sense of "speculation" resonated within the cultural spaces of the theater and stories of romance. In romance, such territorial power could be expressed through magic. Chinon, the hero of the Arthurian derived *Famous Historie of Chinon of England* (1597) (also staged in a now lost play from the 1590s) is rescued through the help of an enchanted mirror. As the story draws to a close, Chinon is lost and must be sought out by the members of the round table. Arthur summons Merlin, "who then liued accounted as a Prophet in England," the narrator tells us, and who can facilitate the travel of these knights to the land of Chinon's captivity. Merlin brings forth a "a speculatiue Glasse" that reveals the location of Chinon and his adventures since leaving England (Middleton M2v). Using his magic, Merlin, through his "cunning," quickly transports the knights to the cave where Chinon is held captive by a giant and enchantress. These speculations, whether in Merlin's mirror or on maps that aspire to scientific representation, cast multiple rays of meaning that point toward stories and representations of romance as well as the mechanical "arts" of geography that was coming into wide practice in the sixteenth century.[7]

Throughout the developing discourse of space in the sixteenth and seventeenth centuries, we find a melding of concrete experience and abstract calculation or "speculation," a word often used to describe the work of geographers and cosmographers. This duality is remarked upon in various treatises on cartography, navigation, and mathematics. Sebastian Münster, writing in his *Treatise of the New India,* calls the work of geography a marriage of experience and imagination "Nought els to say, but that experience to be most certayn which is ioyned with reason or speculation, and that reason to be most sure which is confirmed with experience . . . that neyther practyse is safe without speculacion, nor speculacion with out practyse" (A2v–A3r). William Barlow, the author of *The Navigator's Supply* (1597) and the inventor of new, more accurate navigational tools in the sixteenth century, professed that he had never gone to sea: "even when I was yong and strongest, I altogether abhorred the Sea"(a4r). Nonetheless, Barlow learned "by speculation" the arts of navigation, and confirmed his discoveries with "some of the skillfullest Nauigators of our Land; with such as haue bin principall Actors in our furthest Northeast and Northwest discoueries; with such as haue bin in the South Sea, and at the Cape of *Bona Speransa*; and also with Naturalists of the East Indies"(b1r). Barlow sums up: "For except there be a vniting of knowledge with practise, there can be nothing excellent: Idle knowledge wihout practise, & ignorant pratise without knowledge, serue vnto small purpose"(L1v). This necessary combination of "practise" and "speculation" is personified in another navigational treatise in praise of England's geographical vanguard:

> I am fully perswaded that our Countrie is not inferiour to any for men of rare knowledge . . . for what Strangers may be compared . . . for Thericall speculations and most cunning calculation M. *Dee* and M. *Thomas Heriotts* are hardly to be matched: and for the mecanicall practises drawne from the Artes Mathematick, our Countrie doth yeelde men of principall excellencie, as M. *Emery Mulleneux* for the exquisite making of Globus bodies . . . (Davis ¶ 3r)

Though men like Francis Drake and Walter Ralegh were celebrated for their adventurous exploits on the seas, the figures mentioned in this passage (John Dee, Thomas Hariot, Emery Molyneux) also achieved notoriety for their contributions to expansionist projects.

Even within Gerard Mercator's monumental *Atlas*, the imaginative is part of the new geography's conceptual vocabulary. The final entry in the book is a table of "Technologicall and Geographicall words," divided into two parts: "real" and "imaginary" terms. In the category of the former are land masses (continents, islands, peninsulas) and bodies of water (oceans, bays), all observable physical features. In contrast, the table includes a much more extensive list of "imaginary" geographical constructs: the equator, parallels, longitudinal lines, "climes," the Arctic and Antarctic, none of which constitute places or actual physical features, but are rather ways of conceptualizing and organizing space on the globe. The table's entry for "antipodes" carries the message of this "imaginary" geography most compellingly. Defining antipodes as "people dwelling on the other side of the Earth, with their feet directly against ours," the table moves seamlessly between place and the people who dwell there.

The entry on the antipodes also naturalizes as "technologicall" a term with fabulous origins. The idea of a people opposite to Europeans, not only in geography but in customs, culture, and behavior, dates to ancient times (as its Greek etymology—"feet against feet"—reveals). Richard Eden's English translation of Peter Martyr's *Decades of the New World* shows the story of the antipodes to be another of the ancient disputes that New World exploration solved. He settles the question in a section entitled: "That the Spanyardes haue sayled to the Antipodes (that is) suche as go fiete to fiete ageynst vs, and inhabite the inferiour hemispherie or halfe globe of the earthe, contrarie to thoppinion of the owlde writers" (321r), showing that the Spaniards had proved not only the existence of such lands and peoples, but that their seasons and customs run contrary to those of Europeans. The legend of the antipodes had thus moved from lore and into the vocabulary of geographic writers as a result of a conscious attempt to find the truth in ancient fiction.

Mercator renders the language of the antipodes as "imaginary," a fact picked up humorously in the title of Richard Brome's play, *The Antipodes*, where Peregrine, the protagonist, has become disoriented from reading too much Mandeville and other travel narratives. "In tender years he always loved to read / Reports of travels and of voyages," his father explains, "he would whole days / And nights . . . be on such books / As might convey his fancy round the world" (1.1.131–7). Though amusingly rendered in Brome, the ability of "reports of travels and voyages" to transport their readers (even into madness, in the case of Peregrine) also carries through into the visual representation of space in maps and globes. In the language of Mercator's Table, the uncomplicated flow of fictional story of the antipodes to a realized geographic concept serves as an illustrative example of the mutual interaction of fantasy and experience in the formulation of an early modern geographic project.

For authors and playwrights interested in selling books and plays to the public, there was further reason for trumpeting a connection to exotic places. There were also commercial interests at stake in the expansion of English fiction, drama, and its geography. Thomas Lodge, a poet and author of prose romances, used his experiences as a passenger aboard transoceanic voyages to advertise two of his stories. He had accompanied a Captain Clark on to the Canaries and Terceras islands in 1586, on which voyage, Lodge says, he composed the work for which he is best known, *Rosalynde* (1590), which Shakespeare later dramatized in *As You Like It*. Lodge explains in his dedication to *Rosalynde* his reason for writing the story: "to beguile the time with labour, I writte this booke: rough, as hacht in the stormes of the Ocean, and feathered in the surges of many perilous seas" (A2v). The title page provocatively suggests that the story was "Fetcht from the Canaries." Likewise, while traveling with Thomas Cavendish 1591 to South America, Lodge claims to have penned three more romances. In a letter prefacing one of these, *A Margarite of America* (1596), he again tells of the conditions surrounding the story's composition: "touching the place where I wrote this, it was in those straits christned by Magelan; in which place to the southward many wounderous Isles, many strange fishes, many monstrous Patagones withdrew my senses" (A2r).

In both of these dedications, Lodge plays up the connection between his stories and places where he composed them. He continues in *A Margarite*, "so that there was great wonder in the place wherein I writ this so likewise might it be maruelled that in such scantie fare, such causes of feare, so mightie discouragements, and many crosses, I should deserve or eternize anything" (A2r). *Margarite* was found, Lodge claims, in the Jesuit library at "Sanctum" (Santos, Brazil). His very sentences have the power to transport the reader, as he writes in his address to the readers in *Rosalynde*, where "eurerie line was wet with a surge." In *A Margarite*, Lodge asks the reader to understand that any infelicities in the text are a result of writing aboard a topsy-turvy ship: "pardon an vndiscreete and vnstaied penne, for hands may vary where stomacks miscary" (A4v). Placed as it is within the prefatory materials, Lodge's rhetoric appeals to the readers of this text, and promises them the possibility of becoming enveloped in the foreign place. Lodge concludes *Rosalynde* with a final pitch for a book that would never be printed: if you liked the story, look for another tale spun from the sea, "the Sailer's Kalender" (66r).

Lodge may well have "beguiled the time" by writing these stories at sea, but what is his purpose in sharing this with the reader? Lodge makes his voyages part of the story, perhaps enlarging the appeal of these tales by playing off their exotic origins. Lodge takes boilerplate romances and adds value to the stories by tying them to his maritime adventures. Something similar is at work in the theater with the adaptation of romances with exotic geographies. *Tom a Lincoln,* discussed later, was a play based loosely on Arthurian materials and taken from a popular prose romance by Richard Johnson. As such, it owes its existence to the audience's interest in both romance and the kinds of exotic adventures promised in Lodge. Writers of romance could use the geography of other places to lend validity to their fictions, but they could also summon reader interest and wonder for their tales with allusion to foreign places.

The pleasures of romance derived precisely from this capacity for incorporating the reader into the foreign places (plots) of the narrative. In the 1637 English edition of *Valentine and Orson* (the romance in which Sidney found Pacolet's horse) a prefatory letter from "the printer" (presumably Thomas Purfoot) expresses the qualities of the text that make it appealing to readers: "here are the Countries with the Courts of Kings deciphered, the magnitude of Honors laid open, the true forme of Tournaments described, and combats betweene knight & knight are here most lively portrayed, to the great content of the Reader" (A2v). Furthermore, the writer says, this is not only a text for "courtly" readers: "it gives also a working to the minds of the dull country swaynes, and as it were leads them to search out for Martiall atchievements, befitting many pastimes, & active pleasures" (A2v). Focusing on this final phrase, "active pleasures," we see the rhetoric of this advertisement promoting the fiction as reading designed for action. Though this may be a defensive response to the critics of romance, it also enforces the point that romance as a genre established a relationship between reader and text that implored engaged reading that might ultimately be aimed at more than pleasure. "If you desire to see the cares and troubles of kings, here they are . . . If of the travailes of knightly aduentures, heere they are . . . " the printer writes, employing a language that promises not merely reading, but an experience of the fiction.

Such a rhetoric of presence, a language wrought with promise that the world was imaginatively available and navigable, also characterized discourses of travel and cartography in the period. Terrestrial and celestial globes, available for the first time to a wide market of buyers, provide an illustration of this relationship. Though today we may view globes primarily as maps in another form, in the sixteenth century they had a broader meaning as objects and were used differently by their owners. Globes in the sixteenth century, the historian Elly Dekker has argued, were not merely maps, but were thought of as "representations that facilitate a spatial understanding of things, concepts, conditions, processes, or events in the human world" (136). Beyond simple pictures, globes were tools with which readers could interact to produce new ways of engaging with the world. Emery Molyneux's globe, for instance, in addition to providing maps of territories and oceans with geographic coordinates, plotted out with colored lines the routes that English explorers Drake and Cavendish followed in their voyages. As I will show presently, this form of representation encouraged viewers to use their globes in order to experience these voyages vicariously. Furthermore, they provided the real opportunity to learn the skills of navigation and territorial plotting that globes and maps allowed.

Thinking of the surface of the globe as representational space, an area on which to show the travels of Drake and Cavendish, or to impose grids of mathematical meaning, or even to project imagined territories, gives broader context to the metaphor employed in the naming of the Globe theater. It is reference to this theatrical "globe" that editors use to gloss Prospero's famous speech in Act 4 of *The Tempest*:

>... These our actors
>As I foretold you, were all spirits, and
>Are melted into air, into thin air;
>And like the baseless fabric of this vision,
>The cloud-capped towers, the gorgeous palaces,
>The solemn temples, the great globe itself,
>Yea, all which it inherit, shall dissolve; (4.1.148–54)

Prospero here disenchants the stage, comparing the actors in the scene to the props on stage used to conjure the marriage masque, possibly extending the metaphor to the world outside of the theater. As I have shown in this section, Molyneux's globes (as well as those of Mercator and other cartographers) were associated with imaginative projections, as well. In fact, because of their size, Molyneux's globes were often referred to in the period as "great (i.e., large) globes." Thomas

Blundeville uses this tag ("In the great terrestriall Globe lately put foorth by M. Sanderson and M. Molineux . . . " (242v)), as does Thomas Fale, author of a surveying textbook: "The grauer of the Figures was one M. *Iod. Hondius,* who hath shewed himselfe an excellent workman in the *great Globes* set forth by *M. Mullineux*" (A4r, my emphasis). Hakluyt refers to the "very large and most exact terrestriall Globe" of Molyneux. Geographic representation, like dramatic staging, was limited by space; what both shared were imaginative possibilities that lay beyond their "plots." "The great globe" in this passage surely summons the theatrical space as well as terra firma, but it also argues that the text and images pasted onto Molyneux's "great globe" (the territories, place names, passages of famous voyagers) are no less of a representation than "The baseless fabric" of Prospero's masque. Shakespeare's lines thus acknowledge the imaginative nature of globes, placing them alongside the theatrical spectacle as a representative art.

Several writers in the sixteenth century produced textual apparatuses that were to be used along with globes and maps, teaching readers how to use these objects for navigation.[8] Perhaps the most popular of these were Thomas Blundeville's *Exercises*, published in seven editions between 1593 and 1638. Blundeville states at the outset that his book is motivated by the contemporary explorers of England, "our English Gentlemen, both of the Court and Countrie in these dayes so earnestlie given to trauell aswell by sea as Land, into straunge and vnknowne countries, and speciallie into the East and West Indies . . . " (A4v). Blundeville's contribution to this project, as he sees it, is to educate "young men" in the necessary skills of navigation:

> And because that to trauell by sea requireth skil in the Art of Nauigation, in which it is unpossible for any man to be perfect vnless he first haue his Arithmetick, and also some knowledge in the principles of Cosmographie, and specially to haue the use of the Spheare, of the two Globes, of the Astrolabe, and crosse staffe, and such like instruments belonging to the Arte of Navigation, I thought good therefore to write the Treatises before mentioned . . . (A4v)

One of the sections of Blundeville's *Exercises* contains a description of "a plaine and full description of both the Globes," wherein Blundeville lays out the mathematical principles necessary for using the globe. Thus, like most of Blundeville's book, the treatment of globes is oriented toward practical knowledge: how to properly align the instrument, calculate longitude, tell time, and so on. But Blundeville's treatise also encourages the reader to use the globe to estimate information about other places—for instance, the "second proposition" in the treatise instructs "To know vnder what Clime any place or region is, and of how many houres the longest day is there, and also what latitude any place described in the map hath" (211r, Ee3r). His first example in this section is London, but Blundeville also provides coordinates for Venice and Jerusalem as illustrations. The argument implicit in the pages of this treatise is that it is possible to construct knowledge about any region of the world with a globe and some basic arithmetic. The promised knowledge also combines the imaginative with the experiential: how long is the day in Venice? What is the "clime"?

The copy of the 1594 *Exercises* held at the British Library (Shelfmark C145.c.16.) includes manuscript notes from at least two different early modern readers demonstrating that the book was used for the purpose of creating such an imaginative experience. The opening leaves include carefully constructed tables based on Blundeville's instructions for determining the positions of celestial objects in the sky. What appears to be the hand of a different reader has marked in the margins of Blundeville's discussion of the globe two calculations for the distances from London to the Cape of Good Hope "in Africk" and the East Indies (243v (Ii 3 v)):

> 7440
> miles to ye
> Cape of
> Good Hope
> in Africk
> and 12330
> miles to ye
> Isle called
> Java Major
> in ye east Indies

Blundeville is encouraging his readers to actually use the globe, or even to simply visualize the voyages he writes about. The marginal note above comes in the section of Blundeville's discussion on Drake's and Cavendish's voyages as they are mapped out on Molyneux's globe—noting for the reader the points that each voyager touched in his journeys through the world. Blundeville's treatise, like the globe, encourages an active incorporation of global knowledge, and alignment of mathematics, imagination, and travel narrative. The instruction of his ideal "young men," the voyagers of the future, requires for Blundeville a combination of such practical knowledge with the alluring horizons represented on the globe.

Such a relationship between theoretical or imaginative thinking and actual practice is also illustrated, perhaps humorously, in a 1608 pamphlet, *The Travels of M. Bush*. Most likely written by the prolific pamphleteer Anthony Nixon, *The Travels* tells the story of one William Bush, who "without more helpe than his owne, made a Pynace, by which he past by Ayre, Land, and Water" (B1r). Nixon, who retells the story, apparently patched together from Bush's own narrative of the event, presents the story as a "perfection" of the hope for overseas venturing presented in Barlow and Blundeville. "And how can perfection bee attained," Nixon asks, "but by making use & transporting from place to place, thereby beholding the diversities of daies and nights, with the temperature of the Ayre in sundrye regions, by which the whole course and reuolution of the spheare, is made apparent to mans capacity?" (B1v). Bush never leaves England—his voyage begins in Lamborne and ends at the Custom House in London, but he manages to transport his small handmade boat over land, water, and yes, even through the air by rigging up a system of ropes and pulleys on various castles and public buildings. It is hard to determine Bush's motives in acting out these apparent publicity stunts, but those of Nixon and his publisher Nathanial Butter are easier to descry. They market the voyage Bush undertakes as "aduenturous and strange." Nixon reports that it surpasses the wonders undertaken by those "principal Actors in our furthest North-east, and North-west discoueries: with such as haue been in the South Sea, and the Cape of *Bona Speranza*" (B2r). The undertaking of travels as imagined in Blundeville and Barlow, "making use" of that knowledge, gives the story its market appeal.

Just as Molyneux was adding value to his globes by mapping out the course of Cavendish's and Drake's voyages, Nixon and Butter (like Thomas Lodge before them) found in the story of Bush the chance to tap into reader interest for stories of "strange" adventures. Even though it is a domestic adventure, Butter is exploiting the real commercial possibilities that were available in England for stories of this kind—showing us the reality in Trinculo's famous joke about the marketability of a "dead Indian" to a public hungry for news from abroad. Mapmakers, romance writers, and playwrights alike knew the viability of these enterprises, and as I have argued here, they came to market with something more sophisticated than Trinculo's dull ploy. The lure of the globe as a literal and metaphorical space came in its ability to provide an experience that involved the reader or viewer in the creation of the story. Maps and geographical treatises showed readers that such knowledge was not merely incidental to the act of overseas exploration. It is important to remember the argument shared by Barlow, Blundeville, and other practitioners: "knowledge," in the form of these geographical exercises, was equally important to "practice." I am arguing that there was, in fact, a wide range of arts that could be counted as geographical "knowledge" and that the imaginative materialization of space in these various forms (narrative, cartography, drama) was significant to the expansionist project of the English. Geography could summon worlds abroad, as I will show, but dramas like *Tom a Lincoln* and *The Merchant of Venice* had even more purchase on the imagination. In fact, the movement between the practical and speculative that both geography and drama encouraged, as I will now argue, was foundational in establishing the framework of an early British empire.

Tom a Lincoln and the imaginative geography of English Empire

In Book Three of *The Faerie Queene*, Britomart first beholds Artegall, the object of her quest and desire, while gazing into a magical "looing glasse." Spenser pauses to explain the origins of this "mirror," for its "vertues through the wyde worlde soone were solemniz'd" (3.2.18.9). "The great Magitien *Merlin*" fashioned the glass for Ryence, a Welsh king whose name Spenser found in Malory. Remarkably, and here Spenser found no precedent in Arthurian romance, the looking glass was "round and hollow shaped . . . / Like to the world itself": a "Glassy globe," he calls it.[9] This globe not only looks like "the world itself," it has the power to show its beholder:

> . . . in perfect sight,
> What euer thing was in the world contaynd,
> Betwixt the lowest earth and heuens hight,
> So that it to the looker appertaynd;
> What euer foe had wrought, or frend had faynd,
> Therein discouered was, ne ought mote pas,
> Ne ought in secret from the same remaynd (3.2.19.1–7)

In the following stanza (20), Spenser alludes to the glass tower of Ptolemy, the ancient globe maker, further drawing a geographical lineage for his spherical mirror. Spenser's mirror figures a central idea within early

English expansion. Britomart's mirror allows its beholder to see both what is in the present ("What euer thing was in the world contaynd"), but also that which is not yet materialized: it shows King Ryence foreign invaders "before he hard / Tydings thereof, and so them still debar'd" (3.2.21.4–5).

Though Spenser's globe is undoubtedly touched by Merlin's magic, its description also echoes the excited rhetoric that surrounded the emergence of geographical globes in early modern England. Moving between concrete representation ("speculum") and imaginary projection ("speculation"), Spenser's mirror aligns with the discourse of early imperial and commercial endeavors as it materialized in travel literature, cartography, and drama. Emery Molyneux's globe, the first to be made and sold in England in the late sixteenth century, is heralded by Richard Hakluyt's address to the reader in the 1589 *Principall Navigations*. He admits that his travel narratives could "farre more easily be conceiued of the Readers" with a detailed reference map (˙4v). Hakluyt says, though, that he has only included a small map in his volume, which will be superseded by "the coming out of a very large and most exact terrestriall Globe, collected and reformed according to the newest, secretest, and latest discoueries . . . composed by M. Emmerie Molineux . . . " (˙4v). This real globe will divulge the "secretest" discoveries, a promise tinged with the occult language of Spenser's imaginary artifact: "ne ought in secret from the same [the viewer] remaynd." Molyneux's globe realizes Spenser's fiction; like Merlin's magical looking glass, the terrestrial globe unfolds a geographic vision both widely encompassing and enticingly revelatory.

As John Dee saw it (perhaps the first to use the term "British Empire") the English needed to embrace such imaginative conquests. Writing of the tenth-century King Edgar, Dee expresses what allowed this predecessor of Elizabeth to become such a great emperor:

> This Peaceable king Edgar, had in his mynde (about 600. yeres past) the Representation of a great parte of the self same idea . . . which (from aboue onely, and by no Mans aduise,) hath gratiously streamed down into my imagination: being (as it becommeth me, a Subject) Carefull for the Godly Prosperity of this Brytish Impire, vnder our most Peaceable Queene Elizabeth. (Hakluyt 55)

An empire under the aegis of Elizabeth is expressed here as an act of imagination providentially passed through Edgar and into Dee. As Ken MacMillan, the recent editor of Dee's *Limits of the British Empire*, has argued, Dee possessed an understanding of empire that rested on narratives of past conquests. MacMillan writes:

> Dee's conception of empire was not commercial, cultural, or ideological. Instead, it was historical: His formulation was the ancient empire of three kingdoms founded by Brutus and enlarged to over thirty kingdoms by Arthur. Dee was writing of a lineally descended, recently recoverable, British (Tudor) Empire. (*Sovereignty* 60)

But Dee's fantasy belies the fundamental truth of England's relative incapability as a global authority. By the time Dee's history of King Edgar was published in Hakluyt's *Principall Navigations*, England remained a limited imperial power: unable to establish a foothold in North America or the East, and battling for supremacy in Ireland. At the center of this seeming incompetence is another complicated truth—the English were in the process of assuming territories, taking over trading markets, and establishing footholds on nearly every continent that would eventually unseat the other powers of Europe.

Following the pattern established by Dee, the portrait of Arthur presented in the anonymous play *Tom a Lincoln* is that of a British sovereign whose dominion is not only expanding within his realm (we hear report that he has successfully defeated the Saxons) but also abroad, as the play shows us the British conquest of France and reports, at the end, that Arthur has successfully resisted Roman occupation. Moreover, his renown has reached the ears of Prester John, and through the explorations of his round table, his name emanates throughout the globe. As Brian Lockey has recently shown in his study of romance, law, and empire, early modern romance writers were keenly aware of the legal justifications for expansion and arguments, such as Dee's, for the monarchical authority to lay claim to foreign territory. "Because they could see beyond the insular tradition of nativist common law," Lockey argues, "writers of romance fiction . . . eventually provided ways of thinking about conquest and expansionism in more advanced legal and ethical terms" (9). In this context, it is interesting to note that the play's provenance links it to the Inns of Court, where it may have been presented as part of the Christmastime revels. The play, which lacks a title in the manuscript, is a dramatic adaptation of Richard Johnson's popular sixteenth- and seventeenth-century romance *Tom a Lincoln*, which the twentieth-century editor of the play adopted for its title.[10]

The story begins with King Arthur's liaisons with a beautiful young woman, Angelica, whom he seduces in a convent near the town of

Lincoln. Angelica and King Arthur conceive a child, and in order to hide the shame of their act, their son, Tom, is raised by a shepherd in Lincoln, hidden away safely to conceal his identity as the son of the King. His princely stock cannot be obscured, however, and he grows to be a brave knight, leaving his adopted rustic family to search for adventure. Upon entering the court of Arthur, he is immediately given command of an army that defeats French forces at war with the English.[11] Even after his victory over the French, Tom decides that he wants nothing more than to know his father's identity, so he travels abroad in search of his origins. He goes to Fairy Land, where he beguiles Caelia, the Fairy Queen. Tom abandons Caelia, though, and sails on to the kingdom of Prester John (the legendary Christian ruler of lands in the East), where he falls in love, once again, with a foreign woman, Prester John's daughter Anglitora. Against her father's wishes, she absconds with Tom to England. The play ends with a celebration of their marriage, though with the recognition that Tom has still not found out the identity of his father, thus opening the possibility for the sequel (found in Richard Johnson's prose romance).

Tom travels with Sirs Lancelot, Tristram, and Gawain, to a far-away Fairy Land inhabited by Amazons, then later becomes the first Englishman to enter Prester John's kingdom in the East.[12] Tom's life and travels in his six-year voyage around the globe are narrated to the audience by "Time" who, as in *The Winter's Tale* and *Guy of Warwick*, two other stage romances, serves as the Chorus to the play.[13] The following passage narrates a voyage undertaken by King Arthur's knights of the round table. Its geographic specificity is remarkable, setting out their stops like a series of pins on the globe:

> In wich theyre navigation, they fore past
> Many a monarchs Court & potentate
> Coastinge ore Spaine and frutefull Italy
> Europ & TurKey, with great Affrica
> In wich stands ancient Carthage; Barbary
> Numidia, Mauritania, wich is parted
> In Tyngitania, that hath one the west
> The Curled Ocian, on the north the straights
> of stowte Morocco sowth—Getulia
> Caesariensis—Mauritania hath
> the sea Sardou[line above] leaninge to the North
> the mountayn Libia bendinge to the sowth (1118–29)

Time carefully maps the geography of the Mediterranean and northwestern Africa, citing the Roman names for the various provinces of "Mauritania" (present-day Morocco), noting the ancient division of the region between Tingitana and Getulia. The writer of this passage draws on these descriptions of the region as originally presented by the Roman Martianus Capella.[14] Tom and his companions thus map a trajectory from the old world, represented in the naming of places with Latin nomenclature, toward the more far-flung locations represented in Fairy Land and Prester John's kingdom.

The origin of the text reflects a similar straddling of past and up-to-date present. Despite its medieval setting, *Tom a Lincoln* was written in the sixteenth century by Richard Johnson, a popular writer of prose fiction whose other titles include *The Seven Champions of Christendom*, also adapted into a play in the 1630s. *Tom a Lincoln* thus provides an important illustration, first, of how writers in the sixteenth and seventeenth centuries adapted the materials of romance into contemporary prose and dramatic traditions. Johnson's Arthurian court reflects the imperial ambitions expressed by Dee for early modern England, employing the stories of the past to establish future possibilities of expansion. Although the play begins in the court of Arthur, the central episodes of the play take place outside of England—Arthur hears, for instance, a report that Tom "in yor name [Arthur's] vnhoarst all durst wthstand / yor name or fame wthin the Sophies land of Royall Persia" (2941-3).

The imperative language of Time, the chorus, is notable, as it directly involves the audience in the representation of action. This strategy, similar to the rhetoric of presence seen in cartographic and romance materials alike, here serves the spectacle and the need to break from the stream of plot and time. For instance, in narrating Tom's arrival in "fayry lande," Time offers this encompassing view of the knights' voyage:

> Ye[a] all the spacious orbe he and his mates
> Had well nigh Coasted, Countreys, kingedomes, states
> All, ye all, yet neuer coulde he heare
> The least suspition of his longe sought sire
> But left behinde him still a glorious fame
> Of the rownd table and of Arthures name
> Nowe at the end of six years Navigation
> They have descried a very famowse lande
> Where how they spedde yow pr[e]sently shall heare
> Yf yow but lende them an attentive eare. (1130-40)

The translation of Johnson's prose narrative into a stage play requires the play to account for the six-year gap Tom's travels require. Here Time, as a choric figure, fills out the holes created by the geographic expansiveness of the story with narrative explanation. Moreover, the Chorus involves the audience in this imaginative enterprise. To leap across Tom's childhood and adolescence, for instance, Time asks the audience:

> be yor imaginations kinde spectators
> more swifte then thought, run with me thinke the babe
> hath fully passed sixteen years of age
> the rest he shall performe vpon the stage
> thus with pegasean hast away time flies (205–10)

Though the play does not attempt to capture all the material found in Johnson's narrative (it only covers the action from part one of Johnson's story), it does take Tom, "The Red-Rose Knight," from his birth and through his many adventures, exploring both the fanciful and exotic lands of the Fairy Queen (the "very famowse lande" above) and Prester John's kingdom. The stage must represent England, France, India (where the text locates Prester John), and even Fairy Land.[15] This is all done with the audience's help: "yor thoughts must once more helpe vs thinke you see" (2857). It is through the cooperation and aid of the audience that the stage generates its global spectacle. In this way the dramatic performance of *Tom a Lincoln* provides a more powerful version of the imaginative expansion prompted in Dee's *Limits of the British Empire* or Richard Johnson's prose narrative. The *staging* of the Arthurian Empire is what allows the audience to see in action the "disclosing of your Highnes['s] royal right," as Dee puts it. Like the "cartographic rhetoric" William Sherman notes Dee using in *Limits*, the stage enacts a commanding vision of global British dominion.[16] Medieval romance, as it was transmitted into dramatic representation, made its audience an active participant in the construction of this imagined empire.

What, then, did these knowingly archaic stories provide early modern playwrights and their audiences as they sought strategies and subjects for imagining England's broadening horizons in this period of expanding overseas commerce and exploration? Ultimately, an instructive distinction can be drawn between the writings of Dee and the work of the stage and cartography. Dee's arguments to the queen found little traction with her advisors. While there is an argument to be made that his view of the "British Empyre" eventually became the dominant ideology, it would be inaccurate to overstate the increasingly diminished influence of Dee. The popular articulation of these ideas in drama, travel writing, prose romance, and cartographic representation had a much wider distribution, however. This can be, in part, attributed to the diversity of these sources and the wider accessibility they allowed to the public. Dee's imperial writings sat more or less unread in manuscript, while copies of Hakluyt, globes, and plays reached a wider audience. But the form these popular materials took were also significant in promoting the idea of a British Empire that could legitimately claim territory abroad. This speaks to the lesson contained in Spenser's "Letter to Ralegh": "so much more profitable and gratious is doctrine by ensample, then by rule." I have argued, too, that the specific form of romance on the stage, the way in which the audience is compelled to participate in and complete the imagined travels that the figures of conquest undertake, made these cultural productions an intensely powerful rallying call to empire. While Elizabeth and the political actors within English government may have remained unmoved by Dee's rhetoric, the public received these lessons through another medium that was perhaps more persuasive.

The romance of *The Merchant of Venice*

At the conclusion of *The Merchant of Venice*, Portia hands Antonio a letter containing unexpected news of his lost ships, "There you shall find three of your argosies / Are richly come to harbor suddenly." Intended to amaze, the news achieves its desired effect: "I am dumb," proclaims Antonio in response to the miraculous turn of his fortune. Once he recovers his wits, he unfolds the letter's contents (quoted here from the 1600 quarto): "for heere *I* reade for certaine that my ships / are safely come to Rode" (Kv). All modern editions of the play alter the quartos' (and First Folio's) "Rode" to "road," as in "harbor," ("road," def. II.3.), and thus maintain an emendation first introduced by Alexander Pope in 1723. For nearly a hundred years prior to Pope, however, and beginning with the Second Folio in 1632, Antonio's ships had "safely come to Rhodes."[17] Not only did the Third (1664) and Fourth (1685) Folios follow this reading, but so did George Granville, Lord Lansdowne, in his 1701 adaptation *The Jew of Venice: A Comedy*, the version of the play that held the English stage for forty years in the eighteenth century: "my scatter'd Ships, / Are safely all arriv'd at *Rhodes* / With their whole cargo" (Furness 346, 368).[18]

That multiple readers through the seventeenth and eighteenth centuries saw "Rhodes" as an appropriate rendering of this line reveals an expanded geographic context for the conclusion of the play. It also makes sense to imagine Antonio's ships docked at Rhodes, a way station for merchants traveling between Europe and overland trade routes in the Levant.[19] If we admit Rhodes into the geography of *The Merchant of Venice*, it joins the play's wide-ranging collection of references to scattered ports and points: Antonio's ventures spread through the Mediterranean (the "Tripolis," Barbary), in Europe (England, Lisbon), and beyond (Mexico, the Indies, India). The Prince of Morocco brags that he has seen battle with the "Sophy and Persian Prince," and swaggers that his fellow contestants for Portia's hand cross "Hyrcanian deserts and the vasty wilds / of wide Arabia" (2.7.40–1).[20]

Antonio's ships are the objects of a seemingly magical reversal (we never hear the circumstances of their recovery), a fact that troubled the eighteenth-century editor Ambrose Eccles. He condemned this final moment of fantastical revelation as a "lame, awkard [sic], and inartificial expedient" (Furness 266). Though later redeemed by Arthur Quiller-Couch and John Dover Wilson as a "beautiful example of Shakespeare's dramatic impudence," these editors, too, bring the emphasis to Shakespeare's hand in the turning of Antonio's fortunes (Halio 226). Eccles's use of "inartificial" recalls Sidney's dispute with stage romance and its practical solutions to the problems of staging of its fanciful plot turns. Thus, rather than a flourish of Shakespeare's invention, Portia's mysterious letter might demonstrate Shakespeare following a generic pattern in ushering the story to the stage. "You shall not know by what strange accident / I chanced on this letter." Notably this is a purely theatrical moment—Shakespeare's source did not present this recuperation of Antonio's lost ships. Portia serves as the messenger Sidney called for in presenting stories with many places and many times.

This final moment of *The Merchant of Venice*, with its evocative geographic language and the marvelous recovery of Antonio's ships, raises two points that have not received adequate critical attention. First, the geographic eccentricities of *The Merchant of Venice* suggest the influence of sixteenth-century stage romance on play's generic structure. Originally designated broadly in the quarto editions as *The Comicall Historie of the Merchant of Venice*, the status of the play as "historie" has received little commentary.[21] This is a term that represents generic breadth—history as "story"—but it was also a label often associated with dramatic and prose romance. Considering the play in light of its generic associations, I will connect it to the imperial possibilities that the English found for themselves in the sixteenth century: the hopes (and limitations) of economic expansion through geographic knowledge.

In shifting to the play's genre and treatment of space and geography, I seek to show how the economic representations within *Merchant* are also associated with its geographic and generic engagements. Recent criticism on *The Merchant of Venice* has come to a focal point on the question of economics and trade, its representation of early modern mercantilism, gift exchange, and credit systems.[22] These approaches follow Walter Cohen's influential work calling for a broad reassessment of the play in terms of its engagement with the play's economics.[23] In Mark Netzloff's recent response to Cohen, he refines the point, marking out a salutary distinction between the play's transactions with early modern mercantilism, on the one hand, and a proto-capitalist economics of exchange, on the other. *The Merchant of Venice*, Netzloff argues, offers us a view of the variegated approaches to wealth and exchange that characterized this period; it "naturalizes emergent forms of capital by translating economic innovation into the stable and traditional categories of class hierarchies, landed property, and patriarchal households" (162).

These "emergent forms of capital" also relied upon the systems of geographic knowledge and practice that have been the focus of this chapter. Indeed, the geographers I have cited recognized the importance of their craft in buttressing the mercantile ventures that enriched the British economy. William Barlow, the earlier discussed author of *The Navigator's Supply*, presents the impulse to foreign knowledge and travel as an economic, even political imperative. In order to be proper cosmopolitans, Barlow imagines, the people of London needed to become better acquainted with the origins of their food, the expanse of their trade, and the knowledge that makes all this possible. He writes of this in terms that draw on the specific localities of trade around the globe:

> I know right well, that among the vulgar people, there are many thousands, which going vnto market, doe bring home with them a peniworth or two of Cloaues or Mace nowe and then; and yet neuer asked the question where they grewe, nor by which they were transported from their Natiue countrey vnto vs, whether by the way of *Ormus* through *Persia*, or of *Arabia* by *Carauan* vnto *Alepo*, or by the Red Sea vnto *Alexandria*, and thence out of the *Leuant* vnto vs: or whether they came through the huge Ocean by the *Cape* of *Bona Speransa*. They take no knowledge of such matters: The consideration of any dangers in the Streights of *Cincapura*, or of the Showldes of *Maldivar* neuer troubleth them: And yet it relisheth euen as well and serueth their vses as commodiously, as if they had all the afore mentioned knowledge. (K1r)

Barlow worries that, like the cloudy supply chains that drive today's global commerce, the origins of the goods will remain unknown to London's consumers. Beyond this, Barlow's complaint about ignorant consumers also touches upon the political concerns expressed in those in government. The possibility of consumption without knowledge troubles Barlow, perhaps, because it creates complacency about England's place in this network of exchange.

Shakespeare's *Merchant of Venice* presents a cast of European Christian characters that indeed know the origins and paths of their merchandise. If anything, the worldly traders of Venice are too involved in the knowledge of their overseas risks. It is on this point that Antonio's carping friends open the play with conjecture about the causes of the merchant's sadness: "had I such venture forth," proclaims Solanio, "The better part of my affections would / Be with my hopes abroad" (1.1.15–17). Salerio echoes: "I should not see the sandy hour-glass run, / But I should think of shallows and of flats, / And see my wealthy Andrew, decks in sand" (1.1.25–7). Such knowledge does not bring the comfort Barlow imagined, but uneasy visions of shipwrecks that "scatter . . . spices on the stream" and "enrobe the roaring waters with my silks" (1.1.33–4). Antonio disavows such concerns, "my merchandise makes me not sad," he assures his friends, marking an immediate contrast between the merchant and the common citizen.

In a description that speaks to the contemporary importance of such a worldly point of view, Barlow tells the story of one Londoner:

> dwelling in Bucklers-burie: A man vnskilfull in the Lattin tongue, yet hauing proper knowledge in Arithmetike, and Land-measuring, in the vse of the Globe, and sundry other Instruments: And hath obteined, partly by his own industrie, and by reading of English Writers (whereof there are many very good) and partly with conference with learned men, (of which hee is passing desirous) such ready knowledge and dexteritie of teaching and practising the groundes of those Artes, as . . . I haue not beene acquainted with his like. (K2r)

Here we have John Goodwyn, apparently a self-tutored navigator and expert in the practical arts of geography, who represents to Barlow the exemplar of a new class of London citizen, one who knows and realizes the place of the English in the global marketplace. "And pitie it is," Barlow declares, "that in so populous a place, many such were not employed . . . Surely in all equitie and reason it were fitte, that euery Citie standing vpon merchandise and marine trades, should be ayding vnto those Faculties, whereby the greatest part of their well gotten goodes doeth accrewe vnto them" (K2r–v). A knowledge of and the ability to use maps, globes, and charts is particularly important for the future of London because of its "standing vpon merchandise and marine trades" as a source of consumer goods and wealth.

Barlow is surely attempting to sell books and compasses, the two products that he is bringing to the London market, but there is also a striking tone of national urgency in his remarks. Barlow derisively comments upon the navigators of Spain and Portugal, whom he presents as having an inflated reputation:

> For notwithstanding their first Nauigatours were men of good skill, these now a dayes for the most part are grossely ignorant: And a great folly it is in diuerse of our Nation to haue such confidence in Portugall Pilottages for long voyages, hauing farre more skilfull of our owne Countreymen at home, both better to be trusted, and more valiant and present minded in any danger. (I4r)

Their charts, Barlow claims, are "decked with much Golde and little Arte," and are merely replicated from the experiences of previous sailors (I4v). The English, as Barlow sees it, with their up-to-date technologies and more advanced mathematical knowledge can surpass the Spanish and Portuguese, but only if they cease to rely on foreign navigators. And in a notable moment that speaks to the concerns with race, foreignness, and religion in *The Merchant of Venice*, Barlow writes "wee are very much addicted to admire strangers, and contemne our owne, according to the olde Prouerbe, *For soothe it must needes be true; for I haue learned it of a Iewe*" (I4v). The conclusion of the *Navigator's Supply* sounds a call to both the English gentry and the "commons" (men like John Goodwyn) to stake their claims in the world's mercantile markets. That he chooses to characterize foreignness here in the figure of the learned Jew brings us to the concerns of Shakespeare's play, which presents a complicated version of the relationship between foreign and domestic discussed by Barlow.

Trade in *The Merchant of Venice*, Ania Loomba has argued, helps to distinguish categories of race and religion; it "is . . . portrayed as outward-looking, glamorous, and adventurous, and usury as inward-looking and cannibalistic" (*Shakespeare, Race* 152). This representation, I am arguing, required Shakespeare to alter some of the historical realities of early modern mercantile culture. Barlow's remarks about Jews and navigation underscore Aaron Kitch's recent interpretation of the play, wherein he positions Shylock as a representative of a "Jewish trading 'nation'" (107). That is, rather than being simply a figure of religious or racial "otherness," Shylock and the Jewish community in *Merchant* also stand as a competing force to the Christians within the play's historic economic structure.[24] Following Kitch, I therefore read in Shylock Shakespeare's attempt at domesticating or even taming the economic threat posed by Jewish merchandizing. The play presents a fantasy of economic containment wherein the Christian characters triumph over threats posed by various exemplars of foreignness. The play reverses the geographical orientation of self and other that has been observed in other postcolonial criticism—in various ways, the imperative in *Merchant* is for the native to move *away* from home, not to dwell in it. Travel, as we saw in the cartographic discourse as well as in romance, is understood as an antidote to economic and political stasis.

Such a transformation in the story can be seen in Shakespeare's handling of the source material for the wooing of Portia. Shakespeare found the tale of the casket lottery in the *Gesta Romanorum*, a series of stories that date back to the fourteenth century in England that were still in printed circulation through the sixteenth century. This original version of the story poses the woman as the character who must be tested, and her progression through the caskets is less of a "lottery" than a heuristic exercise that teaches her the moral of the story: God chooses our fate in love and fortune. Shakespeare took the outlines of this story and combined it with the familiar quest structure of romance. In fact, Shakespeare may have been inspired by Greene's dramatic adaptation of the *Orlando Furioso* in staging an international competition for Portia's hand. "the four winds blow in from every coast / Renowned suitors," Bassanio tells Antonio, a circumstance mirrored at the opening of Greene's play:

> From seauonfold Nylus to Taprobany,
> . . .
> From Gadis Ilands, where stowt Hercules
> Imblasde his trophees on two posts of brasse,
> To Tanais, whose swift declining flouds
> Inuirons rich Europa to the North;
> All fetch from out your Courts by beauty to this Coast,
> To seeke and sue for faire Angelica; (3–11)

The suitors to Angelica hail from Egypt, Mexico, Cuba, and the East Indies, an international cast of characters that Greene adapted specifically to his play (Ariosto includes neither these characters nor the scene) and which could have provided a model for Portia's potential mates. Shakespeare even seems to make a nod to Greene's play in Portia's commentary on her various suitors in 1.2: the "County Palatine" (1.2.39) is also the title given to Orlando in Greene, and Portia's dismissal of his dour disposition ("he doth nothing but frown . . . he hears merry tales and smiles not" (1.2.40–2)) might be a glancing allusion to Orlando's famed love-sickness.

From the outset, it is the riches of Portia that define her and her role in the play, an idea Bassanio expresses in comparing her to the Golden Fleece:

> . . . her sunny locks
> Hang on her temples like a golden fleece,
> Which makes her seat of Belmont Cholchis' strand,
> And many Jasons come in quest of her. (1.1.169–72)

Bassanio's flourish marks another parallel between Greene's *Orlando* and the Belmont story in Shakespeare: as he prepares to sail away from Africa, finally victorious in his quest for Angelica, Greene's Orlando boasts that his triumphant peers have outdone Jason and his Argonauts, "Meane while weele richly rigge vp all our Fleete / More braue than was that gallant Grecian keele / That brought away the Colchyan fleece of gold" (1435–7). The story of Jason and the Argonauts, as these allusions suggest, became a trope in discussions of foreign mercantile riches. Marlowe's Faustus places the Golden Fleece in America: "From Venice shall they drag huge argosies, / And from America the golden fleece / That yearly stuffs old Philip's treasury" (1.1.132–4). And Maximilianus Transilvanius, the first reporter of Magellan's circumnavigation, also found the story of Jason to be the relevant classical antecedent for his voyage. He calls the Magellanic voyagers:

> Mariners doubtlesse more woorthy to bee celebrate with eternal memorie then they whiche in owlde tyme were cauled *Argonauti* that sayled with Iason to win the golden fleese in the region of *Cholehic* and the riuer of Phasis in the greate sea of *Pontus*. And the shyppe it selfe, more woorthye to bee placed amonge the starres then that owlde Argo which departynge owt of Grecia, sayled to thende of that great sea. (Anghiera 262)

The story of the Argonauts prompts a boast for these sailors who have circumnavigated the globe. What they have done surpasses the classical example, exceeding the accomplishments of the ancients. The quest narrative of Jason, in all of these instances, serves the story and its audience with a speculative fantasy of foreign riches. The shifting geography of the fleece's location shows that the form of the story is more important than its details. A masculine quest for foreign riches can begin and end virtually anywhere, so long as the movement is from civilization (represented in Shakespeare as Venice) toward spaces that can be shaped by the imagination. In this way, *Merchant of Venice* recalls the argument expressed variously in Dee, Blundeville, and Mercator in their geographic practices. Overseas and formless spaces may be dangerous, but they are also places of possibility.[25]

Yet, as in Barlow's anti-Jewish commentary, Shakespeare's play also raises suspicion about mixing with "strangers." Notably, in all of these sources, the fleece, or the woman who represents it, is distinctly foreign (this is certainly the case in the *locus classicus*, the Medea story of antiquity). Not only do Portia and Nerissa mock the foreignness of the suitors, Bassanio expresses xenophobic sentiments in rejecting the gold casket during the central episode of the play: "ornament is but the guiled shore / To a most dangerous sea, the beauteous scarf / Veiling an Indian beauty" (3.2.97-9). As recent critics have noted, Bassanio's allusion to the "scarf" that veils the "Indian beauty" corresponds, broadly, with Eastern cultural practices.[26] The antithesis implied in the lines turns "Indian beauty" oxymoronic—just as the "guiled shore" might falsely lure sailors from the "dangerous sea" to their ruin, the scarf hides an exotic but false beauty.[27] The terms Bassanio employs here derive from the world of trade and suggest a more nuanced approach to foreign engagement than seen in Barlow and other materials in the chapter. In his caution, Bassanio looks past the obvious rewards of gold and silver (implicitly the "beauteous scarf" of the metaphor) and stakes his claim on what appears to be the least promising venture. Mark Netzloff sees in Bassanio's rejection of gold and silver an "emergent ethos of capitalist venturing," based not on coin and specie but upon credit and investing ("The Lead Casket" 167). In this way, *Merchant* rewrites the rules of chivalric romance into a developing kind of mercantile romance, whereby the questing hero achieves honor and marriage through commercial knowledge and chary speculation.[28]

Bassanio's willingness to venture abroad and take financial risk thus aligns him with the economics of speculation championed within the play. Conversely, we see the play reject the conservative economics of "thrift" embodied in Shylock and expressed through a lack of geographic circulation. I find it instructive that, as much as Shylock is labeled as "alien" to the Venetian Christian community (as he undoubtedly is), he also stands as the most domesticated character in the play. For unlike Antonio, Shylock's business is fully centered on the Rialto. Also unlike Antonio, we are given a view of Shylock's Venetian home, his household servant, and hear mention of his "synagogue" in act three. When Shylock hears of Jessica's prodigality from Tubal, the news arrives from Genoa, and the excessiveness of his daughter's expenditure ("Fourscore ducats at a sitting" 3.1.93) is bolstered by the geographic remove in which it takes place. While other characters in the play circulate through the world (even his "countryman," Tubal, brings tidings from Genoa), Shylock remains in Venice, hewing close to his own motto, "Fast bind, fast find" (2.5.52). His instructions to Jessica from within their home further speaks to this tendency: "Look to my house," "Lock up my doors," "stop my house's ears—I mean my casements," "Let not the sound of fopp'ry enter / My sober house" (2.5.16, 28, 33, 34–5). The Shylockian repetition of "house" in these lines emphasizes a connection to domestic space ultimately rejected in the play. When Shylock asks in the trial scene, "What if my house be troubled with a rat, / And I be pleased to give ten thousand ducats / to have it baned?" the questions sets up a mocking turnabout (4.1.43–5). Shylock's metaphor poses Antonio as the foreign invader to his home, the rat that must be "baned." The cutting irony of Shylock's sentence, then, is that the man who has stood as the most unmoving of Venice's denizens is labeled an "alien."

Shylock's geographic limitation is also expressed in his assessment of Antonio's ventures and the gamble he makes in staking 3000 ducats on a revenge plot. When Shylock calls into question the substance of Antonio's "means," he does so with reference to geography: "Yet his means are in supposition. He hath an argosy bound to Tripolis, another to the Indies. I understand moreover upon the Rialto he hath a third at Mexico, a fourth for England, and other ventures he hath squandered abroad" (1.3.14–18). Shakespeare's choice of the word "supposition" here to describe Antonio's "ventures" reverberates with the "speculative" geography discussed earlier in the chapter. Samuel Purchas used the same word, in fact, to describe the apocryphal stories of lands subsumed by the ocean: "A supposition, that there might be some Ilands or Parts of the Continent in times past, which is now swallowed by the mercilesse Ocean" (Qtd. in "supposition," n. def. 3b.). To Shylock, Antonio's wealth stands on speculation that is weakly supported by material reality: "ships are but boards, sailors but men . . . and then there is the peril of waters, winds, and rocks" (1.3.19–21). But the materiality expressed here in Shylock's thinking, highlighted, even parodied throughout the play ("My Daughter, My Ducats!"), stands in sharp contrast to Antonio's "supposititious" wealth. Ships, to the merchant, are more than the sum of their parts and the men that run them. Indeed, mercantile ventures like those of Antonio relied upon the outrageous multiplication of wealth that global transportation enabled. The materials mentioned by Salerio at the opening of the play, silks and spices, had a value that was significantly compounded beyond their material weight.

Shylock's punishment therefore demonstrates the consequences of refusing to participate in the fantasies of fortune that otherwise govern the economy of Venice. Such an example was also relevant to the London trading community, as well. Anthony Nixon, the hack writer who assembled the story of William Bush's strange journey in a self-made vessel, suggests that it is the imagining of wealth that supplies the merchant his "security":

> the Marchant, although he lye tossed with billowes, and tempest-shaken in the middest of the Ocean, yet is he made merrie at mid-night with the hope of Lucre. He that is mooued with delight in this matter of hope exactly declares his certaine confidence of apprehending the subiect of his hope, & the vndoubted grounds, and probable securitie of obtayning the thinges expected. (*The Trauels of M. Bush* C4v)

As I have shown, the interplay of material actuality with speculative fantasy is a defining characteristic of stage romance, geographic discourse, and the commercial venture. Thomas Heywood's *The Foure Prentises of London*, the anonymous *Tom a Lincoln*, and Robert Greene's *Orlando Furioso* show how the dramatic adaptation of romance responded to audience interest in the commercial and territorial possibilities of overseas expansion. Read in conjunction with this dramatic tradition, *The Merchant of Venice* reveals a complicated adoption of romance, particularly in its geographic movements. Even though in *Merchant* we are no longer in the chivalric courts of Arthur and Charlemagne, its wide-ranging geographic references and representations hearken to the romance tradition. Critics have long noted the play's doubled structure, materialized in movements between the commercial center of Venice and the imagined realm of Portia's Belmont. Cosmopolitan Venice, a place both like and unlike Shakespeare's London, contains the play's tragic forces. It is here that bonds and debts raise the prospect of ruin and death. Beyond the walls of the city, in spaces of speculation and fortune, there is hope that danger and death can be averted.[29]

Understood from the view of geography, the problem of the play is to redeem the speculative practices of the Venetian merchant community. It does so, as Netzloff points out, by conservatively attaching Antonio's merchant wealth to the landed estate of Belmont. *The Merchant of Venice* stages an exchange of wealth derived from capitalist contingency for the fantastical infinite expanses of Portia's treasury in Belmont. Antonio's financial venture and Bassiano's romantic quest (also forwardly financial) constitute a parallel exploration of differing forms of wealth acquisition that are both associated with romance in the sixteenth century—the chivalric quest and the mercantile venture. Read within the genre of romance, *Merchant* thus stages the pleasurable resolution (perhaps only momentarily) of the transition between older forms of wealth and upstart commercial enterprise. Shakespeare's play gives expression to this idea in both form and content. Generically speaking, Belmont (and Rhodes) represents for Antonio a place of salvation from the harsh economics staged in Venice, the place of Shylock. The coding of these places presents an argument for moving beyond the city. Indeed, the possible lost citation of Rhodes with which I began aligns with the fantastical nature of Portia's news: Antonio is granted his "life and living" in Belmont. Like Antonio and Bassanio, the audience takes in this news with amazement. The final situation of Antonio's fortune is not in Venice, but in the broader world of trade that is situated outside of the city. If we imagine Antonio's "argosies" harbored in Rhodes, there is no need to return to Venice. The problems of the city have dissolved in the naming of this geographic place of imagined riches. The final movement from Venice to Belmont maps a transition between commercially moribund spaces to those that are "richly come to harbor."

4
Chronicle History, Cosmopolitan Romance: *Henry V* and the Generic Boundaries of the Second Tetralogy

> Me ne noȝt al telle her / ac wo so it wole iwite
> In romance of him imad / me it may finde iwrite
>
> [All cannot be told here, but whosoever would like to know his story may find it written in the romance.]
> (Robert of Gloucester's *Chronicle*, c.1300)[1]

Romance in its dramatic form, I argued in the previous chapters of this book, helped fill in gaps, expand representations, and reshape the traffic of the early modern stage in the face of new global imperatives. This was the ambivalent admission of Sidney, who saw the early modern stage integrating material previously unknown within English dramatic culture with the help of romance. Such translations of the narrative form required dramatic adaptations that helped reshape the early commercial theater in London. In cartographic culture, as well as in stage romance, the fantasies of English empire and expansion could fill in those parts of the map that were still subject to speculation. As King Arthur's supposed imperial history resurfaced in travel narratives and maps, the knights of the Round Table could be found on the stage prepared for new conquests abroad.

As this final example reminds us, romance, from its very inception, was entwined with history. Arguably the founding text of Arthurian legend, Geoffrey of Monmouth's *Historia Regum Britanniae*, authorizes itself as "history" with the citation of "a very ancient book written in the British language . . . attractively composed to form a *consecutive and orderly narrative* . . . " (51, my emphasis). Both history and romance, here undivided, are materials with a narrative progression that share an "ancient" pedigree. In the passage from Robert of Gloucester above, romance and history are not imagined as competing genres. Romance, instead, fills out history, elaborating on the parts of the story that history cannot provide. Indeed, as Paul Strohm and many others have shown, the medieval conception of "historia" captured in Geoffrey's title is not limited to that of a rigorous factual account.[2] Even into the seventeenth century, the term "history" still signified a broad range of writings: poems, plays, narratives of current events, romances, allegory, and factual stories of the past. These genres, D. R. Woolf has argued, share two commonalities: "they tell stories, true or false, about real or imaginary men and women who lived in the remote or recent past; and they take the form not of a synchronic *inventory* of information but of a diachronic *narrative*" (16–17, author's emphasis). It is only in later stages of historiography that "history" took on the strict meaning that we understand today.[3]

On the early modern stage, romance and history shared more than a lexical relationship. As genres that translated the "orderly and consecutive" narratives of the past into enactment, each carried the burden of compressing profuse material into compressed enactment. Renaissance divisions of genre strictly separated history and poetry. The early modern stage maintained, at least ostensibly, that comedies and tragedies constituted self-evident dramatic genres. But the staging of history as history compelled an act of generic translation on the part of the playwright. Of the three genres listed in the First Folio, only the "Histories" lack classical precedent. The category of "Histories," like drama adapted from romance, required the stage to adapt a new mode of representation that could incorporate long gaps of time and, in some cases, movement over wide expanses of territory.[4]

The geographic expansiveness and travel staged in dramatic adaptations of romance called on the audience's imagination in order to perform its stories, and the employment of bold formal adaptations on the stage corresponded to aspirations for English empires abroad. In *Henry V* (1599) Shakespeare introduces a Chorus who strikingly echoes Dekker's in *Old Fortunatus* (1600): it calls for the audience to "play with your fancies" in imagining the spectacle that will unfold across England and France.[5] Shakespeare's Chorus transports the play's scenes with "imagined wing" that has "no less celerity / Than that of thought," just as Dekker invites "your swift thoughts [to] clap on their wonted wings." The Epilogue to *Henry V* speaks of "Our bending author," who "hath pursued the story, / In little room confining mighty men," words echoed by Dekker's chorus:

> into that narrow roome,
> Your quicke imaginations we must charme,
> To turne that world: and (turn'd) againe to part it

>Into large kingdomes, and within one moment,
>To carrie Fortunatus on the wings
>Of actiue thought, many a thousand miles.

Unlike Dekker's, Shakespeare's Chorus stands in the service of a play drawn from English history—yet in comparing only the two opening speeches of these plays, the naive viewer or reader would be forgiven for not knowing which "history" was, in fact, history.

>For 'tis your thoughts that now must deck our kings,
>Turning th'accomplishment of many years
>Into an hourglass—for the which supply,
>Admit me Chorus unto this history (1.0.29–32)

Both Choruses appeal to the spatial and temporal restrictions that the stage demands in making drama out of narrative: in the case of *Old Fortunatus*, a sixteenth-century German *Volksbuch*, and in *Henry V*, chronicles of English history by Raphael Holinshed and Edward Hall.[6] I begin this chapter, therefore, with the simple question of why two plays derived from seemingly different sources employ similar strategies in dramatizing their stories. What does the parallel structure and language of these speeches show us about the transactions of romance and history on the early modern stage? Moreover, what does the adaptation of this formal characteristic of the stage romance demonstrate about the audience's understanding of the *Henry V*'s genre?

In the past thirty years, as criticism on *Henry V* has become more skeptical of the play as strictly a patriotic set-piece, scholars have also come to question the generic label of "history" for the play, calling our attention to the ways in which "romance" should be considered as part its generic make-up.[7] Anne Barton follows the figure of the disguised king through earlier plays and narratives, as she argues, "the king's disguise demands to be seen as a romantic gesture" (10). Northrop Frye reads the play as "a successfully completed romantic quest" that turns to tragedy in the epilogue with the foreshadowing of Henry's premature death (221). Barton, Frye and others thus find the word "romance" a convenient generic term for indicating how the play incorporates elements not seen in other Shakespearean histories. The final scene of the play, in one critic's estimation, does "violence to [the] genre" of the history play by introducing a "romantic minicomedy" (Hedrick 470). These responses to the genre of the play indicate a continued uneasiness with situating *Henry V* in the category of "history." Yet the body of generic criticism on *Henry V* also produces a sense of the play as idiosyncratic, and less an example to fit within generic tradition than an exceptional artistic expression. Even Joanne Altieri, a critic who detects elements of romance within the play, asserts it as "part of the development towards *The Tempest* and *The Winter's Tale*" and thus reproduces Dowden's thesis that romance develops fully only later in Shakespeare's career (233).

Recent studies in medieval romance have argued that romance and history were not simply combined in undefined amalgamations.[8] Rather, there was a strategic deployment of history in romance and vice-versa. Romance, Geraldine Heng has argued, "transact[s] a magical relationship with history, of which it is in fact a consuming part" (3). The magic of this relationship lies in that distinguishing ability for romance to assume the guise of history, the appearance of truth, within fictive worlds. Writing on Geoffrey of Monmouth's seminal *Historiae Regum Britanniae*, Heng notes:

> in a resourcefully accommodating cultural medium, historical phenomena and fantasy may collide and vanish, each into the other, without explanation or apology, at the precise locations where both can be readily mined to best advantage—a prime characteristic of romance that persists henceforth. (2)

What Heng identifies as a characteristic of Geoffrey's text, the assumption of history into an "accommodating cultural medium," one that silently envelops history into fantasy, I will argue also defines *Henry V*. As plays, pamphlets, travel narratives, ballads, and other popular forms came to incorporate many more stories of journeys into foreign territories, colonial adventures, and the observations of foreign peoples and places, romance provided a means of assimilating the unfamiliar into the familiar. With materials drawn from "chronicle history," romance made the events of the past more easily available and accessible to those who read stories or saw plays. Such a mixing of genres explains, in part, why romance reemerged in the repertoires of early modern theater companies. In *Henry V*, the stage proved itself to be more than a useful ancillary to the telling of history; it could actually enable the story itself. In fact, the advantage of the stage in portraying history (*pace* Aristotle and Sidney) was that it exhorted the audience to both see and imagine—to actually participate in—the creation of the story.

The argument of this chapter is that in order to encompass the imperial and expansionist matter in this history, Shakespeare turned to the stage romance. In determining the materials of this final movement in the second tetralogy, Shakespeare infused what would have been a familiar set of dramatic strategies into the play: the invocation of the audience's imagination, a challenging of classical theory and precedent, and most of all, a commanding visualization of action and territorial conquest through dramatic representations. Choosing a play that is not commonly counted among "romances," I aim to demonstrate a broader influence for the genre within both Shakespeare and English dramatic culture. In the mixing of history and romance, we see the possibilities for staging speculative ambitions within the historical records of the past.

From chronicle history to romance: structuring the second tetralogy

The Bolingbroke of Shakespeare's second tetralogy exhibits a distinctive lack of imagination. Facing his banishment in *Richard II*, he rejects John of Gaunt's pacifying directive to "Call it a travel that thou tak'st for pleasure" and to "suppose / Devouring pestilence hangs in our air / And thou art flying to a fresher clime" (1.3.251; 1.3.256.16–256.18). In Bolingbroke's response, we see that Gaunt's advice about foreign travel amounts for him literally, and trivially, to a flight of fancy:

> O, who can hold a fire in his hand
> By thinking on the frosty Caucasus,
> Or cloy the hungry edge of appetite
> By bare imagination of a feast,
> Or wallow naked in December snow
> By thinking on fantastic summer's heat? (1.3.257–62)

Bolingbroke's summary rejection of these imaginative experiences is also, by analogy, a dismissal of the power of the theater and dramatic representation. Just as Sidney had wondered at the stage's ability to conjure Peru and Calicut, Henry Hereford cannot wish into being the "fresher clime" of his exile. His skepticism in the play about the power of imagination finds its antithesis in King Richard, who fantastically pictures himself "wand'ring with the Antipodes" (3.2.45) upon his return from imperial wars in Ireland, a geographic projection with romance resonances. And unlike his cousin, Richard can conjure a "generation of still-breeding thoughts" to "people this little world" (5.5.8–9) of his prison cell.

Richard's fanciful imaginings, however, are scorned within this play, issuing from the mouth of an "unkinged" king. Yet in the conclusion of the tetralogy in *Henry V*, we find again a king doing the work of empire building in a play that embraces the imagination. The burden is shifted here to the audience; the Chorus begins by asking the audience to conjure "warlike Harry" with "imaginary forces" (1.0.5, 18), reviving the rhetoric of imagination in favor of the new king. In contrast, Bolingbroke's lack of imaginative power presages his political and imperial inefficacy as king throughout the tetralogy. Once he accedes to the throne, the king (and the action of the plays that bear his name) never ranges beyond England, Scotland, and Wales. Despite his desire to mount a crusade in the East, this King Henry never crosses the channel. Instead, the geography of the two *Henry IV* plays maps the civil miasma that infects their plots. In his final moment before death, King Henry is stung by the irony that he will die not on the fields of the Holy Land, but in the Jerusalem Chamber at Westminster. "In that Jerusalem shall Harry die" (4.3.368). Harry Bolingbroke comes not full circle, but is rather inevitably, inexorably, rooted in place as his desire for salvational travel must submit to the broils of succession that dominate these plays.

Shakespeare's second tetralogy is thus initially hemmed in by history. Richard's "wand'ring" in *Richard II* is a marker of his prodigality. Bolingbroke's rootedness, however, proves no solution to his predecessor's extravagance. It is only in the final play in the tetralogy that we find travel employed productively in the new King Henry's imperial theatricality. John of Gaunt calls England, "this little world" (2.1.45) a microcosm "bound in with the triumphant sea" (61), while *Henry V* strives to press beyond, into the macrocosmic view of Britain. Henry V breaks the boundaries of history and geography and travels over Gaunt's "moat defensive" (2.1.48). Taken this way, what we see in *Henry V* is the employment of romance as a means of producing English empire.

In this light, *Henry V* bears a stronger resemblance to another play that stages the romancing of history, Shakespeare's *Cymbeline*, than it does to its predecessors in the tetralogy. Innogen, for instance, expresses a cosmopolitan sense of the world that starkly contrasts with Bolingbroke's earlier quoted speech. Upon learning that she must leave Cymbeline's court to avoid Cloten's unwanted advances, she asks:

> Hath Britain all the sun that shines? Day, night,
> Are they not but in Britain? I'th'world's volume
> Our Britain seems as of it, but not in't;
> In a great pool a swan's nest. Prithee, think
> There's livers out of Britain (3.4.136–9)

While Bolingbroke's narrative must remain firmly tied to the "volume" of history, Innogen wonders at those who separate the British from the "world's volume," a biblio-metaphor that could equally point to historical or geographic representations. For her, there is life (and "livers") beyond the confines of the island. Innogen's speech implicitly critiques the limited imagination of Bolingbroke, but also of her father's queen and Cloten. "Britain's / A world by itself" (3.1.12–13), proclaims the latter, presenting a view of geographical and political isolation hardly celebrated in the play.[9] Indeed, Patricia Parker identifies in the play a "demise of the figures identified with a narrow British nationalism" as *Cymbeline* replaces those figures with broader imperial ambitions ("Romance and Empire" 201).

Cymbeline favorably suggests the possibility of a hybrid Roman and British identity, forged in conquest and burnished by travel between the realms of ancient Britain (including Wales) and a modern-seeming Italy. The avatar of this identity is Posthumus, a middling warrior whose valiance on the battlefield elevates his status by the end of the play. Although Cymbeline initially rejects the match between Posthumus and Innogen, this play's conclusion elides the problem of Posthumus's birth. The dream and prophecy of Jupiter, "such stuff as madmen / Tongue," Posthumus calls it, also contains "The action of my [Posthumus's] life" (5.5.238–9, 242), and the combination of "dream" and life narrative characterizes Posthumus's ascendancy. Redeemed, Posthumus can participate in the "peace" (Cymbeline's final word) that literally ends the play with promises for the "radiant" future of Cymbeline "which shines here in the west" (5.4.474). Romanced history creates imperial visions of the new *Pax Romanum* envisioned in this final moment, or the joining of France and England in *Henry V*. Within the world of romance, the differences in class and nationality that separate Innogen and Posthumus can be smoothed over, much as can the linguistic differences of Harry and Kate. And so it is significant that the Roman and British ensigns, hung "friendly together," oversee the conclusion of the play. The sea does not limit Britain's borders, as John of Gaunt or Cloten would have it. They reach out to a fantasy of imperial expansion like that of John Dee's. Even though it is subjected, it seems, to Caesar, British dominion now reaches beyond the seacoast and into foreign spaces.

Crucially, this external reach is expressed in *Cymbeline* dramatically through the easy and uncomplicated shifts we see in action. Innogen's wish for a "horse with wings" (3.2.49) is not fulfilled literally, but much as the Chorus of *Henry V* is able to whisk its viewers across the channel with "gentle pass" (2.0.39), the action of Cymbeline transports us in moments from the court of Cymbeline to rustic Wales, from contemporary Italy to ancient Rome, all within the course of a few hours. That *Henry V* foregrounds these shifts, while *Cymbeline* allows them to remain implicit, marks an important difference in the dramatic mode assumed in the plays. *Henry V* emphasizes its imperial content through its structure more forcefully. This play, it turns out, connects itself more strongly to romance than *Cymbeline*.

The earliest audiences of *Henry V* would have thus experienced a far different play from the previous installments in the tetralogy. This is a play that frequently points beyond local or regional geography and political affiliation toward world empires.[10] Canterbury, for instance, calls on the King to assume the imperial mantle of Edward III, the King who first brought territories in France under English sovereignty. In a rousing speech, Canterbury tells King Henry to visit:

> . . . your great-grandsire's tomb,
> From whom you claim; invoke his warlike spirit,
> And your great-uncle's, Edward the Black Prince,
> Who on the French ground played a tragedy,
> Making defeat on the full power of France, (1.2.103–14)

The ease with which the clergy determine the English rights to these lands is in lockstep with the straightforwardness of the Chorus in transporting the scene and the English in their miraculous defeat of the French forces. Philip Schwyzer argues, referring to this same passage, "The task imposed on Henry is, in a double sense, that of *revival*—of the dead themselves and of the successful theatrical production staged at Crécy" (*Literature, Nationalism, and Memory* 129–30). In addition to Edward III, his son Edward the Black Prince (the deposed Richard II's father), Alexander, and Essex, the play also conjures the conquering spirits of Caesar (5.0.28), Pompey (4.1.69), Agamemnon (3.6.5), and Antony (3.6.12).[11] Henry is thus, by extension, placed in the long genealogy of these imperial powers.

The subsequent bee analogy proposed in Canterbury's speech is correspondingly imperial—he imagines the collective might of the English empowered to collect, fight, and win. Canterbury describes the state as a divided body aligned in its purposes under the imperial king through an analogy with the honey bees, "Creatures that by a rule in nature teach / The act of order to a peopled kingdom" (1.2.188–9). Book Four of Virgil's *Georgics* has been identified as the *locus classicus* for this simile, but Shakespeare's description of the community of bees is substantially his own.[12] Though Virgil's bees are shown as ready for battle with the "vast passions agitating their little breasts" (83), their battles are mock-heroic, as L. P. Wilkinson observes (101–2). Virgil's bees, rather befitting the genre of the pastoral, are domesticated, "They know a native country, are sure of hearth and home" (155). Contrast this with the appearance in *Henry V* of bees who "like merchants venture trade abroad," or of the soldiers, "arméd in their stings, / Make boot upon the summer's velvet buds, / Which pillage they with merry march bring home / To the tent royal of their emperor" (1.2.191–6). Shakespeare's is an image of the imperial state assembled from different pieces, distinct classes and labors, coming together under "one consent" (206).

Thus, more than the *Georgics*, the bee metaphor in *Henry V* recalls rhetoric like that in this passage from the epistle to Philip Sidney that opens Richard Hakluyt's 1582 *Diverse Voyages Touching the Discovery of America*: "Wee reade that the Bees when they grow to be too many in their own hiues at home, are wont to bee led out by their Captaines to swarme abroad, and seeke themselves a new dwelling place" (¶v).[13] Shakespeare and Hakluyt recast the colony of bees as nature's impetus to empire, a contrast to their simple, domesticated state in Virgil. Shakespeare even sharpens the image—Henry's kingdom of trading merchants and conquering soldiers seek more than a new dwelling place. Their motivation is toward plunder and an aggressive outward extension.

The bee hive is an important metaphor for the play as a whole. The victory at Agincourt is the product of a "band of brothers," as Henry famously calls them, a unit seemingly divided by nationality, class, even speech. And in this initial moment of the play, the diversity of the English stands as a rationalizing justification for war, "as many arrows loosed several ways / Come to one mark" (207–8). There is a parallel logic of unified contraries in romance, as well, as a genre that brings together, in Minturno's phrase, "many things into one bundle." As such, romance becomes an apt expression of empire in these plays, a genre that can align disparate traditions of historiography, chivalric legend, romantic conquest, and foreign quest. Moreover, the vision of empire enacted in the course of *Henry V* is precisely one of alien cultures becoming one under the military power of the English. Though this play raises significant hurdles to that conquest, in the linguistic differences between Catherine and Henry, or instance, or in the suggested racial disparity between the cold northern English and the French, Shakespeare's play successfully eliminates these obstacles in much the same way that the Chorus elides the disparities in space and time created by history. At the very level of dramatic form, the telling of history through drama, *Henry V* enacts its imperialism. Encouraging its audience to imagine what cannot be seen, to capture in the mind's eye the fantasies of conquest enacted on the stage, this play transforms chronicle history into imperial romance.

Henry V also develops the representational concerns with territory spoken by the Chorus within the plot's recurring references to territorial acquisition, places of origin, and general attention to geographic space. In the famously arcane deliberations about land and the politics of land acquisition that open the play, the Archbishop of Canterbury warns that the Parliament's proposed legislation, if passed, would take away properties inherited by the Church:

> If it [the bill] pass against us,
> We lose the better half of our possession,
> For all the temporal lands which men devout
> By testament have given to the Church
> Would they strip from us—being valued thus (1.1.7–11)

Canterbury then offers a list of the titular lands passed to the Church that now stand in contestation. The King, Canterbury promises, will be able to "unloose" the "Gordian knot" of the legislature and win the day for the Ecclesiastical interests (1.1.47). It is worth noting that, though he is not here named, the story of the Gordian knot is a tale about Alexander the Great, who solved the riddle by cutting through it with his sword, thus fulfilling the prophesy that whoever solved the riddle would rule all of Asia. The Gordian knot is the first of many references to Alexander that crop up throughout the play, but here, in the context of empire and territory, it casts the King as the destined conqueror and ruler of an Anglo-French empire.[14] For Canterbury promises, "As touching France, to give a greater sum / Than ever at one time the clergy yet / Did to his predecessors part withal" (1.1.80–2). The Bishop uses this line of argumentation to preserve coveted Church lands while offering to the Crown a "greater sum" of territory than the ecclesiastic properties could provide.

The metaphor of the knot unloosed touches upon the outward reach of the play, which begins with concerns about the constraints of the stage, but unfurls the play's action outward nevertheless. Unique among Shakespeare's histories in this regard, *Henry V* depicts the historical reacquisition of lands conquered by an earlier imperial campaign in France (that of Edward III, referred to throughout the play). On the battlefield, the Welsh Fluellen extols the King's Welsh heritage, and in doing so, connects him, through humorously shaky geographic logic, to Alexander the

Great: King Henry was born in Monmouth, while Alexander was born in Macedon:

> I tell you, captain, if you look in the maps of the world I warrant you shall find, in the comparisons between Macedon and Monmouth, that the situations, look you, is both alike. There is a river in Macedon, and there is also moreover a river at Monmouth. It is called Wye at Monmouth, but it is out of my prains what is the name of the other river—bit 'tis all one, 'tis alike as my fingers is to my fingers, and there is salmons in both. If you mark Alexander's life well, Harry of Monmouth's life is come after it indifferent well. For there is figures in all things. (4.7.19–27)

As David Quint has recognized, Fluellen goes on to comment on Alexander's notoriously bad temper, comparing Henry's order to kill the French prisoners to Alexander's wrathful judgment of one of his officers. While rendered here in comic relief in the exchange between king and soldier, the speech broaches the geographic rendering of empire and history that circulates throughout this play. This speech is not the only place in the play that the audience is invited to see the "figures in all things" and to compare the King and his actions to other historical figures (or, in the case of the Earl of Essex, the "General of our gracious Empress," a contemporary imperial figure). The manner in which Fluellen does so here, however, is notable: the "maps of the world" enable a comparison between places as disparate as Macedon and Monmouth; the visualization that the map corresponds to a transhistorical and macrocosmic yoking of Henry with Alexander and the other empires that surface through the play.

Cosmopolitan romance

Romance on the stage, as I have argued, was cognate with other forms of geographic and imperial imaginings within the period. Indeed, in writings like John Dee's, it becomes difficult to disentangle geography, history, and romance. The intersections of these spheres of experience (the spatial, fictional, and empirical) arose in response to an audience of viewers and readers interested in material that could bridge their understanding beyond the confines of Europe. John Dee's vision of a "British Empire" rested on an expansive conception of history and geography that insisted on the ancient dominion held by the English in the North Atlantic and beyond. William H. Sherman, in his thorough analysis of Dee's reading practices, notes that the historical texts that drew the greatest interest from Dee were those that touched upon King Arthur, the ancient history of *Britannia*, and generally those that related to current debates about the unification and expansion of a Tudor empire (*John Dee*, 91).

This reading materializes in an international political worldview espoused in *The Limits of the British Empire*, as we saw in his discussions of geography and history in the previous chapter. Elsewhere in his writings, Dee extends these ideas. In the *General and Rare Memorials Pertaining to the Perfect Art of Navigation* (1577), Dee offers a "Discourse of the British Monarchy" focused on the Saxon King Edgar, a tenth century prince who provides a model of "cosmopoliticall gouernment."

> I haue oftentymes, (Sayd He,) and many wayes, looked into the State of Earthly Kingdomes, Generally the whole World ouer: (as far, as it may, yet, be yet known to Christen Men; Commonly) . . . to fynde hym self *Cosmopolites:* A Citizen, and Member, of the whole and only one Mysticall City Vniversall: And so, consequently, to meditate of the Cosmopoliticall Gouernment therof . . . (54)

Dee's utopian vision posits a sovereign with reign over "the whole world."[15] He contends, disappointedly, that such a monarchy could already have been realized if only the "British" had followed a path, beginning with "this peaceable king Edgar" some six hundred years earlier. For Edgar, even though a Saxon king (and therefore, not British) would have brought them, in Dee's time, to global primacy. "They mought, very well, ere this, haue surpassed . . . any particular Monarchy, els, that euer was on Earth, since Mans Creation" (54).

Reprinted in Richard Hakluyt's *Principall Navigations*, Dee's small tract fits well into the volume's overarching project: to create an ancient history for English voyaging and, in doing so, legitimate future endeavors.[16] Dee reaches back into pre-conquest history (Hakluyt's headnote to this section cites "Florentius Wigoriensis and Houeden") to find stories and epitaphs of King Edgar, whose prodigious naval fleet and global imagination make him an admirable role model for the present monarch. As we saw him do in the *Limits of the British Empire* previously, Dee forcefully argues that an overseas empire (like a reformed English church) is not an innovation, but a recovery of something the English might have had if they had seized the proper moment.

Hakluyt and Dee present this imperial propaganda through history, or more specifically, in historiography—the writing of past events.

This, however, is a historiography transformed by the imagination. Moving beyond the simple details of Edgar's naval fleet, his conquest of territories surrounding the shores of Britain, and his triumphs over enemies, Dee tells of a ruler who, like Arthur, deserves legendary status as "one of the perfect Imperiall Monarchs of this Brytish Impire" (56). Another document in Hakluyt's collection, a fifteenth-century poem entitled "The Libel of English Policy," does similar work, "exhorting" its extended title says, "all England to keepe the sea, and namely the narrowe sea shewing what profite commeth thereof, and also what worship and saluation to England, and to all English-men" (Hakluyt 187). One of the heroes of the anonymous poem is Henry V, whose voyage to Harfleur is memorialized as a great naval expedition, and Henry as "Lorde round about enuiron of the see" (Hakluyt 203). The poet also compares Henry to "Edgar" and "Edward," but proclaims that he surpassed even them:

> Henry the fift, with whom all my processe
> Of this true booke of pure policie
> Of sea keeping, entending victorie
> I leaue endly: for about in the see
> No prince was of better strenuitee.
> And if he had to this time liued here,
> He had bene Prince named withouten pere (Hakluyt 204)

In turning to Shakespeare's representation of King Henry the Fifth, it is with these contextual illustrations in mind. Henry, as he appears in these paeans, is more than a King of England. He adumbrates British imperial power. Such a portrayal is not far from Shakespeare, whose Chorus asks the audience to imagine Henry's "brave fleet" and "fleet majestical" (3.0.5, 16). "Grapple your minds to the sternage of this navy," the Chorus orders, "And leave your England . . . " (3.0.18–19). The rousing scene the Chorus paints of the stage as a ship connects to this triumphant vision of Henry as a sea captain. Hakluyt and Dee offer precedents for English sea might and therefore naturalize English dominion over the seas.

The hopeful writings in the *Principal Navigations* on this "cosmopolite" government lie parallel to the growing sixteenth-century view of politics that emphasized England's place in a broader international community. "Nation, region, and the world were all intertwined in this period," Alison Games has argued, "as European states and kingdoms struggled for dominance in Europe and turned to overseas holdings to finance or reinforce that power. The power of a state within Europe was necessarily connected to that state's ability to project itself beyond the region" (14).[17] The cultural artifacts of this period embed a contested outlook on this cosmopolitan worldview.[18] In the geographic materials I have examined, the reader is invited into a recumbent adventure that nonetheless enfolds him in a kind of global fantasy—the ability to experience, even seize, the known world. *Henry V*, in its adaptation of English history into romance, and by appropriating the imperial legacy of the conquering Henry, presents its audience with a similar image. The Chorus, using rhetoric similar to that in geographic representations, asks the viewer to envision him or herself as a companion in the journeys of the characters on stage. A version of Dee's "cosmopolites," Shakespeare's Henry seeks to increase English territory, but also invites, and at times impels, the audience to share in that project and cosmopolitan purview.

John Gillies attributes a visualization of "history" to an increasing awareness of world geography precipitated by the publication of global maps. In *Shakespeare and the Geography of Difference*, he argues that at the end of the sixteenth century, the conceptualization of stage representation itself became closely tied to the geographic conception of the world that was spurred by new navigations and discoveries. As Gillies observes, Abraham Ortelius's 1570 *Theatrum Orbis Terrarum* describes maps as being an important tool for relating history: "the reading of Histories doeth both seeme to be much more pleasant, and in deed so it is, when the Mappe being layed before our eyes, we may behold things done, or places where they were done, as if they were at this time present and in doing" (To the Reader). In the "Second Table" of the *Theatrum*, Ortelius prints maps that depict the wanderings of Odysseus and Aeneas, biblical stories, Jason's voyage for the Golden Fleece, and Alexander's conquering path. Ortelius promotes the use of his maps as narrative devices to help the reader visualize "history" in the broadest sense of the term.

But the stage does something different than merely present a picture in which its audience can see history. After all, the stage was not the same as Ortelius's map room, and one could not simply see history unfolding through geography as Mercator's reader could. Such a difference between metaphor and reality are important in this case. The Choruses in Dekker and Shakespeare call on the audience to labor in the service of the illusion. In the first Chorus of *Henry V* alone, the audience must "Piece out our imperfections with your thoughts" (1.0.23), "make imaginary puissance" (1.0.25), "think," "deck," "carry," jump, and turn (1.0.26–30). Likewise, Dekker prioritizes the viewer's involvement, even his courtesy, in creating the world of the play, "Your gracious eye, Giues life to *Fortunatus* historie" (23–4). While the maps of the world, and their narratives, submit themselves to recumbent readers "in the quiet shade of your Studdies," the rhetoric of the stage demands that the viewer become involved in the labor of creating the represented fantasy.[19]

This involvement of the audience separates stage romance from other genres insofar as it places the audience in a working relationship (though fantastical) with empire. These are the moments in which an English audience was shaped, prepared, even, for cultivating English interests abroad. Such a view, according to Allison Games, corresponded with the emergence of actual "citizens of the world," who sought travel and experiences that moved them beyond the shores of England. These men and women were "made not born," and Games calls our attention to the social conditions that allowed for their cultivation (9). Even if they never set foot beyond London, these attitudes and ideas about empire that emanated from the stage played a part in creating the cosmopolitan culture Games explores.

This argument for a cosmopolitan *Henry V* augments a long and now familiar critical tradition that held up the play as the most stridently nationalist of the histories, one that formulates a nascent English identity.[20] Shakespeare's inclusion of Irish, Welsh, and Scottish characters is suggestive of England's contemporary ambitions in consolidating "British" territory, as several recent studies of the rise of English and British nationhood under the Tudor and Stuart monarchies have argued.[21] This body of scholarship has questioned the position that the play exemplifies and champions an unproblematic "Englishness." The Archipelagic turn in *Henry V* criticism, accomplished in important work by David Baker, Willy Maley, Philip Schwyzer, Claire McEachern, Andrew Hadfield, and others, has thus challenged traditional ways of looking at the play's treatment of nation, positing instead what Baker calls "an unresolved political and cultural problem" in the play's assertions of national identities (8).[22] But even these significant contributions maintain the play's insularity, and a proclivity to isolate British identity from Europe and the broader world. As I will argue, the dramatic strategies of romance, as well as the play's envisioning of world empires, contribute to how *Henry V* asks its audience to imagine a British nation. Beyond unifying the ancient three regions of Britain and reaching out to Ireland, the play signals a hopeful view of England's place in imperial history.

Taking the perspective offered by romance opens the definition of nation beyond even the expansive "British" framework. It is this imagined transnational identity that sits at the heart of *Henry V*, and marks its departure from the earlier plays in Shakespeare's second tetralogy. As a genre, romance tends to disrupt the neat parameters of national boundaries perpetuated within political and historical discourse. We saw this in *Tom a Lincoln*, where the Red Rose knight formulates his identity not from his father's lineage, but from his military and sexual feats accomplished abroad. A more hybrid or positional identity often compromises, even trumps, the Englishness (or Frenchness, Germanness, etc.) of the romance hero. Introducing the question of genre to this recent body of scholarship on *Henry V*, and specifically the consideration of the play's entwining of stage romance, demonstrates further how ideas of empire align with the formal imperatives of the stage. *Henry V* illustrates where the generic and geographic boundaries of chronicle history break down, and when romance becomes necessary in staging the past.

Though *Henry V* points momentarily to this celebratory version of such imperial cosmopolitanism, it is certainly not the only imagining of French and English mixture presented. Through much of the play, the two nations are registered as significantly different and mutually inassimilable. The difference between France and England is registered most definitively in a speech among the French in act three, scene five. In it, the French call the English "a barbarous people" (3.5.4) from a "wild and savage stock" (3.5.7). The Constable wonders "Where have they this mettle" (3.5.15), and elaborates by calling attention to the climate of their homeland:

> Is not their climate foggy, raw, and dull,
> On whom as in despite the sun looks pale,
> Killing their fruit with frowns? Can sodden water,
> A drench for sur-reined jades—their barley-broth—
> Decoct their cold blood to such valiant heat?
> And shall our quick blood, spirited with wine,
> Seem frosty? O for honour of our land
> Let us not hang like roping icicles
> Upon our houses' thatch, whiles a more frosty people
> Sweat drops of gallant youth in our rich fields. (3.5.16–25)

This passage resonates strongly with Mary Floyd-Wilson's work on race, ethnicity and climate. Floyd-Wilson contends that early modern English notions of race and ethnicity were rooted in their understanding of "geohumoralism," the connection between the body's humors and the region in which a people lives. "To comprehend the English people's understanding of ethnicity—their own and others'—we must begin with the recognition that they conceived of themselves as and their island as 'northern.' England's northern climate and the English people's northern status colored their perspective on everything from fashion to medicine to politics" (4). The French in *Henry V* see the English as being more northern than they—"a more frosty people" (3.5.24). As a result, the French do not expect the English to be as "valiant" in battle or as "quick" as people from the more southern regions of France. This belief that the English were somehow constitutionally inferior to southern Europeans led to a series of writings, Floyd-Wilson argues, in the English "struggle to stabilize and rehabilitate their northern identity" (4). For, "In facing their northern roots, the English confronted the possibility that they were the barbaric progeny of a dissolute, mingled, and intemperate race" (15).

The Duke of Bourbon captures this in calling the English "Normans, but bastard Normans, Norman bastards!" (3.5.10). As descendents of a conquered people, the English must admit of a history of rape and, therefore, bastardy (in this case, dating to the most recent Norman conquest). The Duke's comments raise the memory of a racially and constitutionally impure past. Notably, the play puts this racially charged language in the mouths of the French, preferring, in the end, a hybrid identity to the purist idea of lineage offered by the French. This idea that the English are subject to intermixing and intemperance surfaces, too, in the conspiracy of Grey, Scrope, and Canterbury. "O England!—model to thy inward greatness, / Like little body with a mighty heart, / What mightst thou do, that honour would thee do, / Were all thy children kind and natural?" (2.0.16–19). The Chorus describes the conspiracy in terms of their bodies, which are rendered monstrous through their dealings. They are not filled with the "mighty heart" of the English, but instead have "hollow bosoms" (2.0.21) that are easily filled with French gold. In saying that the conspirators ("children" of England) are not "kind" or "natural," the Chorus defines a category based on nation and lineage—one that in this instance does not seem to allow for mixing or contamination. King Henry picks up on this same language in his address to the condemned conspirators, calling them "English monsters" (2.2.82) employed in the "practices of France" (2.2.87). As Floyd-Wilson argues, "Having been conquered so entirely by the Romans and then reconquered by the Saxons, the Danes, the Normans, English writers betray a fear . . . that the only thing they have inherited from their earliest ancestors is the tendency to degenerate from their nature and kind" (57).

But meeting the promise of the tetralogy, this Henry can convert "past evils to advantages" (*2 Henry IV*, 4.3.78). Whereas the seemingly xenophobic French see in the English weakness, Henry finds in the marbled characterization of the English undoubted strength. So as the play opens upon a monstrous hybridity, nevertheless it moves toward a less threatening alternative in the marriage match between Henry and Catherine. Or, perhaps more fittingly, the play assuages this initial concern over mixing French hearts with English bodies. *Henry V* thus realigns the idea of "nation" in the conquest of Catherine and the triumph over the French's nationalistic view of race. The final scene of the play, somewhat magically, transforms the conquest of foreign lands, with its attendant bloodshed and ruthlessness, into a romance that resolves the tensions and contradictions brought out by the battles.[23]

Romance here extends to the tradition of medieval courtly love, the language of which suffuses the scene. "Fair Catherine, and most fair, / Will you vouchsafe to teach a soldier terms / Such as will enter at a lady's ear / And plead his love-suit to her gentle heart?" (5.2.98–101). Later, Harry further colors himself as a knight or soldier: "If I could win a lady at leap-frog, or by vaulting into my saddle with my armour on my back . . . I should quickly leap into a wife" (5.2.134–7). Henry coyly poses himself as the inarticulate soldier, who needs education in the "terms" of the "love-suit." "Put off your maiden blushes, avouch the thoughts of your heart with the looks of an empress, take me by the hand and say, 'Harry of England, I am thine'—which word thou shalt no sooner bless mine ear withal, but I will tell thee aloud, 'England is thine, Ireland is thine, France is thine, and Henry Plantagenet is thine'" (220–3). The conquest of land enacted earlier on the imaginary battlefield is transferred here to a love exchange, the territories of Britain standing in as love tokens to be offered in their courtship. And thus, the horror of the war is blushed over in Catherine's "virgin crimson of modesty" (274).

The love match between Henry and Catherine appears, at first, to present no obstacle to Henry's foreign conquest (or to his role as conquering hero). In fact, as discussed above, Catherine is herself termed as "land" and her marriage to the King of England (already ratified when they meet) is part and parcel of his imperial ambitions. But the play raises complicating questions about the marriage of Catherine and Henry and, by extension, the conquest of France by England.

On closer analysis, Shakespeare's *Henry V* underscores the foreignness of Catherine and, therefore, the hybridity of a royal union between France and England. The differences between England and France are made all the more apparent when Shakespeare's *Henry V* is set alongside *The Famous Victories of Henry V* (1594), an earlier play that Shakespeare used in adapting his own version of the story. The most striking thing about the wooing scene in the *Famous Victories* is that it omits the linguistic difficulties the two have in communicating in Shakespeare's play. Like Shakespeare's King, the Henry of *The Famous Victories* opens with a profession of his shortcomings in amorous discourse: "I cannot do as these countries do that spend half their time in wooing. Tush, wench, I am none such. But wilt thou go over to England?" (Sc. XVIII 47–9). The Catherine of that text has no problem in returning his suit with fluent, even quick-witted English: "I would to God that I had your Majesty as fast in love, as you have my father in wars, I would not vouchsafe so much as one look until you had debated all these unreasonable demands" (Sc. XVIII 50–2). Catherine in that version of the story plays the role of ambassador, negotiating on behalf of her father the terms of the treatise that will end war and establish the dynastic marriage between France and England.

Shakespeare chooses to emphasize the difficulty of translation between Henry and Catherine ("I cannot speak your England," Catherine insightfully establishes (5.2.102)), but only as means to showing this as yet another problem that can be bridged. Henry defiantly embraces the hybridity of their proposed marriage: "if you will love me soundly with your French heart, I will be glad to hear you confess it brokenly with your English tongue" (5.2.104–6). Reversing the problem created earlier by the English traitors, Henry sees no trouble in Catherine having a French heart and an English tongue. He also triumphantly imagines their conquering progeny: "Shall not thou and I, between Saint Denis and Saint George, compound a boy, half-French half-English, that shall go to Constantinople and take the Turk by the beard? Shall we not? What sayst thou, my fair flower-de-luce?" (5.2.193–6).[24] Henry's conceit of a "compounded" child stands in metonymically for a unified Christian nation that can produce a king powerful enough to overthrow the Turkish threat to Christendom. Like Dee's cosmopolitan, Henry's son-to-be is a monarch of the world and a powerful symbol of not only a united England and France but, in the broader context of the play, a unified Britain as well. It is in this moment that the play produces its ultimate fantasy: that the overseas excursions and battles of Henry could lead not only to more English territory, but a dynastic union that could produce an imperial prince (and one that would defeat the Turks, for good measure).

Romance enables, in *Henry V*, an alignment of discourses on gender, race, and territory. It is through the staging of English conquest, and the broadening of borders (both imaginary and real) that the theater brings forward questions about English national identity. I have looked at the play's challenges to the idea of a stable identity for the "cold" northern British. But the way in which the Chorus ushers the audience's imagination over borders and the romantic conquest of Kate help, by and large, to cover over these problems of expansion as it presents the conquest of France and the expansion of English dominion from Ireland to Paris. And even though the Epilogue points forward to the decline of English power as it recollects Shakespeare's earlier tetralogy, the play itself seems momentarily to ignore or forget that history in favor of the romantic version offered by Henry.

This is not to say that *Henry V* diminishes the power of monarchy or Englishness. Instead it locates the power associated with those symbols both historically and globally within the theater. Henry's success in the play relies upon his ability to strategically manipulate his own identity, including his national and historical allegiances.[25] The tetralogy as a whole shows, in fact, the difficulty of adhering too tightly to any single position. Family lineage, associative connections based on political allegiances, even purely chivalric connections all fail, in turn, over the course of the four plays. What succeeds, in this final episode, is a malleable, even performative view of these various associations. As I will show presently, this strategic view of identity, inherent in romance, emerges through the facilitation of the Chorus.

Chorus and conquest

At the conclusion of *The Tempest*, the final speech is marked out in the First Folio as an "EPILOGVE, spoken by Prospero" an appellation fit for a Chorus. In the speech, Prospero tells the audience that his flight from the island, a sea voyage, requires their intercession. The change in his speech from earlier in the play is striking, as the power lies not with Prospero's previously magisterial control, but in the audience. His travel back to Naples must await their "hands" and "breath," and more abstractly, "prayer" and "indulgence." This final transaction between the audience and Epilogue recalls the Chorus of *Henry V, Old Fortunatus*, and other plays in the stage romance tradition. The "indulgence" of the audience is more literal here (Prospero wants to end the action of the play), but the obligation placed upon the audience is similar. Prospero's final speech thus turns upon a conventional relationship between audience and stage, one in which the viewer accepts (perhaps even expects) the imaginative commands of the choric figure.

I have stressed throughout this study that the ideas of empire and English expansion encompassed in the stage romance are as important as the formal expression of those ideas. The changes in how stories were represented as romance moved from a narrative genre into a genre of performance sheds light on the cultural changes afoot in early modern England. Robert Weimann has observed a gradual shift in the poetics of Elizabethan drama, marked out by precisely such alterations in theatrical modes of representation within the commercial theater. The break with the allegorical mode and the stage's adaptation of a "postallegorical" approach is monumental for Weimann. In the former, characters used a "narrative type of speech" that was more "descriptive" and "highly stylized" (*Shakespeare and the Popular Tradition* 199). The allegorical mode, Weimann argues, "had provided an altogether different mode of relating the idea (*Wesen*) and the appearance (*Erscheinung*) of reality" (202). In a theater that became increasingly representational, Weimann observes a more complicated relationship between a performer's "gestures, vocabulary, imagery, and even speech rhythm and intonation" and the "meaning" of those gestures and words, whether they be "social, spiritual, or psychological" (202). As Weimann argues, these representational changes were related to a shifting social and historical sphere: "the world of sensuous and individual appearance had become more variegated at a time when their social significance and their historical frame of reference in society (as in trade, nation, government, and ideology) grew more abstract and complex" (202).

The transition that Weimann notes from an allegorical mode of drama to the representational helps explain the transformations I am tracking in the stage's adaptation of romance and history. As the Renaissance stage moved away from the allegorical mode of medieval drama (particularly within the main plot or "locus" of the spectacle, to use Weimann's term) it embraced a mode of representation that relied more heavily on the stage's ability to employ the audience's imagination. The expanding borders of the world (which I would add to Weimann's "historical frame of reference" (202)) pressed the stage beyond the placeless and timeless mode of allegory. What enters into this "different mode," significantly, is "an increased amount of intense imaginative activity" (203), not only on the part of humanist-trained playwrights, as Weimann has it, but on the part of the audience. The correspondence between appearance and experience in such a "postallegorical" world, in Weimann's argument, becomes deeply problematic, requiring the viewer, reader, and playwright to become increasingly "imaginative" and engaged with the spectacle. In the case of the Chorus in *Henry V*, Weimann argues elsewhere, Shakespeare marks a new achievement in the stage's ability to navigate the "distance" between local experience and staged fiction: "for the 'swelling scene' the same distance is both a challenge and a source of strength—provided it can stimulate a larger representation involving hitherto unknown and untried symbolizing, signifying, and 'imaginary forces'" (*Actor's Pen* 71). But was Shakespeare's such an "untried" strategy? In the present section, I consider the development of the Chorus from a classically inflected tool to a staple of stage romance, and how Shakespeare's adaptation of this figure fits within this broader trend.[26]

The Chorus of *Henry V* has largely been viewed as an exceptional, rather than a generic device.[27] For Lawrence Danson, for instance, "The Chorus in *Henry V* is unique," in part because he is unlike other choric figures one finds in Shakespeare (Prospero, Puck, and Vernon's description of Hal in *1 Henry IV* are his examples). If the Chorus in *Henry V* is viewed as "unique" it is because it has been mostly removed from the broader tradition of stagecraft that Shakespeare worked with in composing *Henry V*. The only choric figures critics commonly refer to in these studies are others from the Shakespearean canon—particularly Gower in *Pericles*. Choruses and Prologues were, in fact, quite common in Renaissance drama. These speeches were partly derived from the influence of classical drama, especially Terence, Plautus, and Seneca, where Prologues and Choruses regularly served to offer outlines of the plot.[28] This is reflected, for instance, in Hamlet's comment to Ophelia during the Players' performance in act three, scene two.

OPHELIA: Belike the show [dumb show] imparts the argument of the play.
HAMLET: We shall know by this fellow. [Enter Chorus]

The fourth-century Latin dramatic commentator Donatus said that the Prologue or Chorus could serve the purpose of praising the author, praising the story, telling the plot of the play, or combining all three (qtd. in Butler 98). But it is difficult to generalize about the uses to which early modern dramatists put their Choruses and Prologues. As one critic has argued, Shakespeare inherited a sophisticated, well developed tradition. "Far from establishing any clear rules or even guidelines for the use of such figures, Shakespeare's predecessors in the popular theatre were more intent on varying and adapting the convention, discovering new possibilities in what was provided by tradition and ingeniously extending the guises in which they appear" (Palmer 507). Moving beyond the parameters of classical presenters, Shakespeare and his contemporaries used the Chorus for a range of purposes, including praise and summary, but also in more interactive and involved roles. How the Chorus was used reflects on the genre of the play, and the material that needed to be transposed into action.

In other history plays, Shakespeare used a number of methods for making such a translation of time and geography into action. *I Henry VI*, for instance, extensively employs messengers who, in dialogue, relate events that cannot be contained (or represented) within the bounds of the play. In the opening scene of the play, a group of messengers relay the details of Talbot's battle with the French: "The circumstance I'll tell you more at large" (1.1.109). In *Richard III*, Richard plays the role of his own Chorus, revealing for the audience his plans and assisting in detailing the complicated plot of the story. But the story of *Henry V* required a different kind of intervention. While the plots of earlier plays in the second tetralogy of Shakespeare's histories were focused on internecine warfare (Henry IV can only dream of travel to the Holy Land), *Henry V* moves beyond the borders of England and imagines a foreign conquest. That both Dekker's *Old Fortunatus* and *Henry V* turned to a Chorus to bridge the gap between narrative and enactment reflects the shared burden these stories placed on their adaptation to the stage. As I suggested at the outset, the intriguing parallels in these plays' use of the Chorus gives us reason to further investigate how history, in the case of *Henry V*, might encounter some of the same representational challenges as romance.

Both Choruses must involve the viewer in the production of the spectacle, highlighting the deficiencies of the stage, in one sense, but also its great capacity to transport and help the viewer conceive of different worlds. The Choruses in Dekker and Shakespeare call on the audience to labor in the service of the illusion. *Henry V*'s Chorus's demands on the audience's "fancy" reaches a high pitch when it transports the playhouse to the shores of Dover, gazing at the King's fleet departing for France.

> Suppose that you have seen
> The well-appointed king at Dover pier
> Embark his royalty, and his brave fleet
> With silken streamers the young Phoebus fanning.
> Play with your fancies, and in them behold
> Upon the hempen tackle ship-boys climbing;
> Hear the shrill whistle, which doth order give
> To sounds confused; behold the threaden sails,
> Borne with th'invisible and creeping wind,
> Draw the huge bottoms through the furrowed sea,
> Breasting the lofty surge. O do but think
> You stand upon the rivage and behold
> A city on th'inconstant billows dancing—
> For so appears this fleet majestical,

> Holding due course to Harfleur. Follow, follow!
> Grapple your minds to sternage of this navy,
> And leave your England . . . (3.0.1–17)

In the Shakespearean canon, only the opening scene of *The Tempest* or the storm at sea that witnesses the birth Pericles's daughter, Marina, provide a vision of sea travel as animated and gripping as this one. "Follow, Follow," the Chorus says, inciting the audience with language one might hear on the deck of a ship. The audience is directed to participate in the creation of the spectacle: "Work, work your thoughts, and therein see a siege" (3.0.25). The imaginative force of these lines comes from such incitements, but also from the promise of going away from England—of being transported into France, as the Chorus says earlier, without "offend[ing] one stomach" (2.0.40). This fantasy of physically painless but imaginatively strenuous overseas travel is the same as the vision supplied by the wishing cap in *Old Fortunatus*, by Pacolet's horse in *Valentine and Orson*, and by Ariosto's Hippogryph. Here, however, it is the stage itself that is the magical device for conveying a conquering audience into a foreign land. This act is accomplished by the stirring language of the Chorus, but also by the act of enlisting the imaginary forces of the viewer.

The use of a presenter or Chorus in other plays provides insight about the possibilities for this device. One of the purposes that developed for Choruses was to direct action over wide expanses of geography and time. Shakespeare uses the Prologue in *Troilus and Cressida* in this way, and to apologize for the discontinuity in geography and condensation of time necessarily created by the bringing of history onto the stage (in this case, the story of the Trojan War). The Chorus also brings the viewer into the action of the play, signaling that the play engages the story *in medias res*. "To tell you, fair beholders, that our play / Leaps o'er the vaunt and firstlings of those broils, / Beginning in the middle, starting thence away / To what may be digested in a play" (1.0.25–9).[29] The Chorus's explanation of epic convention is reconstituted here to serve as an excuse for condensing the plot into what the stage can enact. The Chorus thus serves to govern and explain the unfolding of the plot and action as well as time and place.

We also see the device used this way in Thomas Heywood's *Edward IV Part 2* (1599):

> Now do we draw the curtaine of our Scene,
> To speake of Shoare and his faire wife againe,
> With other matters thereupon depending,

You must imagine since you sawe him last
Preparde for trauile, he hath bin abroade,
And seene the sundrie fashions of the world,
Vlysses like, his countries loue at length,
Hoping his wifes death, and to see his friendes,
Such as did sorrow for his great mishaps (913–25)

The Chorus in this case ends with a couplet that should now seem quite familiar in its appeal to the audience's indulgence and generosity, "His and her fortunes shall wee now pursue, / Gracde with your gentle sufferance and view" (928–9). The Chorus has several other features familiar from both *Henry V* and *Old Fortunatus*: it plays the important role of guiding the audience from place to place ("England," and later "abroade"), reminds the audience of the spectacle of the production ("Now we draw the curtain of our Scene"), and calls for the audience to "imagine" that certain events have transpired.

An earlier play, the anonymous *Warres of Cyrus*, published in 1594 but likely performed much earlier, also inserts a Chorus in the midst of its action.[30] Unlike the other Choruses I have discussed so far, this one rejects the "toys" of other dramatic productions. After citing "Zenephon [sic]" (607) as the author of the "tragicke tearmes" (611) of the story, the Chorus turns to a discourse of its own role. It begins by quelling the audience's putative concerns about the function of the Chorus in the play:

. . . our muse
That seemes to trouble you, againe with toies
Or needlesse antickes imitations,
Or shewes, or new deuises sprung a late,
we haue exilde them from our Tragicke stage,
As trash of their tradition, that can bring
nor instance, nor excuse. For what they do
Instead of mournefull plaints our *Chorus* sings,
Although it be against the vpstart guise,
Yet warranted by graue antiquitie,
we will reuiue the which hath long beene done. (612–22)[31]

What the Chorus promises is a play that is not filled with the "new devices" or the "upstart guise" of its contemporary theater, but rather a performance that will "revive" the time of Xenephon in all of its "grave antiquity." It is important that the Chorus cites Xenephon, because in naming the source of its story, the play focuses on its transition from narrative to drama. Although the *Cyropaedia*, on which the play is based, was "writ in sad and tragicke tearmes," it was not a tragedy. In order for it to become appropriate for "Tragicke stage," the playwright must work on the materials and transform them into speeches, scenes, entrances and exits—the stuff of dramatic production. One can only speculate as to what the "new devices," this "trash of their tradition" could refer to in the speech, but techniques such as dumb shows, feigned battles, marches across the stage, and even Choruses, all become possibilities, even necessities, in the adaptation of a narrative source. It is indeed ironic that the Chorus attempts to link its practices to "graue antiquitie," to show itself to be a conservative theatrical gesture. It is, in fact, part of the same "vpstart" theatrical tradition that it derides.

Many critics continue to identify choric figures as being old or vestigial, even though the device had clearly changed through the sixteenth century. One critic calls *Henry V*'s chorus an "archaic device," a remnant of a dying theatrical tradition. But this group of speeches, taken together, shows how the Chorus itself was a method of innovation at the same time that it was highly conventional. Moreover, there are a number of plays written after 1600 (including *Pericles*) that use the Chorus in the same manner as *Henry V* and *Old Fortunatus*.[32] The assumption that Choruses alluded to an antiquated tradition ignores the ways in which Renaissance playwrights adapted them to the needs and exigencies of their materials and strategies of their productions.

Sidney's comments on dramatic representation in the *Defense* can stand as a point of reference for observing the developed state of the Choruses in plays like *Henry V* and *Old Fortunatus*. Sidney's remarks about how the stage represents "Asia of the one side, and Afric of the other" might give us some insight into the changes in dramatic practice from the 1580s through to the time these plays were produced in the 1590s. Interestingly, Sidney is concerned here with the same thing as the Choruses I have discussed—the ability of the audience to imagine or "conceive" of the action on the stage. Sidney famously says that the stage attempts to extend its representation to so many places that "the player, when he cometh in, must ever begin with telling where he is, or else the tale will not be conceived" (243). A play I cited as one of the earliest extant stage romances, *Common Conditions* (published 1576), makes use of such a strategy throughout. Upon entering the stage, Galiarbus narrates in a monologue his arrival in Phrygia:

> For why, though I but [a] knight in Arabia did remayne:
> It was my chaunce and fortune good here in Phrygia for to gayne

A Lordship great, the which the Duke hath now bestowd on mee,
Upon condicion to remayn his subiect true to bee. (494–7)

While this mode of representing travel and boundary crossing (here between Arabia and Phrygia) was sufficiently extravagant for Sidney to object, it carries with it the remnant of the narrative voice. The speech informs the audience without bringing awareness to the relationship between stage action and fictive story.

An early play like *Common Conditions* poses a suggestive fiction that is at a remove from the audience. In contrast, the action of plays like *Old Fortunatus* and *Henry V* actually sweeps the audience into their imagined worlds, molding, even demanding a certain kind of response to the story. We find this same language at work in a place far-afield of the London commercial theater in a series of Old Testament cycle plays written in seventeenth-century Lancashire. This final example of an early modern Chorus reveals the extent of the tradition's influence on drama that conjured expansive worlds. The "Stonyhurst Pageants," which take their name from the Catholic boarding school in which the manuscript is housed, are a series of plays based on stories from the Old Testament. Carleton Brown, the twentieth-century editor of the plays' lone edition, identified several parallels to the Douay-Rheims Bible and thus dated the pageants to 1609. The plays employ a presenter, labeled "Chorus" or "Nuntius" throughout the manuscript, which Brown notes employs language strikingly similar to that of *Henry V*'s Choruses (23–5). In the *Pageant of Joseph*, for instance, the Chorus demands, "You must imagin now that vnto Aseneth Joseph's maryed / & that he perfectly the land of AEgypt hath surueyed" (l. 379–80), or in the *Pageant of Moses*, "You must suppose that moyses ys this while gone vnto Iethro / his father in law, & hath gott his consent that he may go / to AEgipt wth his wyfe & children" (l. 221–3). The insistence that the audience extend its imagination to integrate the geographic and temporal shifts of the Bible are, indeed, remarkably similar to the traditions of romance and history on the early modern stage. Employing the "Chorus," the writers who compiled these plays found in contemporary theatrical practice a means of fitting Biblical stories into a seventeenth century performance idiom.

Helen Cooper has argued persuasively that the use of the Chorus or presenter is a legacy of English medieval stagecraft, an insight that may help to further contextualize the Stonyhurst plays. The cycle plays, in their traveling representations of Biblical stories, relied upon the same kinds of imaginative transactions that the choruses I have discussed here enact. "The practice of embodiment on stage went hand in hand with the exercise of imagination in the spectators . . . " Cooper writes, "Logical impossibilities, like representational ones, were accepted as part of the theatrical experience" (*Shakespeare and the Medieval World* 72–3). But the resources of imagination that were supplied by the theater found new life in the expanding world of the sixteenth century. Cooper admits that in the sixteenth and seventeenth centuries, the stage "tended to move towards a greater specificity of place" (93). By the seventeenth century, the stage had developed in such a way that the narrative excess of the story became the story itself. These plays exploit the pleasure in seeing military feats, travels abroad, large stories "digested" into compact performances. Romance, again, reveals its defining ability to be both archaic and up to the minute, an indelible part of the past and enticingly suggestive of the future.

"To those that have not read the story": staging history and romance

At the opening of act five, the Chorus verbalizes what has been, all along, implicit in the presentation—that the story of *Henry V* is one the audience could have *read* in another source.

> Vouchsafe to those that have not read the story
> That I may prompt them—and of such as have,
> I humbly pray them to admit th'excuse
> Of time, of numbers, and due course of things,
> Which cannot in their huge and proper life
> Be here presented. (5.0.1–6)

In this speech, the Chorus submits himself as a guide to the viewer who has not read the story, but also admits to those who have read the chronicles that the narrative must be abridged, contracted, and otherwise augmented in order to "be here presented" (6). The Chorus is not the only one to remind the audience of the play's roots in the chronicles. Fluellen addresses the King: "Your grandfather of famous memory, an't please your majesty, and your great-uncle Edward the Plack Prince of Wales, as I have read in the chronicles, fought a most prave pattle here in France (4.7.85–7).

Thomas Heywood may have been the first to praise plays drawn from English history for their veracity and ability to teach the lessons of history. In his *Apology for Actors* (1612), he commends the stage for its capacity to make the "unlearned" well versed in "all our English chronicles" (558):

> and what man have you now of that weak capacity that cannot discourse of any notable thing recorded even from William the Conqueror, nay from the landing of Brute, until this day? Being possessed of their true use; for or because plays are written with this aim and carried with this method: to teach subjects obedience to their king, to show the people the untimely ends of such as have moved tumults commotions, and insurrections. (Gilbert 558)

There remains an important thread of criticism on Shakespeare's histories that treats them as part of a historiographic tradition. E. M. W. Tillyard dismissively called the English history play "practical and not very thoughtful . . . It exploited the conscious patriotism of the decade after the Armada and instructed an inquisitive public in some of the facts and legends of English history" (3). More recently, Ivo Kamps argues that "[early modern] dramatists often show themselves to be better expositors of history than the historians" (13).

The examples of *Henry V* and *King Lear* bear out the difficulties of categorization and genre that attended the representation of "history" before 1623. Because on matters of genre we usually accede to the authority of the First Folio over the quartos, it seems odd to anyone today to think of *King Lear* and *Henry V* belonging together under the same grouping. The 1623 collection placed *King Lear* with the tragedies and *The Life of King Henry the Fift*, as the Folio deemed it, in the middle of the "histories." But in 1608, the year the First Quarto of *King Lear* was published, such a difference was apparently less than obvious to its printer. That the two plays came from Holinshed indicated only part of their similarity: the plays also depict onstage battles, dynastic wars, and international political intrigue.

If we look at plays and narratives that are simply called "histories" in this period, we find an amazing array. Many of the plays listed in the Appendix were advertised as "histories": Greene's, *The Historie of Orlando Furioso* (1594, 1599), *The historie of the two valiant knights, Syr Clyomon Knight of the Golden Sheeld . . . and Clamydes the white Knight* (1599), and *Common Conditions*, which the title page bills as "drawne out of the most famous historie of Galiarbus Duke of Arabia" (apparently a fabricated source). Alongside John Foxe's *The first volume of the ecclesiasticall history* (1570), we can place Peter Martyr's *History of trauayle in the West and East Indies* (1577), Richard Johnson's *Most famous history of the seauen champions of Christendome* (1596), and an impressive variety of other narratives and sub-genres.

The varying uses of the term history in the period point, on the one hand, to the elasticity of the term, but also to the centrality of narrative in the conceptualization of history. More broadly, the word "history," and all of its variations, emphasizes something that we have largely lost an understanding of today: that these plays were attempts to turn narrative sources—stories—into a dramatic form. Coleridge, perhaps more attuned to such transformations, called the history plays "the conversion of the epic into the dramatic" (1: 137). History, therefore, presents many of the same problems of theatrical adaptation that romance does—particularly in regards to capturing expansion of territory and dilation of time. In this light, it might be worthwhile to recall Sidney's critique of the stage. Playwrights, he laments, forget that they are not beholden to the "laws of history," nor should they "follow the story," but should bend their source to the greatest "tragical convenience." Sidney closely follows Aristotle in this distinction between tragedy and history. In the twenty-third chapter of the *Poetics*, he distinguishes between how events in history and narrative are organized:

> Concerning narrative . . . it is obviously necessary that, as in tragedies, the plots be dramatically put together, and deal with one action that is whole and complete and has a beginning, a middle, and an end, so that as a complete living creature it may give the proper pleasure. And such works are not put together like histories, in which it is necessary for the composition to deal not with one deed but with *one time*, and to tell whatever happened in that *time* to one or more men, no matter what relation one event has to another. (Gilbert 103, my emphasis)

To put it another way, for Aristotle the organizing principle of tragedy and narrative should be plot, something created by a writer (for better or worse) with a structure resembling other living things in nature—an organic artifact with a beginning, middle and end. History, on the other hand, has no such natural shape or tendency—its sole organizing logic is events in time. As the name "chronicle" indicates, it is *chronos* rather than *praxis* that defines history. To use an example from Aristotle, "the naval battle that took place at Salamis and the battle with the Carthaginians in Sicily at the same time had no relation to the same end, as often one thing comes after another in time but the two do not have the same guiding principle." The two battles are related not causally but chronologically.

Sidney's denunciation of English drama begins with a play he first commends for "climbing to the height of Seneca's style," Thomas Norton and Thomas Sackville's 1565 *Gorboduc*. Though Sidney associates the play with Seneca and the play itself was published twice under the rubric of "tragedy," the material of the play was distinct from that of the ancient. *Gorboduc* was a "King of Britain," as explained by the argument of the tragedy presented at the beginning of the 1570 quarto. His reign, and its dramatic dissolution, had been chronicled in all of the major histories of Britain dating back to Geoffrey of Monmouth's twelfth-century *Historiae Regum Britanniae*.[33] In the story, Gorboduc divides his kingdom between his two sons, Ferrex (the older) and Porrex (the younger). Porrex, out of jealousy, kills his older brother. Their mother, who had always favored Ferrex, avenges his death and slays Porrex. The people of the realm then revolt, killing both Gorboduc and his wife, leaving the land without an heir, and plunging the kingdom into civil war. As the argument concludes, the land was "for a long time almost desolate and miserably wasted." The quarto also prints a description of a dumb show that was meant to begin the performance. According to the text, the dumb show was intended to signify that "[a] state knit in unity doth continue strong against all force, but being divided, is easily destroyed; as befell upon King Gorboduc dividing his land to his two sons, which he before held in monarchy, and upon the dissention of the bretheren, to whom it was divided" (8).

The significance of the story was not lost on Sidney: he calls it "full of notable morality, which it doth most delightfully teach." It therefore achieves "the very end of poesy" as set out by Horace: to edify and delight. The problem for Sidney is that it cannot be "an exact model for all tragedies," because it violates the unities of time and place. Strictly speaking, for Sidney, a play that attempts to represent chronicle history, one that is, perforce, not "tied to the laws of poesy," does not deserve the title of "tragedy." The problem for Sidney, in the first instance, is not the global reach of drama, but the representation of history on the stage. An appreciation of the superiority of poetry to historiography is at the heart of Sidney's objection to *Gorboduc*. If drama is to draw on the events of history, for Sidney, it must do so by organizing the events into a unified whole, reshaping the randomness of history into the order of a properly tragic plot.

What Sidney wanted were plays in the tradition of Greek and Roman drama, told as stories illustrating "the fall of great men" (*de casibus virorum illustrium*). Aristotle allowed for the use of history, particularly historical subjects, names and places, in the production of tragedy, if only to preserve or affect, by identifying with the audience's knowledge of historical figures, the greatest possible audience response to the outcome of the plot. "If the poet do his part aright," Sidney says in this light, "he will show you in Tantalus, Atreus, and such like, nothing that is not to be shunned" (224). But by Shakespeare's time, the intermixing of history and drama allowed for delight and entertainment as much as it did moral instruction. While the didactic function of drama is not entirely lost in the early modern theater, moral imperatives had to compete with commercial interests that pressed the theater to incorporate popular genres like romance and the strategies of representation that they employed.

The same can be said of narratives derived from history more broadly. William Warner's *Albion's England*, a tremendously popular text published in multiple versions and editions from 1586 through 1612, has in its title a seeming paradox that points to the overlapping strategies of history and romance. In the 1592 edition, he calls the book a "history" of the "countrey and kingdom" but also promises an "intermixture of histories and inuention." It is also, according to the title, an "historicall map" that bridges the various components of British history. Following this pattern, the book offers narratives of English history in the tradition of the chronicles, but also stories from Mandeville, overseas travel narratives, and English folklore. Warner sums up the life of Henry V in the following:

> The true perfection of a King was not but in this Land.
> He lead good fortune in a line, and did but warre and winne:
> *Fraunce* was his Conquest: *Scots* but brag and he did beate them in:
> A friend vnto weldoings, and an Enemie to sinne.
> . . .
> In fewe, if any *Homer* should of this *Achilles* sing,
> As of that *Greeke* & *Myrmidon* the *Macedonian* King
> Once noted would I note both Prince and Poet happiest men,
> That for deseruing prayse, and This for well imployed pen:
> For well this Subiect might increase the Worthies vnto ten. (143)

Henry's life, Warner asserts, makes him a candidate for promotion to the status of the "Worthies," the famous heroes (from Alexander to Charlemagne) who were the subjects of many romance narratives. Shakespeare's *Henry V* does just what Warner proposes, as it uses the outlines of history and the strategies of romance to represent a triumphant English nation. Writers living in an age that was attempting to justify global expansion with English history found in the imaginary elements of romance a means of engaging with these new historical developments. But chronicle history had its limits, and as Warner's title page promised, the need "intermixtures of history and inuention" presented a strong appeal.

It is possible to press this point about the intermingling of these genres too far, for it is also clear within the period (and in *Henry V*) that there are distinguishing differences between "chronicle history" and romance. Returning briefly to the Chorus as a strategy associated with romance, the use of these speeches may also shed light on this generic difference. There is an important textual history to *Henry V*, as the play exists in two strikingly different forms. The three quarto editions of the play, published between 1600 and 1619 with only minor alterations between them, contain a much shorter version of the Folio play. In addition to excising the part of the Chorus, the quarto also cuts several other speeches, including the opening conversation between the Bishops of Ely and Canterbury, in which the King's campaign into France receives its complicated ecclesiastical endorsement. The three early quarto editions of the play (1600, 1602, 1619), foreground the transmutation of narrative source into a dramatic performance in their titles: *The Cronicle History of Henry the fift, With his battell fought at Agin Court in France. Togither with Auntient Pistoll. As it hath bene sundry times playd by the Right honorable the Lord Chamberlaine his seruants*. In print, the word "CRONICLE," set in the largest typeface and all in capitals, dominates the page.[34]

The difference between quarto and Folio versions of the play has led some critics to suggest that the Chorus was, in fact, a later addition.[35] This position is presented most comprehensively by Lukas Erne in *Shakespeare as Literary Dramatist*. Erne sees the longer folio text of *Henry V* (as well as first quarto editions of *Hamlet* and *Romeo and Juliet*) as "literary texts" that "correspond to what an emergent dramatic author wrote for readers in an attempt to raise the literary respectability of playtexts" (220). The addition of a Chorus to the Folio text of *Henry V* provides strong evidence for Erne on this point. "The Chorus addresses spectators," Erne admits, "but perhaps less those physically present at the Globe than those spectators of the mind who are imaginatively creating a playhouse performance through 'imaginary audition'" (224).

The differences between the "chronicle history" presented in the quartos and the play version in the Folio hinges on the difference between dramatic and print genres. Notably, the absence of the Choruses from these quarto versions of the play de-emphasizes a key element that would have associated the play with romance to its original audience.

Establishing the play as "Chronicle History," it seems, required a removal of the Chorus's provocative and far-flung language. Building on what I have shown about the integral nature of the Chorus to romance and the enactment of narrative, Erne's argument that the Chorus is a figure written for the purpose of a readership rather than performance needs reassessment. An early date for the Chorus's speeches is all the more convincing when we consider the widespread use of the Chorus as a dramatic device in the sixteenth century, long before these speeches appeared in the First Folio. In arguing for *Henry V*'s place in the tradition of the stage romance, I submit that the play, replete with Choruses, was a text significantly intertwined with the tradition of late sixteenth-century dramatic culture. Importantly, it is precisely the Chorus's invocation of the audience's "imaginative faculties" that connects the play to the strategies of stage romance and to the broader global import of the genre.

Conclusion

The Epilogue to *Henry V* concludes the play with a return to compressed space and time, a "little room confining great men" (3). Expressed as a sonnet, that most compact of poetic forms, the expansive view of the play is once again "pen[ned]" (1) in with the memory of maligned succession and the "small time" of King Henry V's reign. Victorious as this King Henry was, we are reminded, his exploits in the play could not escape the doom set out by historical record, and the plays that preceded this tetralogy—"which oft our stage hath shown" (13). The play thus ends with a movement between chronicle and fantasy that, I have argued, characterizes the tetralogy as a whole. The bright visions of "this star of England" (6) and his "son imperial lord" (8) are eclipsed by the loss of France and the blood of internecine warfare. As Jeffrey Knapp writes, "neither England nor Shakespeare has proven able to shake off England's insular constraints" (107). Unlike romance, with its power to move the audience beyond "this blessed plot," history seems bound to its material and place. *Henry V* provides record for this in the memory of a recent continental empire lost in the French port city of Calais, wrenched from the power of the English throne in 1558.[36]

But all is not lost, as David Wallace argues, "the fertile and unruly France of *Henry V*'s last act now stands in for territories and ambitions further afield" (73). Just as *Cymbeline* ends with promise of a "radiant" future for Cymbeline's court "which shines here in the west" (5.4.474), *Henry V* presses forth the hope for other empires.[37] The imperial vision of the play is not therefore obliterated in its final moment of historical reckoning. Generically speaking, the fusion of history and romance continues to spur its audiences' imaginations even beyond the hard landscape of facts contained in the chronicle. Like the readers of Mercator's *Atlases*, the projections of geography and history enabled, even implored, audiences to reach beyond rigid circumstances. The most powerful suggestion of new worlds in the tetralogy is therefore not the representation of a conquering king, but rather the sense in the play's comings and goings across the Channel that dramatic space can be commanded and controlled. Calais may be lost in truth, but it can still be seen "with imagined wing . . . " (3.0.1).

As I will explore in my discussion of *The Tempest* in the chapter that follows, romance on the stage often explores such oscillations between proliferative representation and hedges of containment. While the stage represents for us the expansive vision of romance in *Henry V* and elsewhere, there are also hints of the opposite need to tighten the scene. Particularly, it seems, when romance touches upon the historical record, when it hints too much at real circumstances, we sometimes find an impulse at containing its narratives. For the strategies of romance, just as they can be used for fantasies of power and expansion, are also capable of dangerous excesses.

5
Containing Romance and Plotting Empire in *The Tempest* and *Pericles*

No play has excited more interest in extending the boundaries of early modern dramatic study than *The Tempest*. Calling it "a touchstone for critical, political and creative work throughout the modern world," Peter Hulme and William H. Sherman observe: "While Shakespeare has been re-invented by every generation and while his plays have been re-staged all over the globe, the stakes involved in *The Tempest*'s travels have been unusually high" (xi). Even beyond Shakespeare studies, *The Tempest* has inspired artistic and critical responses from a range of cultural traditions and scholarly fields. Jonathan Goldberg finds this unboundedness within the very fabric of the play: he writes that its "lack of fixity, this multiplicity of unfixed locations, may well be . . . a condition of possibility for the reinscription of Shakespeare in numerous sites of colonial translation" (1).[1] Scholars of early colonial literature outside of the British tradition have also identified the play as a fecund point of origin. In his important study of Early American literature and cultural geography, Ralph Bauer argues that *The Tempest* shows modernity to be "the product of the complex and inextricable *connectedness* of various places and histories, of the way in which these places *acted upon each other*" (2, author's emphasis).[2] For Bauer, the cultural map of early American literature must be drawn in relation to the *The Tempest*'s prolific boundaries.

In previous chapters, I identified such an outward representational impetus as the element of romance that promoted the values of expansion and empire. In *Tom a Lincoln,* the geographic wanderings of Tom and his companions from the Arthurian court figure as a fantasy of historical English dominion, and *Henry V* moved beyond its chronicle history source by engaging the representational strategies of romance to present a promising (though ultimately thwarted) vision of transnational imperial monarchy. The plots of these plays carried the viewer into the spaces represented on the stage: France, the kingdom of Prester John, and even "Fairy Land." *The Tempest* would seem, if evaluated on such a formal basis, to be a different kind of play altogether—one notably absent of gaps in time and space. Though its island setting conjures the far removed and exotic places of the new geography, it is also the most classically unified of all Shakespeare's plays. Dramaturgically, the island performs the opposite function of the romance stage, as it limits time, space, and plot within strict confines. In this way, it stands out from the other "romances" classified by Edward Dowden in the nineteenth century: *Pericles*, *The Winter's Tale*, and *Cymbeline*. Dowden grouped these plays together firstly because they constituted a chronological group that he associated with the "late stage" of Shakespeare's career. The romances were, in Dowden's formulation, the product of a psychological and artistic unity in Shakespeare's mind as he came to the end of his career. The romances had no antecedents for Dowden, no history aside from the earlier evolutionary steps of plays in the Shakespearean canon, and no distinct formal characteristics.

Such an approach to Shakespearean genre remains even in recent critical framing of *Pericles* and *The Tempest*. In his introduction to the 2003 Oxford Edition of *Pericles*, Roger Warren argues that the late plays of Shakespeare are united by the "spiritual journeys" undertaken by their characters. In *The Tempest*, having Prospero "recall" and "re-experience" the events of the previous twelve years emphasizes that the play is "essentially about his spiritual journey" (8). In all of the romances, Warren says, "the external journeys mirror the psychological journeys of the central characters . . . " (8). Taking this perspective, the peregrinations of Pericles become symbolic:

> Pericles's geographical journeys take him over most of the Mediterranean, from Antioch, Tyre, and Tarsus in the north-eastern corner to Pentapolis in North Africa to Ephesus and Mytilene on the Aegean coast. Although these places still exist, or have modern equivalents, the geography of *Pericles* is as much symbolic as actual; Pericles is on a journey of discovery and self-discovery, in important respects a journey through life . . . (9)

With several quick strokes, Warren writes away the interesting problems created by the play's geographic variety, subsuming those concerns into the psychology of Pericles, and making the play's action revolve around his "journey of self-discovery." While it never cites *Shakspere: A Critical*

Study of his Mind and Art, this reading of *Pericles*, and the "romances" more generally, relies on a conception of genre invented in Dowden's biographical analysis. *Pericles* and *The Tempest* belong together under the same generic heading, Warren attests, because they evince a powerful psychological maturity, "a particularly wide emotional range, focusing on extremes of love, hate, jealousy, grief, despair . . . " which Shakespeare dramatizes "by equivalent extremes of theatrical virtuosity" (Warren 8). This example shows how, in "mind and art" genre criticism, biography can subsume even geographic expansiveness.

Thus with good reason have postcolonial critics remained skeptical of generic readings of *The Tempest*.[3] Yet I agree with Benedict Robinson's claim that "it is impossible to fully historicize the play without thinking about romance" (*Islam* 58).[4] In order to understand the play's engagements with romance, and therefore its historical engagements, I turn in this chapter to question of unity, a topic that has received little attention in recent criticism. I address two plays from Dowden's group, *Pericles* and *The Tempest* to argue that in their configuring of space and time these plays constitute not a unified artistic vision, but disparate trajectories in the tradition of stage romance. The contrast in these two plays' representations of space, time, and action points to differing ways that the stage appropriated historical material into dramatic fiction. *The Tempest*, in this treatment, is a remarkable play not for its evidence of authorial psychological maturity, but because of the formal constraints it places on romance. Although it initially prompts the audience to expect romance, with its doomed ship and remote island setting, the play condenses into a structure of over determined unity. The structure of this plot renders it as anti-romance, an instructive reformulation of the stage romance tradition. Samuel Johnson called the play's unity "an accidental effect of the story, not intended nor regarded by our author" (Furness 355), an attitude that silently prevails among critics who find little to say about the extraordinary unity of *The Tempest*. As I have shown, however, the ways in which drama of the period treated representational time and space were far from "accidental." Moreover, I will argue that this treatment of time and space in the theater reflects on the global interests of the English, and in a play that harnesses the extravagance of stage representation, we see a notable shift in how this history is presented.

A reading of the play's unity therefore enriches our understanding of *The Tempest* and its place within early colonial discourse. The first contacts between England and the expanding world were mediated mainly through narrative: travel logs, pamphlets, and other narrative accounts of foreign countries, peoples, and commodities. The "history" of overseas expansion was written primarily in these documents, assembled, for instance, in the voluminous pages of Hakluyt's *Principal Navigations*. Through the publication of these documents, the expanding globe presented itself as a narrative space. The plays I have been investigating began to reach into these materials and bring elements of the broadening world onto the stage. My interest in this chapter is how *The Tempest* attempts to take on the overseas history of English travels in Virginia and elsewhere while maintaining the integrity of dramatic space. Bridging the burgeoning corpus of overseas "histories" with the representational space of the stage required the condensation of those materials into manageable forms. It is because of the pressing influence of these narratives of overseas expansion and nascent colonization that *The Tempest* must temper its engagement with the excesses of romance and, unlike *Pericles* or *Cymbeline*, limit its representations to an island space.

Staging the "plots" of *Pericles* and *The Tempest*

In *The Political Unconscious*, Fredric Jameson calls for a genre criticism whose purpose is to "sharpen our sense of historical difference, and to stimulate an increasingly vivid apprehension of what happens when plot falls into history" (130). Martin Brückner and Kristen Poole have recently taught us that the word "plot" itself needs historicization: "the basic vocabulary we use for discussing literary texts has remained largely uninterrogated . . . Investigating the semantic origins of 'plot' reveals the degree to which concepts of narrative organization emerged from a sixteenth-century movement to impose geometric order upon the land" (619). "Plot," that is, not only carries a dual meaning of "narrative structure" and "parcel of land," but in the early modern period those two meanings of the word were intertwined; Brückner and Poole identify this as a moment in which "ways of conceptualizing land and narrative were mutually linked" (618).[5]

The spatial concept of "plot," though, need not be limited to the parcels of land in the English countryside and the surveying manuals that interest Brückner and Poole. In his *Theatrum Orbis Terrarum*, Abraham Ortelius includes a map that he titles "Aevi Veteris, Typus Geographicus" (A figure of Geography of the former age) (see Figure 5.1). The map has the form of one of Ortelius's world maps, but only the center of it actually contains any geographic representation. Most of it is emptied of land, replaced with white space and Latin text referring to the classical climatic "zones" of the globe, representing the lack of geographic

147

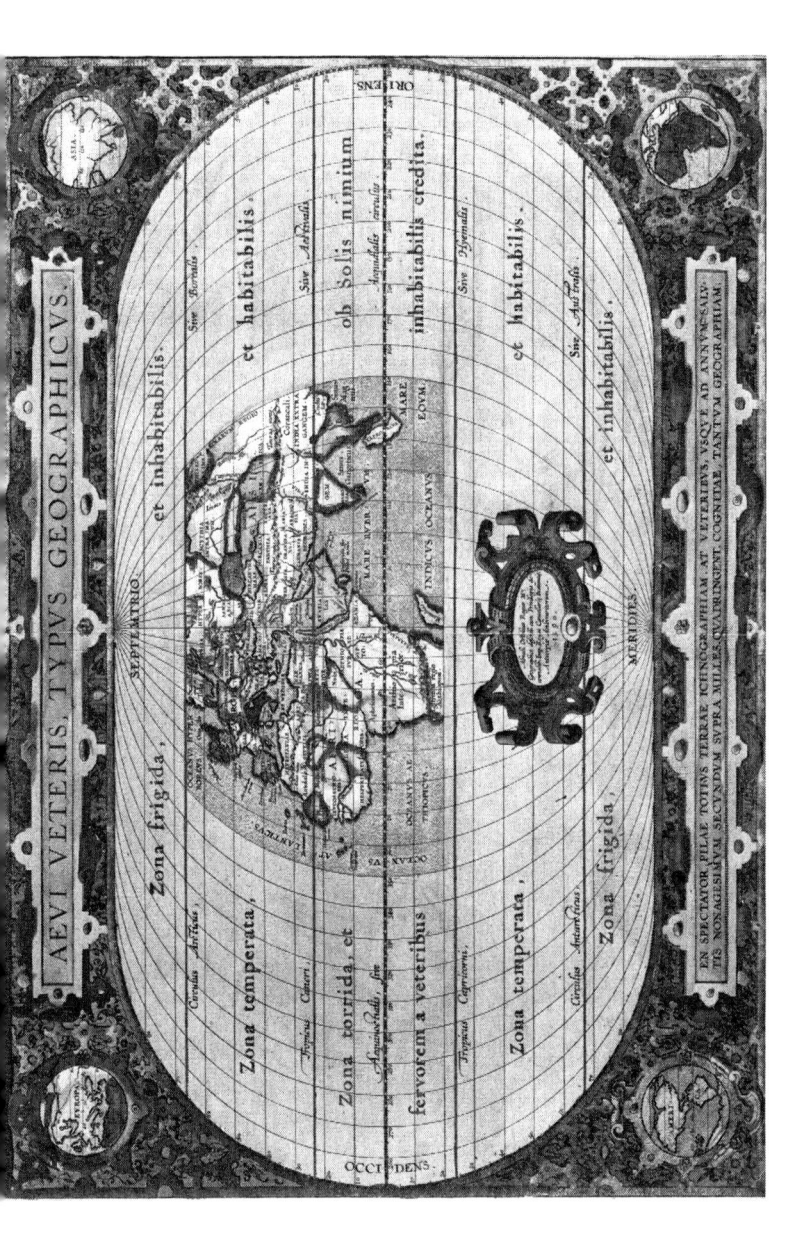

Figure 5.1 Map showing "A figure of Geography of the former age," Abraham Ortelius, *Theatrum Orbis Terrarum* (1590); reproduced by permission of the Huntington Library, San Marino, California

knowledge held by the ancients. He explains this map in a section entitled "A draught and shadow of the ancient Geography":

> Thou hast, gentle and curtuous Reader, in this Mappe a draught (*a plot* or patterne I might call it) of the whole world, but according to the description & ruder Geography of the more ancient authors & of those middle age. For this our globe of the earth was not then further knowen, (a wonderfull strange thing) vntill in the daies of our fathers, in the yeare 1492. Christofer Columbus a Genoway, by the commandement of the king of Castile, first discouered that part of the West, which vnto this day had lien hid & vnknowen. (Fol. vi, my emphasis)

Ortelius is quick to associate the geographical "plot" with the stories of the ancients, which never ranged beyond the confines of the geography framed in the center of his map:

> For *euery storie*, before the forenamed Columbus, written in Latine, Greeke or any other language, exceeded not the limits of the Roman Empire, or the conquests of Alexander the Great, (if you shall only except the trauels of Marcus Paulus Venetus by land, into China: and the nauigation of Katherino Zeni, by the ocean sea, into the North parts, of which we have spoken in the discourse to the Mappe of Mare del zur) which I make no doubt all learned historians and others will easily grant me. (Fol. vi, my emphasis)

The virtual island in the center of the map, Ortelius writes, represents a narrative and linguistic boundary as well as a territorial one. The expansion of the geographic scope of the world both accompanies and necessitates, in Ortelius, new histories that can be written to fill out the empty spaces of the map.

This "plot" of Ortelius captures the relationship between geography and narrative suggested by Brückner and Poole, though it expands the scope of their argument beyond local topography to the level of empire and global geography. Furthermore, these putatively empty spaces of the sixteenth- and seventeenth-century map, as I have argued, were often meant to provoke European intervention in these spaces. The gap between what the ancients knew and what his age knows is astounding to Ortelius. The geography of which they were aware "is scarse the one quarter of the whole globe of the world that is now discouered to vs" (Fol. vi). As I will argue, the difference between *The Tempest*'s restricted dramatic representation and the expansive movement of plays like *Pericles* can be partly explained as separate but related responses to this vast change in geographic comprehension.

Romance, as Helen Cooper has argued, was a genre that created imaginary spaces for its geographic "setting":

> The characteristic setting for a quest romance is most simply described as *somewhere else*. Even if it is given a location, it is in a form its real-world inhabitants might not recognize: water apart, Amadis's England is a legendary land in which marvels can and do happen on a regular basis . . . Quest requires a landscape that follows the coordinates of adventure rather than mappable space—which is why attempts to map the *Faerie Queene* are doomed to failure. (*English Romance in Time* 71, author's emphasis)

We can recognize in this description of romance geography the setting of *The Tempest*, an island whose location is notoriously inexact and multiple. While Shakespeare's Gower and others in the tradition of stage romance celebrated such mobility and mutability, Prospero finds himself continually managing the excesses and dangers that this generic space creates. The realms that romance travels through are remote or unknown, but are made accessible to the reader through the conventions of the genre. This geographic indecipherability gives the writer of romance much greater license than epic, history, or other narrative and dramatic genres tied to specific places and times. *The Tempest*, taken in this context, first appears as a kind of anti-romance, a play that strategically contains the spatial and temporal extension associated with the genre.

Shakespeare used romance strategies as a resource for representing various stories throughout his canon. In Act III of *Cymbeline*, upon hearing that her beloved Posthumus has set up a rendezvous with her at Milford Haven, Innogen immediately wonders how far it is to Wales and how quickly she can get there:

> O for a horse with wings! Hear'st thou, Pisanio?
> He is at Milford Haven. Read, and tell me
> How far 'tis thither. If one of mean affairs
> May plod it in a week, why may not I
> Glide thither in a day? (3.2.48–52)

The antithesis between "plod" and "glide" expresses the difference between literal travel, unrepresentable here in the confines of stage enactment, and the imaginative travel that drama allows. Her "horse with wings" is fantastical, and yet it also figures forth the dramatic tradition that escapes the "plod"-ding of ordinary time. In the sixteenth and seventeenth centuries, "plot" could also be spelled "plod," and it is possible that Innogen puns on the dual meaning of the word in this context where her "plot" to intercept Posthumus requires a week's "plod." ("Plod," v.2). Innogen's questions about distance and time quickly turn to concerns about explaining "the gap" in time that will pass during her absence from court:

> How we may steal from hence; and for the gap
> That we shall make in time from our hence-going
> Till our return, to excuse; but first, how get hence.
> Why should excuse be born or ere begot?
> We'll talk of that hereafter. Prithee speak,
> How many score of miles may we well ride
> 'Twixt hour and hour? (3.2.62–8)

Innogen dwells only momentarily on "the gap / That we shall make in time from our hence going, / Till our return," that is, on what alibi they should concoct to explain the time they must spend away from court in their mission to Milford. She quickly dismisses such consideration, however, determining that it is more important to find their way to Wales than it is to devise an "excuse": "Why should excuse be born or ere begot? / We'll talk of that hereafter." What need is there to premeditate when Posthumous (or the plot) beckons so urgently?

In this moment in *Cymbeline*, travel to Wales is the occasion not only for invoking the winged horse of romance, but also for raising questions about "gaps" in stage representation that, I have argued, are centrally associated with dramatizing a story with a plot as capacious as that of *Cymbeline*. In the following scene, the stage is transported to Wales, and the three exiles of Cymbeline's court ("mountaineers," as they are called in the text) emerge from their cave in the Welsh hills. Innogen appears shortly after. Whatever the distance is to Wales, in *Cymbeline*, as in other dramas in the tradition of stage romance, it can be easily navigated with simple changes in scene. In Shakespeare's *Cymbeline*, despite Innogen's apprehensions, the "gap" in time and place between court and Wales (as well as Rome) is easily traversed.

In writing *Cymbeline* for the stage, Shakespeare, as he did in *Henry V*, adapted a story drawn from the English chronicles. Innogen's wish for a "horse with wings" is perhaps a nod to the stage traditions I have explored, but it is also a coy acknowledgement of the problems created in reworking a play out of a narrative source that included military battles and travel abroad. Shakespeare's Chorus in *Pericles*, performed by the medieval poet John Gower, personifies this transition between narrative and drama. He rises "from ashes" (Sc. 1 l. 2) to "sing a song" (Sc. 1 l.1) that also has been "read . . . for restoratives" (Sc. 1 l. 8). When Ben Jonson famously called *Pericles* "moldy . . . and stale," he was likely noting Gower's presence in the play and the story's roots in medieval romance. The play is straightforwardly a narrative enacted, a fact curiously materialized in the play's early modern print history. Before the six quarto editions of the play (published between 1609 and 1635), George Wilkins published a narrative version of the story: *The Painfull Aduentures of Pericles Prince of Tyre. Being The true History of the Play of Pericles, as it was lately presented by the worthy and ancient Poet Iohn Gower* (1608). The title reverses the common construction seen, for instance, on the play book title pages of *Henry V*, whereby a "chronicle history" is transformed into something that was "played." Wilkins's text, instead, promises to be a "true history" of the drama.[6] Both the print history and the involvement of Gower in this notoriously baggy play draw attention to the hazy distinction between narrative and drama in stage romance.[7]

As in other plays that deploy the strategies of stage romance, Gower directs the audience and implores their participation in the creation of the action. "Be attent, / and time that is so briefly spent / With your fine fancies quaintly eche [eke]. / What's dumbe in show, I'll plain with speech" (10.11–14). Shakespeare used the word "eke" (meaning "fill out," as opposed to the archaism for "also") two other times in his plays. Notably, one of these other instances comes in a parallel context from *Henry V*, where the Chorus invites the audience to "Still be kind, / and eke out our performance from your mind" (3.0.35).[8] "Eke," which the OED defines as "to enlarge, increase, augment," captures the function of both Gower and Shakespeare's Chorus in *Henry V* (Def. 1. and 3.). Gower must manage the episodic plot of *Pericles*, with its ever-increasing multiple locales, as he says in another speech:

> Imagine Pericles arived at Tyre,
> Welcomed and settled to his own desire.
> His woeful queen we leave at Ephesus,
> Unto Diana there's a votaress.
> Now to Marina bend your mind,
> Whom our fast-growing scene must find
> At Tarsus . . . (15.1–7)

152   *Romance on the Early Modern Stage*

This passage celebrates a proliferation in geography—an extravagant expanse in scene and representation. But it is not enough merely to talk about or narrate these places. As Gower shows us, like choruses in *Henry V* or *Old Fortunatus* before, the audience must go along with the narrative, and imagine the stage containing many transported scenes and places.

Gower often boasts about the astounding leaps performed in his play, as he does in this passage:

> Thus time we waste, and long leagues make we short,
> Sail seas in cockles, have an wish but for't,
> Making to take imagination
> From bourn to bourn, region to region.
> By you being pardoned, we commit no crime
> To use one language in each sev'ral clime
> Where our scene seems to live, I do beseech you
> To learn of me, who stand I'th' gaps to teach you
> The stages of our story; (*Pericles* Sc.18.1–9)

Gower's language in this speech is marvelously audacious: he claims to raze time and contract space. His listeners sail the high seas on small boats ("cockles") in their imaginations—they may have anything they want by wishing for it ("have an wish but for't"). As I discussed previously, the chorus could be fashioned in stage romance to assist in the transmission of romance into the stage—something achieved in *Pericles* by bringing John Gower, the actual author of the *Confessio Amantis* onto the stage, to "stand I'th' gaps" and help the audience through "the stages of our story."

The typical story taken from romance did, indeed, require many "stages," a pun that nicely captures the connection between steps in plot and multiple scenes or representational spaces. Thus, the scene in *The Tempest* would seem to work against the scope of geography and narrative represented by *Pericles* and other plays I have discussed. The "stage," in this case is an "an vn-inhabited Island" in the headnote to the dramatis personae at the end of the First Folio text, or "a bare island," as Prospero calls it in the epilogue. In *Every Man Out of His Humour*, Ben Jonson includes, in an exchange about the tradition and form of drama, commentary on that play's island setting:

MITIS: ... What's his Scene?
CORDATIS: Marry, *Insula Fortunata*, Sir.

MITIS:	O, the Fortunate Island? Mass, he has bound himself to a strict law there.
CORDATIS:	Why so?
MITIS:	He cannot lightly alter the scene without crossing the seas.
CORDATIS:	He needs not, having a whole island to run through, I think.
MITIS:	No? How comes it then that in some one play we see so many seas, countries, and kingdoms passed over with such admirable dexterity?
CORDATIS:	O, that but shows how well the authors can travel in their vocation and outrun the apprehension of their auditory. (Induction 266–81)

From this dialogue, it would seem that the choice of a desert island for a drama would not indicate the kind of excess represented by a play where "so many seas, countries, and kingdoms" are "past over with such admirable dexterity."

The Tempest, indeed, is a play that continually calls attention to the *lack* of movement on the island, or the way in which motion is contained and circumscribed. In part this is a result of the island's geographic boundedness, but it also corresponds to the control that Prospero exerts over the various groups on the island. As Margreta de Grazia has argued, his magic is often used to arrest motion ("*The Tempest*" 250–1). She observes a remarkable number of examples of his immobilizing force: Caliban declares early in the play that "here you sty me / In this hard rock, whiles you do keep from me / The rest o'th' island" (1.2.345–7). Prospero threatens to "peg" Ariel in the "knotty entrails" of an oak tree (1.2.296–7), and the scene is littered with the words of physical containment: "manacle" (1.2.465), "subdued" (1.2.493), "obey" (1.2.38, 1.2.375, etc.), and "control" (1.2.443). Ferdinand, too, is almost immediately shackled by Prospero, and later is put under a spell: "My spirits, as in a dream, are all bound up" (1.2.490).[9]

The time of the play is also one of many impositions Prospero (and Shakespeare) press into the island, transforming the way in which the plot of the play is measured and carried out. In his final mention of Caliban's mother, the witch Sycorax, Prospero attributes a profound power to her. She was one "so strong," he says, "That could control the moon, make flows and ebbs, / and deal in her command without her power" (5.1.272–5). Sycorax's "command," here explained as emanating from the moon, is also the power over natural markers of time: the phases of the moon and the turning of tides. Sycorax's prehistorical gauges stand in contrast to the man-made "glasses" that both Prospero and the Boatswain mention (1.2.241, 5.1.226). Prospero asserts time as a mechanized (and manipulable) resource, one that defines his separation from the activities of Sycorax and Caliban. From very early in the second scene of Act One, Prospero raises a heightened awareness of the restricted time, place, and action on the island. Prospero calls himself "master of a full poor cell" at line 20, just a few lines before revealing to Miranda, "'Tis time" (22) to share the story of their arrival on the island, and later, with apparent urgency, "The very minute bids thee ope thine ear" (37). Nothing could be further from Gower's "time we waste": Prospero later sets a time limit on the duration of the action, the "work" (239) and "toil" (243) Ariel must perform: "The time 'twixt six and now / Must by us both be spent most preciously" (241–2). In this long scene, the movements of the two characters never stray beyond sitting (32), rising (170), Miranda's sleeping (186–7) and waking (308), and Prospero's summoning of Ariel and Caliban (189, 319).

The controlled and abbreviated version of past events Prospero narrates in this scene is all the more remarkable because of the amount of time it covers (twelve years) and because of the number of narratives he must abstract: his usurpation in Milan, the subsequent circumstances of their arrival on the island, how he freed Ariel from the "cloven pine," the history of both Caliban and his mother, Sycorax, and, finally, Caliban's failed insurrection. This material is well suited for the kind of protracted story found in narrative romance. *The Tempest* performs its narrative without the assistance of a chorus, and, until the Epilogue, without invoking the audience's intervention or imagination. Prospero performs the function of a Gower or chorus in his opening narrative, supplying the requisite information. Furthermore, he and Ariel both provide markers and cues to the noting the passage of time.

This is not to say, however, that *The Tempest* seamlessly integrates the narrative into its plot. In the urgency of his condensed version of the past, Prospero *underscores* the problems associated with the translation of romance elements onto the stage. Four different times in this scene, Prospero and Miranda use the phrase "tell me." ("You have often / begun to tell me what I am, but stopped . . . Concluding 'Stay; not yet'" (1.2.33–6); "Of anything the image tell me that / Hath kept with thy remembrance" (1.2.43–4); "Mark his condition, and th'event, then tell me if this might be a brother" (1.2.117–18); to Ariel "where was she born? speak: tell me" (1.2.262).) The word "tell" resonates throughout *The Tempest*, highlighting the need for narration created by the play's truncated plot. This need is equally clear in the final scene of the play, when the Italian noblemen repeatedly ask Prospero to tell his story, a request he denies at least four times. "No more yet of this," Prospero says at one point when asked to narrate, "For 'tis a chronicle of day by day, / Not a relation for a breakfast, nor / Befitting this first meeting" (5.1.162–4) The desire to know at the end of this play is powerful, as Alonso finally concludes "I long / To hear the story of your life, which must / Take the ear strangely" (5.1.312–14). This final scene is the perfect reverse of Prospero's narration to Miranda (and the audience). While he expands the narration in the first scene, Prospero here refuses to extend the play's action, and instead rounds off the play with one last reminder of time and place: "And thence retire me to my Milan, where / every third thought shall be my grave" (5.1.311–12). What can explain the play's emphasis on contracted time, action, and space? Why is this play that is so evocative of worlds beyond the English so contained in its dramatic structure?

"Wandring islands": the imaginative geography of romance

When first introduced in Book II of *The Faerie Queene*, the "Bowre of blis" is described as being situated on a "wandring Island." The dying Amavia tells Sir Guyon that her dead lover:

> fortuned (hard fortune ye may ghesse)
> To come, where vile Acrasia does wonne,
> Acrasia a false enchaunteresse,
> That many errant knightes hath fowle fordonne:
> Within a wandring Island, that doth ronne
> And stray in perilous gulfe, her dwelling is. (2.1.51.1–6)[10]

When Guyon and the Palmer commence their sea voyage to the bower, they pass by other "wandring islands," which "haue ofte drawne many a wandring wight / Into most deadly daunger and distressed plight" (2.12.11.8–9). The following stanza elaborates further on the "daunger" of these islands:

> Yet well they seeme to him, that farre doth vew,
> Both faire and fruitfull, and the grownd dispred,
> With grassy greene of delectable hew,
> And the tall trees with leaues appareled,

> Are deckt with blossoms dyde in white and red,
> That mote the passengers thereto allure;
> But whosoeuer once hath fastened
> His foot thereon, may neuer it recure,
> But wandreth euer more vncertein and vnsure. (2.12.12)

The outward beauty of the island, its "fruitfull" abundance and "delectable hew," are but bait for the island's trap, which threatens to ensnare the traveler in an endless maze of uncertainty.

The "wandring island" is an apt metaphor for the sometimes perilous geography of romance, a metaphor, as I will show, that could easily be translated into the dramatic space of *The Tempest*. The "wandring islands" Spenser refers to have many antecedents in both travel logs and medieval and classical literature. In his record of the voyage of John Hawkins, John Sparke notes "certain flitting islands" near the Canary Islands or "Fortunate Islands" (cited in Greenlaw 356). Citations of such islands are not uncommon in the period's travel literature, and reflect a proliferation of free-floating islands, both fantastical and real, on fifteenth and sixteenth-century maps and charts.[11]

Stories of mysterious and magical islands in the Atlantic were passed down to the sixteenth century from well-known medieval tales such as *Mandeville's Travels*. In the Celtic "Voyage of Saint Brendan," a text that circulated in various forms throughout the medieval and early modern period, the title character leads a group of men who explore the unknown waters to the west, and visit the "Island of Joy" and the "land of women."[12] On many early modern maps and charts, one finds fanciful Isles of St. Brendan and Brasil, locations that both derive from the story of the Voyage of St. Brendan. So enduring was the myth of St. Brendan that charts into the eighteenth century continued to map the island of St. Brendan somewhere in the Atlantic Ocean (Quinn 77). In July of 1481, for example, an expedition from Bristol set out "not by cause of marchandise but to thentent [the intent] to serch & fynde a certain Isle called the Isle of Brasile" (Andrews 43–4). This "Isle of Brasile" was also the destination of the Venetian explorer John Cabot. In a letter likely written to Christopher Columbus, an English merchant named John Day reported that Cabot had discovered and explored the mystical Island: "It is considered certain that the cape of the said land was found and discovered in the past by the men from Bristol who found Brasil as your lordship well knows. It was called the Island of Brasil, and it is assumed and believed to be the mainland that the men from Bristol found" (Andrews 46). For centuries before the Columbian voyages, cartographers and historiographers had located several islands, both mythical and real, in the broad ocean beyond the Pillars of Hercules.

Spenser's classical sources for the "wandring island" include "th'Isle of Delos" from Ovid, which he cites in the next stanza.[13] In book five of Ariosto's *Orlando Furioso*, Rogero travels on the Hippogryph to the island of Alcina, a Circe-like witch. In his English translation, John Harington tells the reader that Rogero travels three thousand miles to the island. One of Rogero's companions, Astolfo, also comes to Alcina's mysterious island, which Ariosto ambiguously locates somewhere in an "Indian" sea, where he sees "sundrie Iles, / those called fortunate and others more / That distant are, some few, some many miles" (15.12.2–4). When Rogero escapes in the fifteenth book, Ariosto turns the story into a kind of travel narrative, with Astolfo refigured as a predecessor to Columbus. It is difficult to separate the fictions from the maps and charts that provided evidence of these islands. Spenser may have been citing the Brendan myth directly, or even contemporary travel accounts.[14] But even if he has no specific place in mind for his "wandring island," his narrative exemplifies how romance was a site in which fiction, travel writing, and cartography could fruitfully interact. The placelessness and exoticism, together, provided the kind of imaginative geography that writers such as Spenser and Shakespeare could marshal to their own poetic and historical ends.[15]

Book II of *The Faerie Queene* begins with a similar shiftiness in geography. Spenser's surprising reply to those readers who rate his "happy land of faery" as a "painted forgery" is to recall that many of the newly discovered regions of the world "were neuer mentioned" by ancient authorities. He asks in the Proem, "Who euer heard of th'Indian *Peru*? / Or who in venturous vessell measured / The *Amazons* huge riuer now found trew? / Or fruitfullest *Virginia* who did euer vew?" Although his tales of romance, his "famous antique history," may not be immediately verifiable, he appeals to the reader's knowledge of geography to curtail incredulity. In doing so, Spenser places his fairy land in the same geographic coordinates as the remote Peru, Virginia, and the Amazon river. History, in the case of Spenser's narrative, helps to enable his fiction and even make it more exotic. Spenser verifies the fantastical tales in his narrative by invoking recent discoveries in the west (including England's fledgling Virginia colony).

But we would be mistaken to see this remote and fantastical geography as unproblematic for Spenser. While other romances or travel accounts may infuse geography with fantasy (and celebrate the narrative mobility it enables) Book II, by and large, casts such spaces as perilous.

Amavia at first calls the bower a "cursed land where many wend amis" (2.1.51.8). The bower presents to the adventurer the danger of becoming lost, a possibility that lurks throughout Book II. What we see in the bower's hazards, I will argue presently, is the genre incorporating the geographic novelty of the island and a romance topography transformed by the sea.[16]

Cooper argues that "[t]he westward voyages of exploration posed new challenges not just to the explorers themselves but to the imaginative conception of the unmapped; but that was a challenge that romance was well adapted to take up" (*The English Romance* 73). Though the motifs of romance predate New World discovery and the European "Age of Exploration," those same strategies and motifs took on new significance as the world expanded. *The Faerie Queene* registers these differences, for instance, in contrasting the mode of travel traditionally used by knights (horses) with voyage by sea. Spenser begins the *Faerie Queene* with a "Gentle Knight . . . pricking on the plaine," riding on his "angry steede." The first stanza ends with a vision of a knight in his proper disposition: "Full iolly knight he seemd, and faire did sitt, / As one for knightly giusts and fierce encounters fitt" (1.1.1.8–9). Book I ends, however, with the invocation of a strikingly different place:

> Now strike your sailes yee iolly Mariners,
> For we be come vnto a quiet rode,
> Where we must land some of our passengers,
> And light this weary vessell of her lode.
> Here she a while may make her safe abode,
> Till she repaired haue her tackles spent,
> And wants supplide. And then again abroad
> On the long voiage whereto she is bent:
> Well may she speede and fairely finish her intent. (1.12.42)

Whereas the opening stanza has the reader out on the ramparts "pricking" along with Red Cross Knight, in this stanza, Spenser sends the reader out, metaphorically, onto a "long voiage" at sea. The characters of his narrative are "passengers" who board or disembark during the travel, but the reader is always on the journey "abroad." Guyon, too, does not stay on the "plaine" in following his adventure. Red Cross wishes him well, telling him "to the wished hauen bring thy weary barke," (2.1.32.9), foretelling that it is Guyon's destiny to travel by sea.

Romance, from its origins in medieval feudal culture, was a genre closely tied to the land. Knights were defined by their lands of origin, feats performed at tournaments, and, not least of all, their horses.[17] The topography of medieval romance, its castles, forests, plains, and heaths, continually draws the reader's attention to the land. The very definitional categories of romance (the "matters" of Britain, France, and Rome), as well as stories of travel to the Holy Land and pilgrimage all rely on their connectedness to a place or the land on which the stories unfold. Travels by sea are not unknown in medieval romance—there are examples, for instance, from the so-called Vulgate Cycle of Authurian romance that depict shipwrecks, travels to remote islands, and other sea voyages.[18] But even in these examples, the sea registers as a space of unease. The seas are unpredictable and difficult to navigate. Much like the forest on land, the sea in romance serves as a space of fortune, chance, and wilderness.

Such is the condition invoked in the many sea voyages of *Pericles* and at the opening of *The Tempest*. This scene introduces immediately the struggles for authority that carry through the play. "What cares these roarers for the name of king?" the Boatswain cries, chastising the nobility for interfering with the sailor's efforts to save the ship (1.1.15–16). The "tempestuous noise" (1.1. stage direction) of the first scene of the play sets the stage on contested ground, as the storm subverts the order of hierarchy, requiring shipmen to give orders to kings. But the irony is that, at sea, there is no real ground (beyond the boat) to contest, as Gonzalo reminds us in the last speech of the scene: "Now would I give a thousand furlongs of sea for an acre of barren ground: long heath, broom, furze, anything. The wills above be done, but I would fain die a dry death" (1.1.58–60). The play comes back to the desire for a "dry death" repeatedly. Gonzalo's sentiments are comically echoed in Stefano's drunken sea song, "I will no more to sea, to sea, / Here shall I die ashore" (2.2.39–40). Ariel sings to Ferdinand "Full fathom five thy father lies" (1.2.400), imagining the transformations "rich and strange" (1.2.405) brought on him by the sea. Alonso mourns Ferdinand, "thou mine heir / Of Naples and of Milan, what strange fish / Hath made his meal on thee?" (2.1.111–13). Later, Alonso again thinks about having his grave in the sea: "I wish / Myself were mudded in that oozy bed / Where my son lies" (5.1.152–4).

Similarly, in *Pericles*, the sea provides an unfit place to lay a "monument" to Thaisa, who dies (it first appears) while giving birth at sea. Pericles laments having to give her body up to the sea:

> . . . nor have I time
> To give thee hallowed to thy grave, but straight

> Must cast thee, scarcely coffined, in the ooze,
> Where for a monument upon thy bones
> And aye-remaining lamps, the belching whale
> And humming water must o'erwhelm thy corpse,
> Lying with simple shells (Sc. 11 57–63)

The word "grave" itself is closely tied to the land; its etymology traces back to the Old English word "grafan" meaning "to dig" (OED). But there is only "ooze" at the bottom of the ocean—no dirt to dig. The sadness Pericles expresses in this passage as he "casts" his bride into the sea comes, in part, from his not being able to perform proper burial rites on land. The implication of the speech is that she is not blessed ("hallowed"), as the passage also turns on the notion that a true grave at sea is impossible. The close connection between dry land and burial is enshrined in the familiar language of Christian burial: "Ashes to ashes, dust to dust." Marina also, as her name suggests, has no affiliation to the land because she was born at sea. She later tells Pericles that she is not "of any shores" (Sc. 21 93).

The unpredictability of the ocean is also foundational to the story of *The Tempest*. Prospero admits at the beginning of the play that it is fortune that has brought his enemies to him, rather than his power. "By accident most strange, bountiful Fortune, / Now my dear lady, hath mine enemies / Brought to this shore" (1.2.179–81). As much as Prospero's plot is traditionally understood to rely upon his magical powers (his "art"), Prospero allows that his plan is predicated on chance. "I find my zenith doth depend upon / A most auspicious star, whose influence / If now I court not, but omit, my fortunes / Will ever after droop" (1.2.182–5). Though Prospero exercises a great deal of control over his island and his "plot," the vagaries of "accident" and "fortune," also the guiding forces of romance, continue to bear on the story throughout the play.

Dramatic unity and the dangers of romance

The excesses of *Pericles* materialize, as Lori Humphrey Newcomb has shown, in the play's mixed authorship and multivalent use of sources.[19] *Pericles* is widely regarded today as the product of collaboration between George Wilkins (the author of the aforementioned prose version of the play) and Shakespeare. Gary Taylor's edition of the play for the Oxford *Complete Works* increased the influence of Wilkins by adding interpolated text from *The Painfull Advuentures* in moments that seemed like gaps in *Pericles*. The play itself is an amalgamation of several versions of the Appollonius of Tyre story, and as Newcomb concludes, part of the pleasure for seventeenth-century audiences must have come from the weaving together of these various textual strains: "It called on early modern audiences to listen carefully for patterns of repetition and difference . . . to draw on romances' resources to travel an expanding sea of narrative meaning" ("Sources of Romance," 41). The proliferative meanings of romances stem from the sometimes brash intertextuality of their plots. In *Pericles,* we find Shakespeare and Wilkins adding another layer to the play's intricate "pattern" of sources, for instance, in the unexpected appearance of Pericles in a suit of armor and the chivalric plot that follows. After his shipwreck in Pentapolis (suffered when Pericles flees Tyre for fear he will be slain after unfolding the riddle of Antiochus's incest) Pericles finds salvation in his father's suit of armor, salvaged from a fisherman's net (2.1). The discovery serves a dramaturgical need, as Pericles must wear his "rusty armour" in order to joust in the following scene and win audience with Simonides and Thaisa, his future wife.

That Shakespeare and Wilkins chose to insert a chivalric tournament in the middle of the ancient Mediterranean world (there is no precedent for this in the Latin or medieval sources of the play) speaks to the influence of both contemporary print and stage romance on the play. Suzanne Gossett notes in her Third Series Arden Edition of the play that the discovery of the armor and subsequent tournament may have been borrowed from Sidney's *Arcadia*, which records a similar episode in the trials of Pyrocles, or from the popular play *Mucedorus* (also derived, ultimately, from Sidney), where we find another knight who must disguise himself in order to enter the heart of a young princess (72–3). Indeed, it may have been the replication of such stories that Wilkins and Shakespeare were after in the creation of this scene, an opportunity to stage popular spectacles from stage romance.

Such a profusion of sources, even when they require anachronistic juxtapositions of time and culture, were certainly part of the pleasure of romance on the stage. In contrast, *The Tempest* enacts a departure from the narrative entanglements and romance spectacle of *Pericles*. *The Tempest* is therefore precariously situated. It unfolds on a romance island whose dangers and enticements must continually be managed, because it is the only space on which Prospero is able to carry out of his plot. At the same time, the final outcome of the play necessitates a departure from the island, both as a geographic space and as a generic one. While the island enables his plot, it is not the space on which Prospero's dynastic vision can, ultimately, be achieved. The dynasties of

Milan and Naples are, after all, tied to a land that they do not inhabit. In order to create his new empire, Prospero must continually manage the forces of romance (both narrative and dramaturgical) in order to write the "unified history" of the play that will return them to the European seats of power.

As I have been arguing, there is a close association between how *The Tempest* situates itself geographically and its generic classification. The play itself prompts this observation, as its geography is coordinated by references to sources like the *Aeneid*, but also to travel narratives that take the island out of the Mediterranean and bring it toward the Western horizon. Romance, as David Quint has argued, is construed in classical literature as the generic "other" of epic. Part of the articulation of this "otherness" is expressed geographically, as the spaces of romance lie outside of the imperial centers of the stories. Locating itself outside of the locus of political control and in unmappable space allows romance its characteristic license in representation and narrative.

Much has been made in recent years about the connections between *The Tempest* and Virgil's *Aeneid*.[20] This analysis rests, in particular, on an elliptical exchange between Antonio, Gonzalo, and Adrian at the opening of Act Two:

GONZALO: Methinks our garments are now as fresh as when we put them on first in Afric, at the marriage of the King's fair daughter Claribel to the King of Tunis
. . .
ADRIAN: Tunis was never graced before with such a paragon to their queen.
GONZALO: Not since widow Dido's time.
ANTONIO: Widow? A pox o'that! How came that "widow" in? Widow Dido!
SEBASTIAN: What if he had said "widower Aeneas" too? Good Lord, how you take it!
ADRIAN: "Widow Dido" said you? You make me a study of that: she was of Carthage, not of Tunis.
GONZALO: This Tunis, sir, was Carthage.
ADRIAN: Carthage?
GONZALO: I assure you, Carthage. (2.1.68–84)

As Jerry Brotton notes, the references to the *Aeneid* are strikingly geographic, highlighting for him the play's "Mediterranean geography" (24).

Indeed, the strongest evidence in attempts at identifying the geography of Prospero's "vn-inhabited island" come from these references to Tunis and the imagined route that the Italian nobles would take between Naples and Africa for Alonso's daughter's wedding (the occasion of their voyage). For Brotton, these references indicate "that *The Tempest* is much more of a politically and geographically bifurcated play in the negotiation between its Mediterranean and Atlantic contexts than critics have recently been prepared to concede" ("Carthage," 24). Brotton sees the geographic "bifurcation" of the play as suggestive of a transitional moment in England's overseas ventures and interests. As he puts it, "the play is precisely situated at the *geopolitical bifurcation* between Old World and the New, at the point at which the English realized both the compromised and subordinated position within which they found themselves in the Mediterranean, and the possibility of pursuing a significantly different commercial and maritime initiative in the Americas" ("Carthage," 37, author's emphasis). Following my analysis thus far, we can see how the geographic ambiguity of the "bifurcation" comes, too, from its roots in the romance tradition. Romance writers often evoke inexact and unstable geography to create a locale that allows for its wide-ranging plots.

David Quint's discussion of the *Aeneid* in *Epic and Empire* provides further evidence of the significance of Dido and Carthage to the play's engagement with romance. His treatment of Latin epic and its relationship to romance will help provide a framework for further understanding how the dramatic structure and geography of *The Tempest* operates generically. In his insightful treatment of the genre, Quint posits that romance and epic are dialectically related, a relationship played out in the narrative structure of the *Aeneid*. The wanderings of Aeneas that open the epic and the long retelling of the fall of Troy are, in Quint's account, elements of romance that the narrative must extinguish in order to move toward its epic conclusion. Epic, for Quint, is the "victors'" genre, and attempts to represent fiction as a unified, teleological whole that celebrates empire (in the case of the *Aeneid*, the triumphant origins of imperial Rome). Quint writes,

> The narrative shape of this history-as-triumph bears an affinity with the well-made literary plot—the plot that presents a whole with its linked beginning, middle, and end—defined by Aristotle in the *Poetics* (7c) . . . If the plot of imperial history projected by Virgilian epic may already be modeled upon a classical idea of literary form, it, in turn, seems to lend its linearity and teleology to the epic narrative

itself, which typically recounts a critical, founding chapter in that history. (33)

In this unified vision of history, there is no room for the delays and "dalliances" (a word I turn to shortly) of romance, which always works in epic, Quint argues, as "mere historical accidents" and "deviations from the straight line of imperial triumph" (34).

In Quint's analysis of the *Aeneid*, Dido's Carthage is such a space that raises the danger not just of foreign corruption, but also of Aeneas starting the wrong kind of empire: one that follows a different path than the Augustan Empire that is the narrative end of the *Aeneid*. It is only when Aeneas and his men leave Carthage that they set out on the right generic path. Quint writes: "The process by which the Trojans go from being losers to winners thus matches the movement in the poem from one narrative form to another, from romance to epic" (50). Christopher Marlowe and Thomas Nash's reading of the *Aeneid* in *Dido, Queen of Carthage* follows precisely these lines. After one of Aeneas's crewmen tells him "This is no life for men-at-arms to live, / Where dalliance doth consume a soldier's strength," (4.3.33–4), another Trojan insightfully comments, "Why, let us build a city of our own, / And not stand lingering here for amorous looks. / Will Dido raise old Priam forth his grave, / And build the town again the Greeks did burn?" (4.3.37–40). An empire raised in Carthage cannot replicate the lost empire of the Trojans. Only a new city, one "of our own," can complete their narrative.

Latin epic, in Quint's account, must write away romance in order to establish its imperial teleology. In English romance, Patricia Parker argues, the narrative structure that produces the form's pleasure must also be managed. In her analysis of *The Faerie Queene*, Parker alights on the word "dilation" as a central figure of the narrative's structural and eschatological meaning. "This term," she writes, "and the etymological complex which includes not only 'deferral' and 'dilation,' but 'difference' provide a revealing perspective on the structure of Spenser's romance" (*Inescapable Romance*, 59). That structure, whereby a middle period of delay sits between monumental events, Parker argues, coincides with the organization of Christian temporality. "The time between First and Second Coming is itself a respite or 'dilation,' an interval in which the eschatological Judgment is held over or deferred a period of uncertain duration when the 'end' already accomplished in the Advent is, paradoxically, not yet come . . . " (58). Parker thus uses her structural analysis of Spenser's narrative to insert a theological argument about how romance narrative comments on and engages with theological issues of time and redemption. Parker shows us that, just as the exotic geography and "wandring islands" are constitutive motifs of romance, so, too, are the structural narrative elements.

The temperance of Guyon may be read, in this context, as a metaphor for the necessity of neither progressing too quickly, nor becoming ensnared in the narrative excess of romance. When Guyon sets out in the opening canto, Spenser emphasizes both the direction and pace of his movement:

> Then Guyon forward gan his voyage make,
> With his blacke Palmer, that him guided still.
> Still he him guided ouer dale and hill,
> And with his steedy staffe did point his way:
> His race with reason, and with words his will
> From fowle intemperaunce he ofte did stay,
> And suffered not in wrath his hasty steps to stray. (2.1.34.3–9)

This attention to Guyon's "steps" appears again later when he must go without his horse. "The whiles on foot was forced for to yeed, / With that blacke Palmer, his most trusty guide; / Who suffred not his wandring feete to slide" (2.4.2.3–5). Both Guyon's feet and the meter of Spenser's poetic feet are true and steady, governed by proper narrative temperance. Guyon's voyages and adventures leading up to the Bower of Bliss prepare him for the steady forward march that he must take in order to avoid the delights that would derail his aim.

In the Bower, Guyon's forward progress becomes so central as to be over-determined. He "forward did proceed" (12.37.3) and "marched fayrly forth" (12.38.7). So jarring is the moment in which his progress is temporarily halted by the "Mermayds" that Spenser marks it with what A. C. Hamilton calls an "unusual syntactical break" in the enjambment, falling on the word "still": "And now they night approched to the sted, / Where as those mermayds dwelt: it was a *still* / And calmy bay . . . " (12.30.1–3). But Guyon's forward movement belies the intense temptation that arises all around him. At one point, we know that the Palmer "much rebukt those wandring eyes of his, / and counseld well, him forward thence did draw" (12.69.2–3). This tension between the narrative delight of romance (symbolized here, interestingly, in the *visual* excesses of the Bower) and the need for governance is a central tension in *The Faerie Queene* specifically, but romance more generally. As Parker argues, "A look at *The Faerie Queene* . . . suggests that Spenser was quite consciously engaging in the delights as well as the dangers of this form" (62). She also points out that the problem for Spenser is in "giving shape to a form as potentially endless as that of romance, without reducing it" (61).

There is a close relationship, I want to suggest, between the uniform direction and motion that Spenser gives to his romance and the tight structural boundaries of Shakespeare's *The Tempest*. On his "wandring island," Prospero must contain the romance elements that threaten to erupt at nearly every moment. The play grants all of these outcomes a significant political charge, particularly the plot of Antonio and Sebastian against Alonso. Antonio tells Sebastian that that his usurpation of Prospero, narrated for us in the opening of the play, should inspire further action, "to perform an act / Whereof what's past is prologue, what to come / In yours and my discharge" (2.1.248–50). "Thy case, dear friend," Sebastian tells Antonio, "Shall be my precedent. As thou got'st Milan, / I'll come by Naples" (2.1.286–8). Disrupting the past, and establishing a new dynastic line, is Prospero's central concern. Such action clearly cannot occur in the Old World of the play. In order to perform the actions necessary to undo Prospero's past, and to do so without repeating the cycle of violence that brought his brother into power, the architecture of Prospero's plan must be constructed beyond the realm of Italy and in the space allowed by the island.

But while the island allows Prospero to avenge his enemies and reestablish his dynastic line, *The Tempest* shows that the boundlessness of romance space also allows for other trajectories and possibilities. The geography of romance, in which characters inhabit indeterminate spaces, is central to the genre's capacity for multiple episodic story lines. In *Pericles*, for instance, the play's frequent movement between places allows for multiple and overlapping story lines in each. Indeed, part of the entertainment in the play derives from its digressiveness. The instability of this island's location, its romance geography, allows for a potentially explosive set of plots. Competing visions of empire and dynastic union crop up at almost every turn: from Caliban, Stefano and Trinculo's comic kingdom of three to Gonzalo's utopian vision of the island as a "plantation" (2.1.143) unhindered by Old World hierarchical structures. The island opens a space for a multitude of possible outcomes, from the heterogeneous republic of an island "peopled" (1.2.353) by Caliban and Miranda's Creole children to the homogenous union of Ferdinand and Miranda.[21] In the end, dissolving these "rival narratives," as Quint calls them, requires that Prospero relinquish his magic and the control of the island that allowed for his plot to unfold.

Dalliance, the masque and the dissolution of spectacle

Just before celebrating the union of Miranda and Ferdinand with some "vanity" of his "art," Prospero issues a warning to Ferdinand: "Look thou be true; do not give dalliance / Too much the rein; the strongest oaths are straw / To the fire i'the blood: be more abstemious, or else, good night your vow!" (4.1.53–4). Prospero's speech is ironic, I would suggest, because it is in this moment that he allows dalliance into his plot in the form of the masque. Although the expressed purpose of the marriage masque is to stem the erotic impulses of Ferdinand and Miranda, and thus to ensure the legitimacy of their marriage and offspring, it is in this moment that the other "plots" of the play threaten to erupt. Prospero's warning about "dalliance" is connected broadly to the tradition of romance, both in its narrative and dramatic forms. The forces of delay that loom over Prospero's plot are represented in the threatened emergence of competing narratives. The geography of *The Tempest* locates it, in one sense, near Dido's Carthage, but that link is solidified in the play's concern with a straightforward narrative, chastity, and empire. That the island of *The Tempest* is geographically close to Dido's Carthage but never partakes of the narrative excess associated with that space is a testament to Prospero's success in staging and carrying out his play. Prospero and his spirits must always stave off dalliance and delay in order to execute their plot. Thus, in *The Tempest*, we see competing generic impulses at work. Although the play presents a classically unified dramatic production, it is also continually working against the excesses represented by Caliban, Miranda and Ferdinand, and Stefano and Trinculo.[22]

The masque scene usefully encapsulates and incorporates the generic tensions I have been discussing. Prospero doesn't simply want to create a memorable spectacle, he somewhat surprisingly says that it is obligatory: "It is my promise, / and they expect it from me" (4.1.41–2). But the spectacle must also be tempered by the exigencies of the situation. Prospero wants to celebrate the couple's hoped-for fertility, but not to the point that he incites their desire. He attempts to both delight and instruct the young couple, all the while stressing the importance of keeping "dalliance" at bay. The action of the masque is sealed off from the rest of the island, a fact emphasized by the repeated references to the staging space. During the masque, Iris asks Ceres to descend "here on this grass-plot, in this very place" (4.1.73). This stress on the space of enactment appears elsewhere in the masque, where the stage is called "this short-grassed green" (4.1.83) and "this green land" (4.1.130). The masque is, of course, interrupted when Prospero remembers "[t]he minute" of Caliban's "plot / is almost come" (4.1.141–2). The competing plot of Caliban's insurgency potentially thwarts the "green-plot" of Prospero's masque in this moment.

Caliban's disruption of the masque is the crucial moment of the play in Peter Hulme's influential reading.[23] In this instant, Hulme contends, "[t]he Atlantic material, seemingly at the periphery, proves to be at the center" (*Colonial Encounters* 133). Much has been argued about the importance of these "Atlantic materials" to *The Tempest*, but Hulme's focus on plot and sub-plot and the influence of dramatic structure to understanding the place of these materials provides a model for further investigation.[24] We might be able to refine Hulme's thesis, though, by considering Caliban's threatened overthrow as an expression of a formal disruption of narrative over the dramatic. "The *minute* of their *plot* is almost come," Prospero remembers, emphasizing again the overwhelming concern in the play with managing time and space and preventing incipient plots, narratives, and histories from expanding into the dramatic space of the play.

When Caliban instructs Stefano and Trinculo on the plan to overthrow Prospero, his "plot" (3.2.103) is described in narrative terms: Stefano twice refers to Caliban's "tale," (3.2.46, 78) and promises, when Caliban is through, that he "remember[s] the story" (3.2.142). Caliban does not simply tell Stefano to kill Prospero, he instructs him to "knock a nail in his head" (3.2.59). The Norton editors cite a reference to the biblical story of Jael and Sisera in *Judges* 4.18. In that narrative, Sisera, a captain of an enemy army of the Israelites, is killed in his sleep by Jael, a servant woman. She "tooke a naile of the tent, and tooke an hammer in her hand, and went softly vnto him, and smote the naile into his temples, and fastened it into the ground" (4.20).[25] But this biblical story is not the only narrative source for insurrection on the island. The letter from William Strachey that offers "the true repertory of the wreck and redemption of Sir Thomas Gates . . . upon and from the islands of the Bermudas," perhaps the most widely-cited Atlantic source for the play, contains details of an aborted conspiracy against the life of the governor, Thomas Gates: "Yet there was a worse practice, faction and conjuration afoot, deadly and bloody, in which the life of our governor, with many others, were threatened, and could not but miscarry in his fall" (Orgel, *The Tempest*, 216). The story of conspiring "mutineers" (a word Stefano uses (3.2.34)) who threaten to destabilize the governance of the island in a strange and remote space is another narrative that threatens to unfold from Caliban's attempted plot.[26] Just as

Prospero must abridge his own narrative (as well as that of Caliban and Ariel) at the opening of the play, he also must disrupt all plots that threaten to impinge on his ploy.

But this is not the only impending disruption that the masque reveals. Just as Prospero continually limits the potential for amorous involvement, Ceres wants to ensure that "Venus or her son" (4.1.87) are not invited to participate. To which Iris responds, "Here thought they to have done / Some wanton charm upon this man and maid," (4.1.94–5). Finally, the spectacle is so alluring to Ferdinand that he proclaims, "This is a most majestic vision, and / Harmonious charmingly . . . Let me live here ever! / So rare a wondered father and a wise / Makes this place paradise" (4.1.118–23).[27] Ferdinand's fascination threatens to dissolve the purpose of Prospero's masque, and his plot on the island. "Let me live here ever!" cannot be the resolution of the masque or the play, which perhaps helps us to understand why Prospero, with the moment of his second usurpation apparently at hand, offers his famous poetic demystification of the spectacle.

> And like the baseless fabric of this vision,
> The cloud-capped towers, the gorgeous palaces,
> The solemn temples, the great globe itself,
> Yea, all which it inherit, shall dissolve;
> And, like this insubstantial pageant faded,
> Leave not a rack behind. (4.1.151–6)

Prospero promises that nothing shall be left of the performance, or the stage, just as there is nothing to be left behind on the island. The spectacle is but instrumental to Prospero's plot: it is not the plot itself. The stripping away of the scene at the end of the play culminates with Prospero standing on "this bare island" (Epilogue 8), once again returning the audience to the sparse conditions of the open stage. Unlike *Pericles*, for instance, where Gower introduces the last scene with promise of "pageantry," "feats," "shows" and "minstrelsy," and elicits the audience's imagination to fill out the spectacle ("that you aptly will suppose"), Prospero signals his departure from the scene, contingent on the audience's applause and approval.

Significantly, Prospero's abbreviated masque is more than a mechanical demand brought on by the play's adherence to unity. As in *The Faerie Queene*, the threat of delay looms large for Prospero and his plans to create a new dynasty out of his daughter's marriage. The central plot of Prospero is not to exact revenge, but to assure that his heirs will be rulers of Milan and Naples. When Caliban famously plots at first to take control of the island by "peopling" it with his and Miranda's offspring, he iterates perhaps the most injurious plot against Prospero. Prospero continually tries to preserve the virginity of his daughter, as he explains quite explicitly, so that she can produce legitimate progeny. The closely governed structure of *The Tempest* also helps to stem the possibility of amorous digression that romance invites. The ambling plot of *Pericles*, for instance, is founded on the opening revelation of incest in the court at Antioch, a moment of sexual transgression that surfaces through the end of the play. The travels of Pericles lead him not to a spiritual awakening, as was suggested by the modern editor I quoted at the outset of this chapter, but into decadence. His journey transforms him into a spectacle of oblivion—mute, unshaven, and in sackcloth: "behold him, this was a goodly person / till the disaster of one mortal night / Drove him to this" (21.28–30). *Pericles* exposes the pitfalls of a genre that allows for such an expansion of geography, plot, and matter. Gower advertises at the opening of the play that "lords and ladies in their lives / Have read it for restoratives" (Sc. 1 7–8). The play's purging of excess, however, also introduces digressions that threaten to subvert its moralizing objective. It is these deviations that *The Tempest*, ostensibly, controls.

In naming of *The Tempest* a "specimin of the romantic drama" in the nineteenth century, Samuel Taylor Coleridge declared that it was the *ahistorical* nature of the play that entered it into this class: "the interests of which are independent of all historical facts and associations, and arise from their fitness to that faculty of our nature, the imagination" (1:118). Coleridge furthermore makes an odd observation about this play that draws so close to the neoclassical unities: "[it] owns no allegiance to time and place,—a species of drama, therefore, in which errors in chronology and geography . . . are venial, or count for nothing" (1:118). Though for historicist critics today Coleridge's Shakespearean criticism represents an artifact of a earlier age, there is something in his discussion of *The Tempest* that remain influential in our current criticism. Coleridge offers the imagination, *a priori*, as the logical antithesis of history. For Coleridge, Shakespeare elevates his drama beyond the concerns of contingency ("chronology and geography") through the use of artistic imagination. "Romanticized" in this way, the imagination becomes a force beyond the horizon of the historical discourses of early modern drama. As I have shown, far from being removed from the historical concerns of geography and chronology, the imaginary impulses of romance were in fact defined by the speculative engagements prompted by these plays. Thus, like Sidney before him, Coleridge's commentary in this discussion of *The Tempest* is fascinating not only for what it gets wrong, but for its ability to point us to terms and methods that are indeed relevant to the early modern theater.

Earlier in this chapter I cited Fredric Jameson's directive to pay attention to "what happens when plot falls into history." I would suggest that *The Tempest* points us to a consideration of the converse: what happens when history falls into plot, when the unshaped mass of narrative offered by travel narratives and fiction must be contained within a more rigid structure. As much as romance could supply writers with the tools for engaging with worlds abroad, we see in *The Tempest* that the genre also became increasingly weighted by the demands of history, particularly in the form of the incipient narrative of English colonization in Virginia, but also in a host of other narratives recognized in recent criticism—from Irish persecution to cross-cultural miscegenation. Despite Prospero's attempts at containing within his magical circle the romance elements of the island, what resonates today for critics is not the play's boundedness, but, recalling Ralph Bauer's words, its "inextricable *connectedness*." As these responses to *The Tempest* show us, the real history to which the play is prologue is not one in which Caliban will "seek for grace" (5.1.299), but one that sees the irrepressible energies sitting below the surface of the play, the romance of it, disrupting the historical prospects that Shakespeare's play sought to manage.

6
Milton's Imperial *Maske*: Staging Romance on the Border of Wales

The Trinity Manuscript version of John Milton's 1634 *Maske Presented at Ludlow Castle* (commonly known as *Comus*) includes a passage in which the Attendant Spirit describes the location of his "mansion" (Sprott 46) in strikingly cosmographical terms:

> Amidst the Hespian gardens,
> Bedew'd wth nectar & celestiall songs
> Aeternall roses & hyacinth
> & fruits of golden rind, on whose faire tree
> the scalie-harnest dragon ever keeps
> his uninchanted eye, & round the verge
> & sacred limits of this Isle blissfull
> the jealous ocean that old river winds
> his farre-extended armes till wth steepe fall
> halfe his wast flood ye wide Atlantique fills (Sprott 46)

The place he tells of is "amidst the Hespian gardens," on an "Isle blissfull" surrounded by "ye wide Atlantique" (Sprott 46). The Spirit concludes, however, that "I was not sent to court yor / wth distant worlds, & strange removed clim[e] / yet thence I come . . . " (Sprott 46). Milton must have decided that he, too, did not want to summon "distant worlds" in the opening lines of his masque, because the passage is crossed out in the manuscript and never became part of either the Bridgewater Manuscript (a copy of the likely production text) or the first printed edition in 1637. Milton's *Maske* is, instead, an expressly local affair. Its title, as it appears in the 1637 edition, grounds the performance in the specific place of Ludlow Castle and ties it to the specific time of "1634: On Michaelmasse night." The action of the masque mainly takes place, as the opening stage direction states, in the "wild wood," a scene that is evocative of the lands that surrounded the Castle and the region around Ludlow. We also know from the Bridgewater Manuscript that the three children in the *Maske* played themselves, and that Henry Lawes, the family's court musician, played the part of the Spirit.

Thus, in its very form, Milton's *Maske* stands outside of the conventions and traditions of the popular theater generally and the stage romance specifically. Stage romance was an art form suited for the commercial theater, where companies required material that could be easily adapted into various performance spaces. Such a dramatic form prompted metaphorical representations, a stage for a ship, in *The Tempest,* or a handful of men for an army, as the Chorus to *Henry V* lamented. The court masque, in contrast, relied less upon such metaphorical representations. While the stage romance beckoned the audience's imaginative involvement in filling out the scene on its bare stage, the masque deployed elaborate set designs, costumes, and theatrical effects in creating its drama. As is the case with *Comus,* masques were commonly commissioned for specific occasions, and those occasions informed the content and structure of the performance. The masque was, to use Stephen Orgel's characterization, "the most ephemeral of Renaissance genres" (*Authentic Shakespeare* 49). Masques were expensive and elaborate one-time affairs, not intended for repeated performance.

"One of the greatest differences between drama and royal entertainment or masque," Helen Cooper helpfully observes, "lies in the interpretation given to the acting area and its relationship to the audience" ("Location and Meaning" 135). In contrast to the plays of the stage romance tradition, where time and geography tend to be indeterminate and non-localized, the 1637 title page locates the performance in rather precise coordinates: "A Maske Presented at Ludlow Castle, 1634: On Michaelmasse Night, before the Right Honorable, John Earle of Bridgewater . . . Lord Praesident of Wales" (Milton *A Maske*). The immediate occasion for Milton composing *Comus* has long been known. John Egerton, Earl of Bridgewater, whom Charles I appointed President of the Council of Wales and Lord Lieutenant of Wales and the four English border counties in 1631, commissioned the performance for his family's arrival at their new residence in Ludlow.

The design of the masque is intended, according to Cooper, "to break down the division between the fictive world of the action and the real world of the audience. The playing area is symbolically as well as physically continuous with the floor of the hall where the King sits" ("Location and Meaning" 137). The end point of a masque was always to integrate its audience into the representational space of the spectacle: "Every masque moved toward the moment when the masquers descended and took partners from the audience," Orgel observes, "annihilating the barrier between the ideal and the real, and including the court in its miraculous transformations" (*Authentic Shakespeare* 49). This integration of local place in Milton's *Maske* is important, I will argue, because of the heightened awareness the masque brings to the difference between the court at Ludlow and its surrounding environs. In the central debate between Comus and "the Lady," Alice Egerton, this distinction is central. It distinguishes Comus, as Orgel has argued, as the crass raider who sees the land as something to use, and the imperial Egertons who must dwell on the land.[1] In *Comus*, Milton thus uses the tradition of romance both to summon the generic space of Wales, but also to pursue the integration of English culture into foreign spaces. Though the romance plot is usually designed to bring the foreign traveler home, in this masque, there is no return.

For all of its formal differences from stage romance, the *Maske Performed at Ludlow Castle* also shares affinities with the stage plays I have included in this study. As I will argue, Milton's remote and "wild" space of Wales and the Marches belong to the same kind of expansionist landscape that we see in other romance narrative and drama. The drama of the *Maske* shows romance moving into another mode.[2] Even in the masque form, however, romance is used and still functioning as a strategy for moving England beyond its geographical boundaries through representations of the exotic, unknown, and imaginary. In this case, though, the masque enacts the translation of actual (rather than imagined) political dominion into this foreign space.

What happens to romance, I ask in this chapter, when it is localized, "confined and pestered in this pinfold here" (7)? Is the genre limited when it takes on specific historical and political exigencies? What requirements did the formal constraints of the masque place on romance and its attempts to project England into spaces abroad?

"Of dire chimeras and enchanted isles": romance in the *Maske*

The children in *Comus*, we are told, were "nursed in princely lore" (34) and follow a path that leads them through a Spenserian plot, replete with a magical enchanter, temptations that strain their temperance, and beastly foreign creatures.[3] The Attendant Spirit tells the boys that they are in a place where their "lore" could prove true:

> . . . 'tis not vain or fabulous
> (Though so esteemed by shallow ignorance)
> What the sage poets taught by the heavenly Muse,
> Storied of old in high immortal verse
> Of dire chimeras and enchanted isles,
> And rifted rocks whose entrance leads to hell,
> For such there be, but unbelief is blind. (513–19)

Milton's masque adapts general situations, structure, and even verbal details from the romance narratives of Spenser and Ariosto. In particular, Ariosto's episode on Alcina's island in book six of the *Orlando Furioso* serves as an important intertext for Milton's *Masque*. Book six finds Rogero sailing through the skies on the back of the winged "Griffeth horse" (6.18.1) and "farre from Europa" (6.17.5). After traveling many miles, he descries a beautiful island. He finds the noble Astolfo, a descendant of English kings, transformed into a tree by the enchantress Alcina. Rogero resolves to find Logistilla, "a virtuous Lady, chast, discreete, and milde," (6.57.6) who has the power to unloose the spell that Alcina has cast on Astolfo. But the way to Logistilla's piece of the island is beset by "A thousand kinds of hindrances and lets" (6.55.8) set out by the wicked Alcina. In his endnote on the "Moral" of the episode, Ariosto's English translator John Harington explains: "In Rogeros traveling three thousand miles and then resting at Alcynas we may observe how the thoughts of men raunging abrode into a thousand matters lastly abide in the pleasantest." That last clause, "into a thousand matters lastly abide in the pleasantest," describes the danger Harington sees in travel abroad. Travelers, weary from their efforts (recalling the period's ever-present "travel/travail" pun), are disposed to the "pleasantest" diversions, and are thus susceptible to the charms of an Alcina, Circe, or Comus.

On his adventure, Rogero encounters a rout of monstrous figures who have fallen under the power of Alcina.

> A foule deformd, a brutish cursed crew,
> In bodie like to antike worke devised,
> Of monstrous shape and of an ugly hew
> Like masking Machachinas all disguised:
> Some look like dogges and some like apes in vew,
> Some dreadfull looke and some to be dispised,

>   Yong shamelesse folke and doting foolish aged,
>   Some nakd, some drunk, some bedlem like enraged; (6.61)

E. G. Ainsworth pointed out many years ago that Comus's "rout of monsters" resembles Ariosto's "brutish crew"—much more, in fact, than it does Circe's enchanted menagerie (91–2). The members of Comus's crew are "headed like sundry sorts of wild beasts," and otherwise human in form (unlike Circe's men, who are wholly transformed into swine). The word "antic" also resonates through to Milton's text. In the stage direction from the Trinity manuscript of the masque, Milton has them entering in "a wild & antick fashion" (Sprott 58). Later, when Comus leads the group in their "light and fantastic round" (157), the "measure" is described in both the Trinity and Bridgewater manuscripts as "a wild, rude, and wanton antic" (Sprott 64–5). The word "antic" has a rich variety of usage in the period, registered nicely here in these various expressions from Milton and Ariosto. The monstrous creations of Alcina resemble "antike worke," or figures drawn in a grotesque fashion (the OED lists this as the primary definition of antic (A.1.)). Like those artistic figures, the dance performed in *Comus* is also gross and "antic." "Antic" could also describe a performance (OED B.3.) or the performers themselves in such a production (OED B.4, B.4.b). All of this points to the identification of this group of revelers on Alcina's island with a kind of performative troupe—a metaphor that is further developed in the stanza: "Some nakd, some drunk, some bedlem like enraged."

Perhaps the most interesting detail here in Harington's translation of Ariosto is his comparison of this group to "masking Machachinas all disguised" (4). This simile is Harington's interpolation, and draws upon his knowledge of a continental folk tradition adapted in English theater. The "machachina" or matachin was a sword dance, like a Morris dance, that involved intricate costuming and represented a fight or a duel (OED I.1.a.).[4] In his 1596 *Metamorphosis of Ajax*, Harington reports having seen Machachinas in "stage-plays," suggesting its currency as a form of interstitial entertainment. The "antic" performed by the rout in Milton is thus prefigured by the monstrous troupe—compared here to the players of a raucous masque.

The time and place of *Comus*

But Milton's text, though it makes use of many conventions of romance, the pastoral, drama, and court entertainments, was also drawn to meet the specific circumstances of the performance.[5] As stated earlier, the title page of the first printed edition of the *Maske*, dated 1637, presents the circumstances for its performance: "A Maske Presented at Ludlow Castle, 1634: On Michaelmasse Night, before the Right Honorable, John Earle of Bridgewater . . . Lord Praesident of Wales." Ludlow was the administrative and governing center of Wales and the "Marches," the four English western counties of Worcestershire, Gloucestershire, Herefordshire, and Shropshire (where Ludlow itself is located). The castle was not only the residence for the President, it also was the seat of government in the West—the place where the Council of Wales held its meetings and the legal courts heard cases. Egerton's arrival at Ludlow was delayed some two years, apparently while the castle received much-needed repair and other business detained him in London.[6] He and his family first arrived in Ludlow in July, but as the title page indicates it was not until Michaelmas (September 29) that the masque was performed (Brown 6–7).

Why Michaelmas? Critics have noted the influence that the liturgy of the day had for Milton in composing the masque.[7] The celebration of Michael and the Angels does indeed seem relevant to the story, as the angel-like Attendant Spirit oversees the production and helps conduct the children through the perils of the forest. Others have noted the political significance of Michaelmas as the date on which the court calendar would begin for the year. Stephen Orgel makes the point that "the holy day would . . . have marked the beginning of the viceregal administration *in situ*" ("Case for Comus" 33). Orgel also concludes that "the masque does not have the look of a public celebration: on the contrary, performed by the family children, organized and composed by their music teacher, who also played in it, it is very much a family affair" ("Case for Comus" 33). But certainly the political and ceremonial importance of the day would have weighed heavily on the mind of Egerton and the court in planning for the masque—it is difficult to imagine that the President of the Council, having been absent from Ludlow for three years, would spend this important occasion outside of public view. As John Creaser has shown, the Ludlow Bailiff's account of 1633–34 registers items that were purchased for "the officers when wee were invited to the maske" (131. n. 15), suggesting that important members of the community were present at the performance.[8] The Spirit's speech after seeing the Lady freed from Comus's spell seems to indicate the presence of other members of the court, as well:

> And not many furlongs thence
> Is your father's residence,
> Where this night are met in state

> Many a friend to gratulate
> His wish'd presence, and beside
> All the swains that there abide,
> With jigs, and rural dance resort,
> We shall catch them at their sport,
> And our sudden coming there
> Will double all their mirth and cheer; (945–54)

It is notable that the Spirit further mentions "swains that there abide," the rustics who are later integrated into the masque's final procession and dance. Whether or not these were actual villagers and local farmers or merely actors is impossible to know. What this does finally indicate, though, is another context for Michaelmas. David Cressy writes that Michaelmas was "a crucial date in the secular calendar. It stood at the opposite side of the year from Lady day, and was the most important of the annual, half-yearly or quarterly days for the payment of rents and dues. Farm leases fell due at Michaelmas, at the end of the agrarian year" (29). As well as marking the beginning of the government's year, September 29 was the end of the harvest, and thus would have been the occasion for many farmers to settle their dues in town. In addition to being a date of much celebration and revelry, it would have been a time, in other words, for two worlds to come together: landlords and renters, the courtly and the rustic, the governors and the governed. The date was significant in representing Egerton's jurisdiction over the territory. Creaser also notes that, "The date itself associated government and divinity and, like the choice of Ludlow and its castle for the final scene, is an affirmation of authority" (114).

"A haughty nation proud in arms": Wales and romance

In taking the commission to write a masque for the opening of business at Ludlow Castle in the Marches of western England, Milton was saddled with staging his drama in a contested space—the history of which Milton carefully integrated into his drama. "The first scene discovers a wild wood" is the opening stage direction of the masque. In portraying the landscape of the area as "wild," Milton was deploying conventional language used for describing both the land and the people of Wales and the border country. In the opening scene of Shakespeare's *1 Henry IV*, the Earl of Westmorland reports dreadful news from the Marches of England:

> . . . the noble Mortimer,
> Leading the men of Herefordshire to fight

> Against the irregular and wild Glyndŵr,
> Was by the rude hands of that Welshman taken,
> A thousand of his people butchered,
> Upon whose dead corpse' there was such misuse,
> Such beastly shameless transformation,
> By those Welshwomen done as may not be
> Without much shame retold or spoken of. (1.1.37–46)[9]

Glendŵr is "irregular" in that his reported brutal actions do not conform to "rule, law, or moral principle" (OED Def. 2.). As such, he stands in for the "wild" and "rude" Welshmen and women who have allegedly performed this act. Shakespeare's description largely echoes Edward Hall's account of Glendwr and the Welsh people in his 1548 chronicle, *The Union of the Two Noble and Illustrious Fameliies of Lancaster and York*.

> Owen Glendor a squire of Wales, perceiuyng the realme to be vnquieted, and the kyng not yet to be placed in a lure and vnmouable seate, entendyng to vsurpe and take vpon hym the principalitie of Wales, and the name and preheminence of the same, what with faire flatteryng wordes and with large promises, so enuegled entised and allured the wilde and vndiscrite Welshmen, that thei toke hym as their prince and made to hym an othe of aliegeance and subieccion. (Henry IV, Fol. XVIIv)

Shakespeare's characterization of Glyndŵr as an "irregular" and "wild" Welshman corresponds to a broad body of discourse from the sixteenth and seventeenth centuries that characterized Wales and the Welsh as uncultivated and barbaric.[10]

Ludlow first became a satellite of English government in the West in 1471, when Edward IV appointed his young son Edward as the first "Prince of Wales" and established the Council to oversee affairs in the Marches and in Wales. In 1473, Prince Edward (only twelve years old) took up residence at Ludlow as Parliament and the King expanded the powers of the Council in the region.[11] Narrating the establishment of Edward V as the first Prince of Wales and the creation of the Council of Marches, Hall asserts in his chronicle, "The younge kynge at the deathe of his father kepte houshoulde at Ludlowe, for his father had sente hym thether for Iustice too bee dooen in the Marches of Wales, too the ende that by the autoritee of his presence, the wilde Welshemenne and eiuell disposed personnes should refrain from their accustomed murthers and outrages" (King Edward V, Fol. Vr).

By 1634, Wales had officially been a part of Henry VIII's imagined English empire for almost a century. England assumed legal power over Wales in 1536, consolidating it under the rule of the Council of the Marches and redrawing its administrative and political boundaries. This and subsequent Parliamentary acts effectively integrated Wales into England, breaking down the boundary between Wales and the Marches. The acts did so by organizing the territories of Wales into shires that came under the jurisdiction of Justices of the Peace established on the English model of common law (Smith, *Emergence of a Nation State*, 36). The whole territory also came under the governance of the Council of the Marches (which was then expanded into the Council of Wales). In a remarkable statement of English imperial power over Wales, the Act of 1536 writes out any historical boundary between England and Wales, naturalizing their union:

> Albeit the dominion principality and country of Wales justly and righteously *is and ever hath been* incorporated, annexed, united and subject to and under the Imperial Crown of this realm, as a very member and joint of the same, whereof the king's most royal majesty . . . is very head, king, lord and ruler; yet notwithstanding, because that in the same . . . principality . . . divers rights, wages, laws and customs be far discrepant from the laws and customs of this realm, and also because that the people of the same dominion have and do daily use a speech nothing like nor consonant to the natural mother tongue used within this realm, some rude and ignorant people have made distinction and diversity between the king's subjects of this realm and his subjects of the said dominion and principality of Wales. (Smith, *Emergence of a Nation State*, 392, my emphasis)

The logic of this opening statement is simply that the rule of law must now follow the lay of the land: Wales has always been a part of England ("a very member and joint of the same"), therefore an extension of English law into the realm is not merely to be presupposed, but required. In order to effectuate this geographic claim, the Act redrew the boundaries of Wales. The Marcher Lordships that had governed the land for centuries were replaced with five new shires, while other lordships were absorbed into the English border shires (Williams, *Recovery, Reorientation, and Reformation*, 268).

But the geographical continuity between England and Wales did not mean that the English and the Welsh were the same, for, in the document, the "speech" of the Welsh is not "consonant" with the "mother tongue" of the English—a cultural difference staged, for instance, in the Welsh speech of Glyndŵr's daughter in *1 Henry IV*. The Act also states that its purpose is to "extirp all and singular the sinister usages and customs differing from the same [England]" (Smith, *Emergence of a Nation State*, 392). Thus, at its very origin, the union of England and Wales enacted a paradox. Wales "is and ever hath been" a part of the "Imperial Crown," yet it was also markedly dissonant in its culture, laws, customs, and very speech. Though Tudor authors such as Spenser, Dee, Sidney, and even Shakespeare tapped into Anglo-Welsh history and myth as means of legitimating British empire, Wales also remained situated as a remote and (to use Milton's word) "dim" space.[12] Philip Schwyzer notes the persistence of this perception of Wales and the Welsh into the seventeenth century, "the Welsh borderlands remained one of the most unruly parts of Britain, a running legal and cultural sore giving rise to endless wrangling and occasional outbursts of violence" (Schwyzer, "Purity and Danger," 31). Milton's forest is, consequently, hostile; it "threats the forlorn and wandering passenger" (39). The separated siblings, alone and wandering in the "tangled wood," must face the test of this land before joining their parents. Milton's descriptions of the forest draw out the notion that the woods are a place of trial, as he composes his setting with "perplexed paths" (36), "blind mazes" (180), and compares it to a "leafy labyrinth" (347) and a "dungeon" (348). When Spenser first describes the cave of Mammon, he places it in a similar landscape: "At last he came vnto a gloomy glade, / Couer'd with boughs and shrubs from heauens lights, / Whereas he sitting found in secret shade" (2.7.3.1–3). In Spenser, as in Milton's masque, the "gloomy glade" reflects the spiritual depravity of the place and Mammon, its inhabitant.

Andrew Hadfield has maintained that Wales be considered England's first colonial project (2). Ireland, he maintains, can only hold that inauspicious claim "if colonised territories have to be overseas" (2). Gwyn Williams has likewise argued that Edward I's conquest of Welsh territory in the thirteenth century marked the first colonial endeavor of the English.[13] This notion of Wales as a colonial space finds some corroboration in John Doddridge's 1630 *History of the Ancient and Moderne Estate of the Principality of Wales*, though Doddridge dates the establishment of "English Collonies" in Wales to an even earlier period.

[I]t appeareth by diuers ancient monuments that the Conqueror [William] after hee had conquered the English, placed diuers of his Norman Nobility vpon the confines and borders towards *Wales* . . . and gaue power vnto the said persons thus placed vpon the borders, to make such conquests vpon the Welsh, as they by their strength could accomplish . . . And here upon further ordained that the lands so conquered, should be holden of the Crowne of *England in capite*, and vpon this and such like occasions diuers of the Nobility of *England* hauing lands vpon the said borders of *Wales* made roades and incursions vpon the Welsh, whereby diuers parts of that Country neere or towards the said borders were wonne by the sword from the Welshmen, and were planted partly with English colonies . . . (36–7)[14]

As Doddridge sees it, by the seventeenth century, Wales and the Marches were literally marked with "diuers ancient monuments," signifying a history of conquest that dated back to the Norman invasions. Ludlow Castle was itself founded in the eleventh century by the Lacys, a family of Norman barons.[15] Along with these physical markers of empire, we can add the legislative acts under Henry VIII's reign, and perhaps most significantly, the discursive work performed by writers like Hall and Shakespeare in perpetuating the notion that Wales and its inhabitants were "wild" and "incivil." As I have shown, the English actively promulgated this ideology throughout the period, in much the same way that other "colonies" and nascent "empires" were characterized. We can register the difference, even alterity, of the region in these descriptions. But we can also see how these putatively empirical or historical descriptions work to create Wales as a generic space—one that can lend itself easily to dramatic or narrative adaptation.

Milton uses this discourse about Wales to give his scene the kind of expansionist landscape encountered elsewhere in romance. In Milton, this space in the West is not far removed from the paradoxical description of it in Henry VIII's 1536 proclamation. Milton makes it both an integral part of the English Crown (it is under the "new-entrusted scepter" (36) of Bridgewater), but also a place that is remote, wild, and consequently dangerous to those who enter it. At the same time that the action of the masque encompasses the landscape in its representation, it cannot fully avoid its foreignness.

The Egerton family must not only survive in this space, but in the case of Bridgewater himself, govern the "wild" countryside. Such a situation, in which the virtuous must be tempted, strongly evoked romance for Milton. "That vertue," Milton argues in his *Areopagitica*, "which is but a youngling in the contemplation of evill, and knows not the utmost that vice promises to her followers, and rejects it, is but a blank vertue, not a pure" (*Selected Prose* 213). To know virtue, for Milton, it is necessary to also have a deep knowledge of evil. To illustrate his point, Milton reaches back again into romance, specifically to Spenser, and draws on the example of Guyon: "Which was the reason why our sage and serious Poet *Spencer*, whom I dare be known to think a better teacher then *Scotus* or *Aquinas*, describing true temperance under the person of *Guion*, brings him in with his palmer through the cave of Mammon, and the bowr of earthly blisse that he might see and know, and yet abstain" (*Selected Prose* 213). Guyon's temperance is true because it has been hardened by trial and experience. Milton makes a famous error in this version of the story: in Spenser's account, Guyon proceeds to the bower of bliss alone, "hauing lost his trustie guyde" the palmer (2.7.2). But throughout the *Maske*, the children rely on various intervening forces (the Spirit, his magical "haemony," Sabrina, and ultimately the safety of Ludlow Castle) to help them foot the "tangled" terrain of the country. Indeed, it is when the Lady finds herself alone that she is tricked by Comus into captivity. Milton's intriguingly inaccurate recollection of this episode raises several questions that will further motivate my analysis in this chapter: How can the traveler protect himself from the dangers of alien spaces? Does the presence of a godly force (the Palmer in Spenser or the Attendant Spirit in *Comus*) preserve one's chastity and honor?

Elsewhere in his writing, Milton connects these kinds of concerns to the expansionist policies that had guided England in the sixteenth century. In his *Brief History of Moscovia*, Milton assembles a précis of travel writing that documented the history of English expeditions into Russia. In the *Brief History*, Milton mostly paraphrases reports previously printed in Purchas and Hakluyt. However, in one bit of editorial interpolation, Milton offers the following:

> The discovery of Russia by the northern Ocean, made first, of any Nation that we know, by *English* men, might have seem'd an enterprise almost heroick; if any higher end than the excessive love of Gain and Traffick, had animated the design. Nevertheless that in regard that many things not unprofitable to the knowledge of nature, and other Observations are hereby come to light, as good events ofttimes arise from evil occasions. (524)

The "enterprise" of the English in Russia is "almost heroick," but tainted by the "excessive love" that those pioneers had for "Gain and Traffick." Milton's enthusiasm for overseas venture is not entirely lost, however, as indicated by the language in this paragraph of "higher ends" and "things not unprofitable to the knowledge of nature." But the "knowledge" that Milton promotes in his *Moscovia* tract is of a different kind than what the terrain of Wales requires of the children. Milton hoped that merchants and explorers in Russia might record their experiences and increase England's knowledge of the natural world. The children in the *Maske*, on the other hand, are sent to Wales as part of a colonial entourage. Their travel through the forest allows them to gain knowledge of the topography and resources of the land that could be used, as I will argue in the case of Sabrina, to help secure and extend English power over the region.

The language Comus uses in his attempt to persuade the lady into drinking from his cup seems to align him with those who are moved by "the excessive love of Gain and Traffick" in Milton's *Moscovia* commentary. Indeed, Comus promotes a view of the land and its "fruits" that could have come from a colonial advertisement.

> Wherefore did nature pour her bounties forth,
> With such a full and unwithdrawing hand,
> Covering the earth with odours, fruits, and flocks,
> Thronging the seas with spawn innumerable,
> But all to please, and sate the curious taste? (709–13)

In the Lady's response, she calls for Guyon-like "temperance" (766) in appropriating the gifts of nature.

> If every just man that now pines with want
> Had but a moderate and beseeming share
> Of that which lewdly-pampered Luxury
> Now heaps upon some few with vast excess,
> Nature's full blessings would be well-dispensed
> In unsuperfluous even proportion. (767–72)

Orgel has recently characterized this debate as a staging of the pros and cons of New World exploration and colonial management: "This argument looks a little different when we realize that it is a version of the standard English argument against the behavior of Spain in the New World . . . " ("Case for Comus" 37). To extend this idea, for Milton, it seems that the entire enterprise of overseas expansion, whether English or Spanish, needs to be motivated by the kind of virtue expressed by the Lady—an ethic, it is worth saying, that is informed by the imperial project that brought the Bridgewaters to Wales.

Importantly, Comus's magic is not only spiritually deleterious, it also transforms the bodily appearance of his victims, thus altering human travelers into monstrous beasts. The Spirit narrates the changes that occur to anyone who drinks of Comus's cup:

> The express resemblance of the gods, is changed
> Into some brutish form of wolf, or bear,
> Or ounce, or tiger, hog, or bearded goat,
> All other parts remaining as they were,
> And they, so perfect is their misery,
> Not once perceive their foul disfigurement,
> But boast themselves more comely than before
> And all their friends, and native home forget
> To roll with pleasure in a sensual sty. (69–78)

Their change is also ontological: from "the express resemblance of the gods" into an animal. The unfortunate travelers who encounter Comus, in their "foul disfigurement," forget their "native home." In addition to the spiritual corruption and physical disfigurements suffered by Comus's victims, the danger of forgetting "native home" must be taken quite seriously in the context of the masque. Remembering "native home," is, in effect, the role that the governor must play in his office, as he works as a conduit for the Crown to exercise control over the region.

The fear that their sister might, in a compromised state, "forget" wracks the two boys as they contemplate her fate: "What if in wild amazement, and affright, / Or while we speak[,] within the direful grasp / Of savage hunger, or of savage heat?" (355–7). Repeated throughout the *Maske* are these sentiments that the unknown and foreign can alter one's moral, and therefore, physical appearance. Milton finds a model for such transformations in narrative and dramatic romance going back to Spenser. Here is Guyon's first vision of Mammon in *The Faerie Queene*, a knight who has coveted only worldly goods.

> Whereas he sitting found in secret shade
> An vncouth, saluage, and vnciuile wight,
> Of grisly hew, and fowle ill fauour'd sight;
> His face with smoke was tand and eies were bleard,
> His head and beard with sout were ill bedight,
> His cole-black hands did seeme to haue ben seard
> In smythes fire-spitting forge, and nayles like clawes appeard. (2.7.3)

In *Comus*, the Elder brother similarly describes the transformations that overcome those who let "lust" and "sin" into their bodies: "The soul grows clotted by contagion, / Embodies, and imbrutes, till she quite lose / The divine property of her first being" (467–9). John Fletcher's *The Sea Voyage*, a rewriting of *The Tempest*, reproduces this same discourse of moral tests and transformation in strange places.[16] Upon making landfall on a western desert island, French pirates and gallants encounter Nicusa and Sebastian, Portuguese sailors who have been stranded on the island for an unspecified but extended time. Upon seeing their ghastly appearances, the French call them "sea-calves" (1.3.95) and wonder "Are they human creatures?" (1.3.93–4). They are also described as animals: "They have horse-tails growing to 'em, / Goodly long manes (1.3.94–5, 98–9). The characters' geographic displacement from Europe onto a "wretched island" (1.3.122) is measured here in their physical appearance. Sebastian tells the newcomers of the perils of the island:

> These many years, in this most wretched island
> We two have lived, the scorn and game of fortune.
> Bless yourselves from it, noble gentlemen!
> The greatest plagues that human nature suffers
> Are seated here: wildness and wants innumerable. (1.3.122–6)

Sebastian alludes not simply to the physical challenges the island poses, but the greed and desire for fortune the island represents. Pointing to the pile of treasure they brought with them from their ship, Sebastian says: "Look, ye that plough the seas for wealth and pleasures, / That outrun day and night with your ambitions, / Look on those heaps. They seem hard, ragged quarries" (1.3.160–2).

In Milton's *Comus*, as in *The Tempest*, the susceptibility of the individual to foreign spaces is expressed in similarly moral terms, but more specifically through the virginity of Miranda and the Lady. Frail virginity becomes a metaphor in both of these texts for the precarious existence of a foreigner who must tread into unknown spaces. In "An Apology for Smectymnuus" (1642), Milton describes romance as a genre that celebrates "honor" and "chastity," and elaborates on how his early encounters with the genre influenced him:

> I betook me among those lofty Fables and Romances, which recount in solemne canto's the deeds of Knighthood founded by our victorious Kings; & from hence had in renowned over all Christendome. There I read it in the oath of every Knight, that he should defend to the expence of his best blood, or of his life, if it so befell him, the honour and chastity of Virgin or Matron. From whence even then

I learnt what a noble vertue chastity sure must be, to the defense of which so many worthies by such a dear adventure of themselves had sworne. (*Selected Prose* 63)

Chastity and virtue were, for Milton, generic features of tales of adventurous knights and their trials. Furthermore, chastity itself is, in Milton's eye, the guiding value of romance, despite its reputation as a genre that promotes "wantonnesse and loose living": "So that even those books which to many others I have bin the fuell of wantonnesse and loose living, I cannot thinke how unless by divine indulgence prov'd to me so many incitements as you have heard, to the love and stedfast observation which abhorres the society of Bordello's" (*Selected Prose* 63).

The central question of the masque, I would argue, is whether one's virtue can stand the test of the "society of Bordello's" represented by Comus and his crew of hybrid misfits. This is the topic of the debate between the Elder Brother and Younger Brother after they are separated from their sister. The Eldest takes the position that the Lady's virtue will guide her through the forest unscathed:

> No savage fierce, bandit, or mountaineer
> Will dare to soil her virgin purity,
> Yea there, where very desolation dwells
> By grots, and caverns shagged with horrid shades,
> She may pass on with unblenched majesty,
> Be it not doen in pride, or in presumption. (425–30)

As I have argued, the temptations of the weary traveler are many: thirst brought on by long travel, losing one's self on a meandering path, the riches of the land, sexual temptation, and, most generally, the temptation to stray from the structure of society in the chaos of the wilderness. Readings of *Comus* often allegorize these elements of the masque, turning the production into a kind of Platonic morality play. But I think it is also important to see Milton turning the occasion and circumstances of the court at Ludlow and the Council of Wales into a political allegory. The emphasis throughout the *Maske* on temperance, virtue, and chastity must be read as a result of one of the most important features implied in the masque: the Egerton family must remain in the Marches. They must find a way to integrate themselves into the landscape without falling to its perils.

I want to return, then, to Orgel's proposition that the debate between the Lady and Comus, a debate that resonates into many other corners of the masque, raises questions that are similar to those pertaining to the New World. "What is our relation to newly discovered lands and their inhabitants—do they become ours, or have they an integrity that must be respected? Is the New World an extension of ourselves, or is it the Other? . . . What legal claim have Europeans to land in the New World? What claims do we have on nature?" ("Case for Comus" 37). These are the same questions, Orgel maintains, posed by Shakespeare in the relationship between Caliban and Prospero. In the *Maske*, these questions gain a new and even stronger resonance as they are transported into the political spectacle of the Ludlow court. They are also all the more pressing given the geographic proximity of Wales and its historical association with England. The English made claim on these lands in the West almost a century before the court staged this masque, but the performance shows how relevant the imperial relationship between England and Wales remained.

Romance quest and travel stories almost always present a model whereby a voyage into the unknown is followed by a return home. Such is the case in *Cymbeline*, for instance, as the reunification of the boys with their biological father, the King, closes the circuit of their travels. They have returned home stronger and better prepared to be rulers of the land. Prospero, too, always presents the island merely as an extended parenthesis to his broader plans. In some sense, the plot of *Comus* attempts to mimic this pattern, with the children supposedly returning to their parent's home. Upon their arrival, the Spirit sings:

> Noble Lord and Lady bright,
> I have brought ye new delight,
> Here behold so goodly grown
> Three fair branches of your own,
> Heaven hath timely tried their youth,
> Their faith, their patience, and their truth,
> And sent them here through hard assays
> With a crown of deathless praise,
> To triumph in victorious dance
> O'er sensual folly, and intemperance. (965–74)

But the Spirit's speech hides the foreignness of their new home. The homecoming that the Spirit announces is, in fact, no return home at all. It is not entirely clear from the masque whether the children ever resided in Ludlow. The speech also fails to mention the means by which they are able to arrive "so goodly grown" to their parents—the *deus ex machina* that ultimately prevented the Lady from Comus's ravishing.

I am referring to the intervention of Sabrina, the spirit of the river Severn who frees the Lady from Comus's spell. The Brothers and Spirit are ineffectual in their attempts to overthrow Comus, requiring the intervention of a local resource. Sabrina, as the patron of the river that straddles the border counties of England and Wales, is closely related to the land itself. The Spirit tells the boys that "the shepherds at their festivals / Carol her goodness loud in rustic lays, / And throw sweet garland wreaths into her stream" (847–9). But Sabrina is also tied to a Roman and British heritage that Milton is keen to summon. She was "sprung from old Anchises line" and was "the daughter of Locrine, / that had the scepter from his father Brute" (826–7).[17] When the boys fail to break Comus's wand, the Lady must be released by summoning this local power. Sabrina thus finally enables the *translatio imperii* that has been envisioned since the beginning of the masque. Her magic overcomes that of Comus, whose aspiration it was to marry the Lady and thus subvert the power of Egerton ("I'll speak to her," Comus says before approaching the Lady, "and she shall be my queen" (263–4)). Sabrina provides the fulfillment of the masque, in which the children arrive at Ludlow Castle triumphant over the native forces that threatened them. Inhabiting and governing outlying territory requires the integration and adaptation of local customs, but in this case, Sabrina is a local transplant with the right kind of genealogy (unlike Comus, the son of Bacchus and Circe, whose cup is filled with an "orient liquor" (65)). As a conduit of an imperial genealogy that stretches from Troy to Rome and into Wales, Sabrina helps legitimize and celebrate the power of the Egerton family on their arrival at Ludlow.

Despite the trials that the children face through the action of the *Maske*, in its form, the conclusion of the masque is as inexorable as the imagined westward translation of empire. Comus and his "antic" rout might momentarily threaten the progression of the narrative, but the children's arrival at their parents is dictated by the form. As a masque, the rival worlds of court and wilderness must, and do, resolve themselves into a harmonious denouement.

Conclusion

Sir Thomas Smyth, a diplomat in the court of Elizabeth, having organized a group of colonists to establish a settlement in Ireland in 1573, composed a list of rules and orders to guide their conduct in the colony. He punctuates his orders with these remarks: "Two things do I wishe most specyallie avoyded now at the beginynge of this Colony, superfluity of fare or delicatres, and excesse of apparel. For yow be com to laye the foundation of a good and (as it hoped) an eternall Colony for your posteritie, not a may game or a stage playe."[18] I have tried throughout this study to distinguish between the imaginative work done by audiences and playwrights in presenting the expansion of England through travel abroad, exploration, conquest, contact with foreign people, and increased involvement in foreign trade. For Smyth, quite clearly, the actual labor of colonizing a place should be nothing like a "stage playe," emphasizing, I suppose, the word "play" as jocularity, imagination, and, most importantly, ephemerality.

What, if anything, distinguishes the masque from a "stage playe"? What is it that allows the masque to serve as a form that enables, rather than disrupts, what I have characterized as England's imperial dominion over Wales? We might begin to answer this question by looking at how the masque constrains romance and its projections into spaces beyond the locality of England. In the episode from Ariosto's *Orlando Furioso* that I detailed earlier, Rogero's flying horse inconveniently takes him to places that he does not want to visit. Rogero's lack of control over the Griffeth leads him far away from home and onto the dangerous island of Alcina. The Griffeth thus functions as the aerial version of David Quint's "boat of romance," the vessel that magically transports its passengers to unknown locations and through far flung adventures with no discernable path or destination.[19]

The voyagers in Milton's masque, though unaided by the enchantments of a magical horse, find themselves, like Rogero, in a place full of temptations that both literally and metaphorically threaten to transform them into hybrid monsters. Unable to control their way to the final destination, Ludlow Castle, they must rely on the "courtesy" of local inhabitants. But unlike in Rogero's episode on Alcina's island, the form of the masque does not allow for a departure. The locality of the genre constrains their movements, and, furthermore, their return "home" is, in fact, an arrival to a new space that is hardly native. The aim of the children is not to return "home," as it was for Rogero (or Prospero and Miranda on their island, Guyon in the Bower of Bliss, and nearly every traveler encountered in romance), but to find a way to implant themselves into this foreign space.

In this way, the conclusion of Ariosto's episode on Alcina's island is illuminating. After defeating the forces of Alcina's monstrous fleet (Ariosto has them assailing Rogero from sea on ships), Rogero is able to escape the island with the assistance of Alcina's chaste and virginal sister, Logistilla.

What she teaches Rogero, and what allows him to leave the island, is the knowledge of how to control and govern his magical flying horse.

> *Rogero* mounted on the winged steed
> Which he learnd obedient now to make
> Doth deeme it were a brave and noble deed
> About the world his voyage home to take,
> Forthwith beginneth Eastward to proceede,
> And though the thing were much to undertake,
> Yet hope of praise makes men no travell shunne
> To say another day: we this have donne; (10.58)

Rogero's flight home is thus planned, allowing him to fly over and visit a host of foreign and exotic countries ("the Indian river Tana," "Catay," "Russia," "Quinsay" (10.59)). The pleasures of romance (travel, delay, wandering) are heightened for Rogero because of his new-found control over his magical horse.

John Harington, in explaining the Allegory of Rogero's episode on Alcina's island, says that the horse's flight represents imagination.

> we may understand the Griffeth horse that carried him to signifie the passion of the minde contrarie to reason that carries men in the aire, that is, in the height of their imaginations, out of Europ, that is, out of the compasse of the rules of Christian religion and feare of God, unto the Ile of Alcyna, which signifieth pleasure and vanities of the world. (Ariosto 79)

I have argued that stage romance moved beyond the classical dictates of representation insofar as it moved "out of the compasse of the rules." Furthermore, romance on the stage elicited and demanded an intense participation on the part of the audience in the creation of the drama. In doing so, drama played its own part in expanding the imaginations of its audiences and further pressing the boundaries of the globe, as well. *Comus*, however, in encompassing the "vanities" into a dramatic space that is by its very form more contained and circumscribed than that of the commercial stage, manages to control the "passion of the minde" that Harington describes and stage romance celebrated.

The masque in its spatial and temporal specificity and dependence on elaborate stagecraft rather than imagination, provides a safer space in which to unfold the extravagance of romance. Milton was still drawn by the attraction of the genre and its capacity to evoke fantasy and "foreign wonder" (264), but those fancies are also tempered and constrained by the requirements of the masque form. Rather than a fantasy of unencumbered overseas travel and exploration, the genre is pressed, in the *Maske*, into the service of imagining how an exogenous force can maintain order in hostile conditions. Such a possibility is performed most assuredly in the requisite conclusion of the masque, where "country dancers" are allowed to occupy the stage, only to be pushed aside by the Spirit, who heralds the arrival of "lighter toes" (961). The formulaic conclusion of the masque in dance, Blair Hoxby has argued, may be read as Egerton's performance of his dominion over his own children and household, and by extension, the new territory. "For there was no more basic model of rule than a father's governance of his household and no more basic expression of concord and order than dance" (96). In the tradition of the masque, one has to imagine the entire court, even "Ludlow Town," being integrated into the final movement and dance, thus expressing in choreography the unity between foreign and native, rulers and ruled, that is hoped for throughout Milton's *Maske*. While romance provides the fantasy (and danger) of expansion, the rigor of this performative genre infuses the moment with a structure that can maintain empire. In staging this performance, Milton's *Comus* stresses the capacity of the masque, as a form, to do the political work that it was called to in Ludlow Castle, on Michaelmas, 1634.

Coda: Global Romance after Shakespeare

In 2012, more than four hundred years after Martin Frobisher carried a copy of *Mandeville's Travels* with him to the Arctic Circle and dramatizations of the *Travels* first hit theaters, Mandeville returned to the London theatrical scene. This time, however, it was on a global stage in the midst of the opening ceremonies for the games of the thirtieth Olympiad. This "Mandeville" was a wonder of a different kind, a cartoonish one-eyed mascot conjured for marketing the games to its worldwide audience. As Anthony Bale noted of these opening ceremonies, titled "Isles of Wonder" by director Danny Boyle, the spectacle drew on a range of medieval and early modern cultural resources: "it was shot through with references to the medieval and early-modern past." Indeed, the leitmotif for the performance was Caliban's line from *The Tempest*: "Be not afeard. The isle is full of noises" (3.2.130). Printed at the top of the ceremony's program, etched on the bell that signaled the games' opening, and called out in the voice of Kenneth Branagh, Shakespeare's words seemed to call the "Isles of Wonder" into being.

Boyle's Olympic fantasy was (at least in part) an expression of the cultural legacy established by Edward Dowden, whose invention of the "Shakespearean romance" remains an indelible part of our critical vocabulary. "Caliban and Ariel, Prospero and Miranda," Dowden wrote in the nineteenth century, are "creatures of an enchanted world over which time owns no sway, they belong to the life of humanity, and are borne onward with the stream of that life from generation to generation" (*Essays* 351–2). Boyle's production replicated the sense of cultural teleology expressed in Dowden's formulation, "the stream of life," as it promulgated a vision of economic and social progress that stretched from the agrarian to the digital age. The program's narrative promised "A ceremony that celebrates the creativity, eccentricity, daring and openness of the British genius by harnessing the genius, creativity, eccentricity, daring and openness of modern London" (Boyle 11). Both nostalgic and proleptic, the ceremonies perfectly replicated what Dowden supposed to be Shakespeare's artistic genius at the close of his life. Shakespeare's *Tempest* stands in for the twilight of the massive (and messy) cultural history of a British Empire that could hardly be imagined in the seventeenth century.

In arguing for a more historically responsible account of the cultural influence of romance in the early modern theater, this book encourages a re-reading of these symbols that clearly remain relevant to our contemporary global society—for it was not only Shakespeare and Mandeville who were reformulated for these Olympic Ceremonies, but King Arthur and Avalon, Milton and Blake, Voldemort and Mary Poppins, as well. Thinking generically, placing these authors and traditions within a longer arc of literary and cultural history, allows us to revise Whiggish pronouncements like Dowden's. The purpose of this book has been to rediscover the host of strategies, tropes, and motifs that characterized the earlier tradition of romance, and to see how these cultural signifiers gave expression to early colonial and economic expansion. This project aligns with Elleke Boehmer's analysis of how new worlds were adapted through the language and stories of the old:

> with the onset of European migration and colonization, people experienced an intense need to create new worlds out of old stories. On few other occasions in human history did so many encounter such diversity of geography and culture in so short a time-span. It was necessary to give that diversity conceptual shape: known rhetorical figures were used to translate the inarticulate . . . To decipher unfamiliar spaces—what were to all intents and purposes airy nothings—travellers and colonizers relied on and scattered about them the stock descriptions and authoritative symbols that lay to hand. (13)

In conclusion, I want to ask what happened to these "stock descriptions" and "authoritative symbols" once they began circulating in the world. "The old generic categories do not . . . die out . . . but persist in the halflife of the subliterary genres of mass culture," Fredric Jameson observes, as he calls for a "new, historically reflexive, way of using categories, such as those of genre . . . " (107). What was the afterlife of the generic language of romance in subsequent moments of geographic expansion and British Empire?

To consider this question in brief, I turn to a seventeenth-century travel narrative that provides a view of the legacy of romance. In the autumn of 1681, a group of buccaneers led by Captain Bartholomew Sharp had just departed from the port of Paita in northwestern Peru. After many months of raids on Spanish ships, silver mines, and battlements along the west coast of South America, the crew was heading home to England. But the ship could not find its bearings toward the Straits of Magellan, and instead came upon "a place *incognito*"—a group of mysterious uncharted islands (Ringrose 178). Disoriented, the sailors took harbor in the islands for several days and searched for provisions. What we know about Captain Sharp's voyages comes from a member of his crew, Basil Ringrose, who kept a journal of the expedition's proceedings.[1] In it, he records the following incident involving the inhabitants of the islands:

> In the evening of this day, our Canoa which was gone to search the adjacent places for *Indians*, or what else they could find, returned unto the ship, with a *Doree* at her stern . . . In it were three *Indians*, who perceiving themselves nigh being taken, leapt over-board to make their escape. Our men in pursuing them did unadvisedly-shoot one of them dead. A second, being a woman, escaped their hands. But the third, who was a lusty boy about eighteen years of age, was taken, and him they brought on board the ship. He was covered onely with a Seals skin, having no other cloathing about him: His eyes were squinted, and his hair was cut pretty short . . . His Language we could not understand. (Ringrose 182)

Ringrose describes the "boy" as "very innocent and foolish" and says that by his "carriage," his appearance and behavior, "I was also perswaded that he was a Man-eater" (183). Finally, as the ship is set to depart, the Englishmen decide to keep their "Indian" captive: "As for the Indian boy . . . we kept him still prisoner, and called him *Orson*" (185).

Although Ringrose does not provide the source of their captive's new name, it comes from the same romance we encountered in Chapter 2's discussion of Sidney's magical horse: *Valentine and Orson*. By this time in the seventeenth century, the tale of Orson's redemption from the wilderness was current enough not to necessitate citation.[2] In the Ringrose narrative, the name "Orson" functions as shorthand for a wild and uncultured man (Orson was the brother who was lost in the wilderness), but it also registers the story as a kind of romance itself, with the proverbially "innocent" native cast in the familiar romance narrative that has the Europeans as crusaders and redeemers of their "Man-eater" brethren. This was an allusion with some currency—Peter Heylyn's *Cosmographie* (1652), too, says that there are some men living near the Andes mountains in Brazil who are "hairy all over like Beasts, such as *Orson* is fained to have been in the old *Romance*" (165).

I end here with Ringrose's appropriation of the story because it links the travel narrative generically to a series of similar stories, including *The Tempest* and *Cymbeline*. Ringrose's rendition of the story is also strikingly similar to an earlier set of tales from the narratives of European expansion that provided some material for Prospero's island. In its first telling, a member of Magellan's crew recorded the following incident off the coast of South America.

> Two weeks later they saw four of these giants without their weapons, for they had hidden them among the brambles, the captain kept two of the youngest and best proportioned, through a ruse, by giving them knives, scissors, mirrors, bells and glass beads. And having both hands full of these things, the captain two sets of chains brought, of the sort that is put on the feet, and they placed them at their feet, indicating that they wanted to give them to them . . . and when they bolted the irons around their legs, they began to be suspicious, but the captain reassured them in order to keep them still. When they saw that they had been deceived, they roared like bulls. And they cried aloud for Setebos to help them. (Pigafetta 15)

This story, quoted here from Antonio Pigafetta's journal of Magellan's circumnavigational voyage, was reprinted and retranslated many times through the sixteenth and seventeenth centuries. After its first printing in French in 1526, it appeared again in Peter Martyr's Decades, Richard Eden's *History of Travayle in the West and East Indies* (1577), and Purchas's *Pilgrimes* (1625). The name Setebos even appears later in accounts of Francis Drake's passing through South America on his journey around the globe. But perhaps most famously, Shakespeare used the name "Setebos" as the name of Caliban's "dam's god" in *The Tempest*. Through all of these stories (the early travel accounts, *Valentine and Orson*, Ringrose's narrative), one can easily see the correspondences with Shakespeare's story: in Prospero's eventual enslavement of Caliban and Ariel, Prospero and Miranda's attempts at teaching Caliban language, Prospero's baiting of the hapless Trinculo and Stefano with "trumpery," and even the setting of ships and exotic lands.

The sub-plot in *Cymbeline* that brings Innogen to the wilderness of Wales, too, resonates with the story of siblings who are separated at birth. The exile of Belarius and the boys to a "cell of ignorance," a "pinching cave" anticipates Prospero's sojourn on the island. The story of Innogen's travel into Wales itself, whereby two brothers raised in the wild are reunited with their sister (disguised as a boy), is another version of the *Valentine and Orson* narrative. Shakespeare perhaps refers to this tradition in several of the conversations between Fidele, Arviragus, and Guiderius, as the two boys call Fidele "brother" throughout.

But *Cymbeline* also provides an important twist on the story of Valentine and his "wild" brother Orson. In that story, Valentine liberates his brother from the savage wilderness, teaching him how to speak and, eventually, returns to court and turns him into valiant warrior. Separated from the court and chivalric values at birth, Orson forgets the ways of the civilized world and becomes as beastly as the animals that live with him in the forest. It is only through Valentine's efforts to teach him language that he can reintegrate into the courtly world. *Cymbeline* inverts this model, as the brothers prove to be more virtuous by the very fact of their wildness. Belarius wonders here, as he does throughout the play, at the kingly behavior evinced in the boys:

> How hard it is to hide the sparks of nature!
> . . .
> though trained up thus meanly
> I'th' cave wherein they bow, their thoughts do hit
> The roofs of palaces, and nature prompts them
> In simple and low things to prince it much
> Beyond the trick of others. (3.4.79–86)

Having honed their battle skills outside of the world of the court, they prove to be superior warriors to their British brethren, and play the pivotal role in defeating the Roman forces in Wales and establishing a fantastical *Pax Britannia*. Thus, in *Cymbeline*, the remoteness of the land provides a forge where the boys can harden their mettle. Belarius's language throughout the play celebrates the wilderness for its relative simplicity and even nobility.

Ringrose's story in which an "Indian" boy is given the name Orson comes from a collection entitled *The History of the Bucaniers of America*. One bibliographer writes about this collection, "Perhaps no other book in any language was ever the parent of so many imitations, and the source of so many fictions as this" (Sabin 310). While there were, no doubt, many imitators of Ringrose's adventure stories, the reference to *Valentine and Orson* reveals *The History of the Bucaniers* as itself a descendent of a long generic history. The conflict between Valentine and his wild brother, Orson, is an example of an important romance motif: the confrontation between the civilized and educated and the barbaric "other." This is a particularly interesting example, because Orson and Valentine are brothers who were separated at birth. And Valentine attempts not only to educate Orson, as Miranda does Caliban, but also to redeem and baptize him.

When I first cited *Valentine and Orson* in Chapter 2, it was in reference to Sidney's allusion to "Pacolet's Horse," a figure drawn from the same narrative (or, perhaps, play). In Sidney's treatise, invoking a magical flying horse in the context of "Peru and Calicut" lends an element of the fabulous to these exotic geographies. It also reflects the extent to which, in the late sixteenth century, the English saw the hazy margins of the global map as the realm of the fantastical. Romances, with their "feyned no where acts," as Thomas Nash derisively called them in the sixteenth century, provided resources for representing these spaces (Smith 2: 323). One hundred years later, as English exploration became more surefooted in its incipient overseas empire, Basil Ringrose's adaptation of the romance still offered a way of understanding global engagements and casting them into the realm of the fantastic. The repetition of this story through history demonstrates for us the centrality of the imaginative resources of romance in the putatively empirical documents of overseas exploration. In Sidney, the figure of Pacolet's horse is also deployed as an aspersion, a critique of the ridiculous strategies the stage employed to encompass an expanding world. In Ringrose, however, the romance model offered by *Valentine and Orson* validates the brutal exchange of slavery and death between the English and Orson. This encounter had been rehearsed and enacted before in drama, fiction, and the "historical" documents of sixteenth-century expansion. The romance provided a narrative structure into which the enslaved Orson could be imaginatively integrated into the world of the Europeans as they journeyed onward.

In this way, Danny Boyle's 2012 Olympic ceremonies may also have shared in the kind of romance that has been the topic of this book. For although Caliban's line "the isle is full of noises" served as the organizing principle of the performance (and arguably the London games as a whole), Caliban himself was absent from the proceedings. In his place stood Isambard Kingdom Brunel, performed by Sir Kenneth Branagh with cigar and top hat, the Victorian industrialist responsible for the creation of the Great Western Railway (*Media Guide* 21). Romance, the genre that arises in moments of cultural and economic contradictions (as Fredric Jameson reminds us) elides the problems that attend such a performance. The conversion of Shakespeare's "abhorréd slave" (1.2.354) into a stock character from the early capitalist age assimilates Caliban's difference into a sweeping narrative of modern progress; metaphorically, Caliban (like Orson) could be reincorporated into English history through romance. Boyle, also similar to early dramatists who adapted popular romances into their stage idiom, recognized the importance of space and geography in creating his spectacle. Standing on the hill of the Glastonbury Tor, the reputed site of Arthur's Avalon, Branagh's performance drew on a powerful host of symbols and images, including the visage of the actor himself (familiar to the international audience for his portrayals of Henry V, Hamlet, and other iconic figures of English literature). Although far removed from a largely forgotten genre of the early commercial theater, these "isles of wonder" brought a fleeting return to Avalon, a globalized postscript to the long tradition of romance.

Appendix: Titles and Dates of Stage Romances

The following table collates play titles taken from several sources: Harbage, Greg, Fleay, Ellison, Foakes, Cooper (*The English Romance*), Hays, and Littleton. I have also extensively utilized two electronic resources to identify possible origins for the titles of these plays: Literature Online and the TEAMS Middle English Text archive.* This is not intended to be comprehensive, but rather to give a sense of the extent of the tradition of dramatic romance in the period.

Play title	Origin	Year	Author	Source/status
Cloridon and Radiamanta	Characters featured in Ariosto's *Orlando Furioso*	1572	Unknown	Revels (Lost)
Paris and Vienna	Late medieval French romance by the same title (Caxton printed translation in 1485)	1572	Unknown	Revels (Lost)
Chariclea (Theagenes and Chariclea)	Heliodorus's *Aethiopica*	1572	Unknown	Harbage (Lost)
Herpetalus the Blue Knight and Perobia	Unknown	1574	Unknown	Revels (Lost)
Common Conditions	"The most famous historie of Galiarbus Duke of Arabia" named on title page—an unknown and possibly apocryphal source	1576	Anon	Extant
The Red Knight	Possibly Medieval English *Sir Perceval of Galles*	1576	Unknown	Harbage/Schoenbaum (Lost)
The Irish Knight	The Irish Knight could possibly be Sir Marhaus from the Arthurian Cycles	1577	Unknown	Revels (Lost)
The History of the Solitary Knight	Many Middle English romances feature the figure of the solitary knight, see Herzman	1577	Unknown	Revels (Lost)
Queen of Ethiopia	Heliodorus's *Aethiopica* (?) Possibly the same play as Chariclea (1572)	1578	Unknown	Harbage (Lost)
The Knight in the Burning Rock	Unknown	1579	Unknown	Revels (Lost)

(*continued*)

Appendix Continued

Play title	Origin	Year	Author	Source/status
The Soldan and the Duke of ...	Possibly *The Siege of Milan*, *The Sultan of Babylon*, or one of the many medieval romances featuring the figure of a Sultan	1580	Unknown	Harbage/Schoenbaum (Lost)
Clyomon and Clamydes	*Perceforest*, a French Romance	1583 (Printed 1599)	Anon	Extant
Ariodante and Genevora	*Orlando Furioso*	1583	Unknown	Harbage/Schoenbaum (Lost)
Destruction of Jerusalem	*Siege of Jerusalem*—medieval romance	1584 (records exist of two separate performances in 1584)	Unknown	Harbage (Lost)
Misfortunes of Arthur	Arthurian Legend	1587	Hughes	Extant
The Rare Triumphs of Love and Fortune	Unknown	1589	Anon	Extant
Orlando Furioso	Ariosto	1591 (Printed 1594 and 1599)	Greene	Extant
Titus and Vespasian	*Siege of Jerusalem*—medieval romance (perhaps same as Destruction of Jerusalem (1584))	1592 and 1619	Unknown	Harbage (Lost)
Sir John Mandeville	*Mandeville's Travels*	1592	Unknown	Henslowe (Lost)
Huon of Bordeaux	Popular medieval romance, early sixteenth century English translation by John Berners	1593	Unknown	Henslowe (Lost)
1 Godfrey of Bulloigne, with the Conquest of Jerusalem (possibly an earlier version of Heywood's *Four Prentices*)	Many medieval and early modern sources with stories of Godfrey	1594	Unknown	Henslowe and Stationers' Register 1594 (Lost)
2 Godfrey of Bulloigne		1594	Unknown	Henslowe
Palamon and Arcite	Chaucer's *Knight's Tale*	1594	Unknown	Henslowe (Lost)

(*continued*)

Appendix Continued

Play title	Origin	Year	Author	Source/status
Valentine and Orson	Fifteenth-century French romance	1595, 1598, 1600	Anon	Henslowe and Stationers' Register (Lost)
Chinon of England	Arthurian Legend (Christopher Middleton wrote 1597 narrative, *The Famous Historie of Chinon of England*)	1596	Unknown	Henslowe (Lost)
Uther Pendragon	Arthurian Legend	1597	Unknown	Henslowe (Lost)
Arthur's Show	Arthurian Legend	c.1597	Unknown	Mentioned in *2 Hen. IV* (Lost)
Mucedorus	Possibly Sidney's *Arcadia*, which also includes a character named Mucedorus	1598 (and sixteen subsequent editions through 1668)	Anon	Extant
Arthur, the Life (and death) of, King of England	Arthurian Legend	1598	Hathway	Henslowe (Lost)
Jerusalem	Possibly *Siege of Jerusalem* (see 1584 above) or Godfrey of Bulloigne material	1599	Unknown	Harbage (Lost)
Tristram de Lyons	Middle English Romance, possibly Malory	1599	Anon	Henslowe (Lost)
The Seven Wise Masters	Version of *The Seven Sages of Rome*, a popular medieval Romance	1600	Chettle, Day, Dekker, and Haughton	Henslowe (Lost)
Old Fortunatus	German Romance *Fortunatus*	1600	Dekker	Extant
Conquest of the West Indies	Unknown	1601	Day, Haughton, Smith	Harbage/Henslowe (Lost)
The Four Sons of Aymon	Medieval romance of the same title—Caxton printed English translation in 1489	1603	Robert Shaw (?)	Harbage (Lost)
Trial of Chivalry, with Cavaliero Dick Bowyer	Unknown	1604	Anon	Extant

(*continued*)

Appendix Continued

Play title	Origin	Year	Author	Source/status
Sir Giles Goosecap, Knight	Unknown	Printed 1606 and 1636	Anon (attributed to Chapman)	Extant
The Knight of the Burning Pestle	Parody of Heywood's *Foure Prentises of London*	1609	Beaumont	Extant
Tom a Lincoln	Richard Johnson romance of the same title	1608–1615	Heywood (?)	Extant in MS
Four Prentices of London with the Conquest of Jerusalem	Godfrey of Bulloigne	Printed 1615 and 1630	Heywood	Extant
Guy, Earl of Warwick	*Guy of Warwick* Tradition	Performances recorded in 1618 and 1631 (printed 1661, but unclear whether this is the same play)	Ascribed on title page to "B.J.," but possibly Day or Dekker	Extant
Baiting of the Jealous Knight (Fair Foul One)	Unknown	1623	Smith	Harbage (Lost)
Fairy Knight	*Sir Degare*, a middle English romance, features a Fairy Knight, as does *Tom a Lincoln*	1624	Dekker & Ford	Revels (Lost)
Invisible Knight	Unknown	1633	Unknown	Mentioned in *A Bird in the Hand* (1633) (Lost)
Seven Champions of Christendom	Multiple sources	1638	Kirke	Extant
St. George for England		Before 1642	Unknown	Harbage, Cited in Warburton (Lost)
Knight of the Golden Shield	Version of *Clyomon and Clamydes* (?)	n.d.	Unknown	List of Printed Plays from Goffe, *Careless Shepherdess* (1656) (Lost)
The Birth of Merlin	Arthurian Legend—related to *Uther Pendragon* (1597) (?)	1662	Rowley (ascribed on title page to Shakespeare and Rowley)	Extant

*I am also grateful for Jonathan Hsy's help in locating Middle English sources for these plays.

Notes

Introduction: Romance and the Globe

1 Collinson's edition of Frobisher's voyages for the Hakluyt Society includes a complete record of these purchases.
2 *The voiag[e] and trauayle, of syr Iohn Maundeuile* . . . (STC 17250) was published in 1568. Earlier extant English editions were printed in 1496, 1499, 1503, and 1510. The reputation of Mandeville remains as clouded today as it was in the sixteenth and seventeenth centuries. For a summary of the skeptical responses to this figure (particularly in the theater) see Gordon McMullan, "Stage-Mandevilles." Charles W. R. D. Moseley argues that readers had a range of responses to the *Travels*, from skepticism to outright belief, and Michael Householder argues for the canonicity of *Mandevilles Travels* as an early modern colonial text.
3 Ralegh included *Mandeville's Travels* in a list of geographical and cosmographical texts that were apparently part of his library. See Walter Oakeshott, who compiled the list from a manuscript believed to be Ralegh's commonplace book (320).
4 For further discussion of Ralegh's *Discovery*, geography, and the work of fiction, see especially Benjamin Schmidt's excellent introduction to his Bedford edition and Mary Fuller, "Ralegh's Fugitive Gold: Reference and Deferral in the *Discovery of Guiana*."
5 Henslowe records items in his inventory that could have been used for the staging of *Mandeville*: copper and wooden targets (shields), engraved armor, a gilt spear, and, most quizzically, a "chayne of dragons" (Foakes 320). These items are noted in the playhouse inventories that Edmond Malone transcribed from Henslowe's papers, which are now lost. Malone's transcription can be found in Foakes, who notes with caution, "little reliance is to be placed upon the connecting of a property with a specific play" (317). Charles W. R. D. Moseley discusses this lost play in "'Whetstone leasings,'" see especially 36–8.
6 See especially Gillies, *Shakespeare and the Geographies of Difference;* Helgerson, *Forms of Nationhood;* Donald Smith, *The Cartographic Imagination;* Sanford, *Maps and Memory in Early Modern England;* and Raman, *Framing "India."*
7 See also Hulme, *Colonial Encounters* for his analysis of Columbus's writings.
8 Buscoducensis is the Latin name for today's s'Hertogenbosch in the Netherlands. The modern translation of the Latin text of the cartouche is provided in MacMillan and Abeles.
9 According to Mercator, the friar's travels were recorded in a lost book, the *Inventio Fortunatae*. For a discussion of the possible existence of this narrative, see E. G. R. Taylor, 62–6.
10 Mercator's letter to Dee was transcribed and translated from the British Library's Cotton MS Vitellius IV by Taylor and printed in *Imago Mundi* in 1956. Quotations from the letter are taken from her translation.

11 Further discussions of Dee and his expansionist arguments in *The Limits of the British Empire* are to be found in William Sherman, *John Dee* (especially 182–92), Parry, and Artese, all of whom concur that Dee's arguments were largely insignificant in actual policy—Dee himself lamented that his labors were made "little accownt of" (qtd. in Sherman, *John Dee* 200).
12 E. G. R. Taylor, who seems to believe in the veracity of Mercator's story, speculates that the Cnoyen book may have come from Ortelius.
13 Translated from *De Oratore*, Book Two: "Historia vero testis temporum, lux veritatis, vita memoriae, magistra vitae, nuntia vetustatis." For a discussion of Cicero and early modern historiography, see Woolf, *The Idea of History in Early Stuart England* 13–23.
14 Gillies describes the contrast between an "old geographic poetic" represented in the works of classical antiquity and the "new geographic poetic" embodied in the work of sixteenth- and seventeenth-century cartography, see especially 34–9. Though he includes Mandeville briefly in this discussion, Gillies understanding of the older tradition focuses mainly upon Greek and Roman conceptions of geography and "otherness." For a recent critique of this model of spatial understanding, see the epilogue, "Re-enchanting Geography," in Kristen Poole's *Supernatural Environments in Shakespeare's England*.
15 Gillies is utilizing the concept of "imaginative geography," a phrase coined by Edward Said in his influential *Orientalism*. Interestingly, Said uses the metaphor of the theater to illustrate how the West constructed images of the East, see especially 63. For insightful adaptations of Said's work in cultural geography, see especially Derek Gregory, "Imaginative Geographies" and *The Colonial Present*.
16 See especially Barker and Hulme, "Nymphs and Reapers Heavily Vanish: The Discursive Con-texts of The Tempest"; Greenblatt, *Marvelous Possessions: The Wonder of the New World*; Hulme, *Colonial Encounters: Europe and the Native Caribbean, 1492–1797*.
17 Walter Cohen, "The Undiscovered Country: Shakespeare and Mercantile Geography"; David J. Baker, "'The Allegory of a China Shop': Jonson's Entertainment at Britain's Burse."
18 For recent work in this vein, see the essays in Sebek and Deng's *Global Traffic*, and particularly Daniel Vitkus's, "'The Common Market of All the World': English Theater, the Global System, and the Ottomon Empire in the Early Modern Period." See also the foundational work of Kenneth Andrews, *Trade, Plunder, and Settlement: Maritime Enterprise and the Genesis of the British Empire, 1480–1630* as well as Crystal Bartolovich, "'Baseless Fabric': London as World City"; Jerry Brotton, *The Renaissance Bazaar: From the Silk Road to Michelangelo*; Valerie Forman, *Tragicomic Redemptions*; Jonathan Gil Harris, *Sick Economies*; and Aaron Kitch, *Political Economy and the States of Literature in Early Modern England*.
19 On the East, see especially Archer, *Old Worlds: Egypt, Southwest Asia, India, and Russia in Early Modern English Writing*; Barbour, *Before Orientalism*; Brotton, *The Renaissance Bazaar: From the Silk Road to Michelangelo*; Burton, *Traffic And Turning*; Dimmock, *New Turkes*; Maclean, *Re-Orienting the Renaissance* and *Looking East*; Matar, *Turks, Moors and Englishmen in the Age of Discovery*; and Vitkus, *Turning Turk*. Jane Degenhardt provides a particular focus on issues

of sexuality and religion in *Islamic Conversion and Christian Resistance on the Early Modern Stage*.
20 As Cohen points out, this thesis extends from J. H. Elliot's analysis in *The Old World and the New*.
21 Robert Markley also discusses the importance of "fantasy" in the development of trade in the East in *The Far East and the English Imagination*, 30–70. He writes, "The Far East thus serves as a fantasy space for mercantile capitalism because it allows for the rigorous externalization of costs: profits can be tallied (or future profits imagined) without calculating (to take only two examples) either the value of lost lives, ships, and cargoes, or the value, in devastated local ecologies, of the deforestation necessary to build ships for the British navy and East India Company (EIC) fleets" (4).
22 Jyotsna Singh offers a thorough account of this critical tradition in her introduction to *A Companion to the Global Renaissance*. For other studies that bring attention to the question of form in the history of empire and geographic expansion, see especially Valerie Forman, *Tragicomic Redemptions*, Jean Howard, "Shakespeare, Geography, and the Work of Genre on the Early Modern Stage," and Roland Greene, *Unrequited Conquests*.
23 For further discussion see Fuchs, "Imperium Studies," and Fuchs and Baker, 339–40. This work develops from the foundational study of empire in English culture by David Armitage, *The Ideological Origins of the British Empire*; for other examples of this approach, see Hadfield, *Literature, Travel, and Colonial Writing in the English Renaissance, 1545–1625* and Netzloff, *England's Internal Colonies*.
24 See, for instance, Stanley Wells, "Shakespeare and Romance," which begins by posing the problem of naming plays from the period "romance," and Stephen Orgel, who maintains that romance is a "modern invention" ("Introduction," 4).
25 Though the terms "romance" and "tragicomedy" are sometimes conflated in Shakespeare studies, I maintain some distinction between the two. Unlike romance, tragicomedy had a theatrical history that, although checkered, reached into both continental and English traditions. For an examination of tragicomedy as a genre, see Gordon McMullan and Jonathan Hope, eds., *The Politics of Tragicomedy* and Valerie Forman's *Tragicomic Redemptions*, which also argues for the connections between dramatic genre and economics.
26 Richard Johnson's prose romance and its continuations appeared in six different editions before the printing of the 1638 play. It continued in popularity through the eighteenth century.
27 Romance outside of Shakespeare has received attention as a dramatic genre, but mainly in its connections to the Shakespearean canon. See Barbara Mowat's important work in calling attention to these "early dramatized romances," recommending them for their value in understanding later Shakespearean drama (143). See also Christopher Cobb's study, which also treats these earlier plays, but again only as a means of showing their impact on Shakespeare's writing.
28 There is a significant body of scholarship on romance within medieval studies that has usefully catalogued the range of motifs and stories that comprised this tradition, demonstrating a deep cultural familiarity with the genre. Yin Liu suggests that we think of the Middle English romance as a

"prototype genre," whereby single examples can be extrapolated to define the wider whole. Liu shows that middle English romance was a more capacious category than has previously been recognized, a collection of stories that ranged from Arthurian materials and insular romances like *Guy of Warwick* and *Richard Coer d'Lyon* to materials not generally thought of in the medieval canon of romances (Charlemagne stories, the Siege of Troy, etc.). See also Helen Cooper, *The English Romance in Time*, and Paul Strohm.

29 In her recent book, *Shakespeare and the Medieval World*, Helen Cooper interprets the plays of Shakespeare as an extension of the medieval tradition, including works of romance. See especially 176–8, and "Staging the Unstageable." I agree that the romance genre marks an important continuity between medieval and early modern culture, though I maintain that the movement into the commercial theater was an important generic change within the history of genre.

30 For further discussion of materiality and form, see Douglas Bruster's informative essay in the volume *Shakespeare and Historical Formalism*.

31 A comprehensive study of Dowden's creation of the "late plays" and the notion of Shakespeare's late work can be found in Gordon McMullan's *Shakespeare and the Idea of Late Writing*.

32 Rosalie Colie's *The Resources of Kind* remains a seminal study of Renaissance genres and genre study. See also Jean E. Howard, "Shakespeare and Genre."

33 See Fuchs, 66–98, for a relevant discussion of how critical attention to "Shakespearean Romance" neglects the wider range of possibilities for romance in the period.

34 Dowden's categorization lives on in both the *Norton Shakespeare* and the *Riverside Shakespeare*, today's standard classroom texts.

35 Important theoretical scholarship has developed around attempts at defining "New Formalism." For an overview, see especially Marjorie Levinson's helpful survey "What is New Formalism?" In early modern studies, specifically, this question is pursued in the volumes *Shakespeare and Historical Formalism*, ed. Stephen Cohen, and *Renaissance Literature and Its Formal Engagements*, ed. Mark David Rasmussen.

36 See also Lori Humphrey Newcomb (*Reading Popular Romance*), who shows in her remarkable study of Robert Greene's prose romance *Pandosto*, the source for Shakespeare's *Winter's Tale*, how publishers found an eager readership for small, quarto editions of chivalric romances and other stories that shared similar plot structures, motifs, and strategies with those medieval tales.

37 Quotations are taken from the *OED Online*, 2nd edition.

38 Although there is evidence that minstrels and court readers gave oral performances of Middle English romances (see Karl Reichl, "Orality and Performance"), I would argue this is a substantially different tradition than the sixteenth-century stage romance. The narrative bias toward romance remains in contemporary criticism: the genealogy of the novel, our ascendant narrative form, has been rooted firmly in romance by the influential work of Ian Duncan, Michael McKeon, and Fredric Jameson.

39 There is evidence for a sixteenth-century performative tradition of romance before the opening of the commercial theaters. Puttenham writes of the "*cantabanqui*," the "bench songs" he says were popular entertainment at "Christmas dinners and bride-ales" (173), those same songs that Sidney

admits in the *Defense* moved "my heart more than with a trumpet" (173 n. 8). These songs, however, delivered by a single speaker or singer, are more closely aligned to a narrative tradition than dramatic.

40 Here my use of "ideology" echoes David Armitage's definition in *The Ideological Origins of the British Empire* as both "systematic" and "contestable," and therefore open to critique (4–5). Richard Helgerson offers a seminal reading of spatial representation in geography and its construction of national ideology in *Forms of Nationhood*, especially 105–46. See also Jonathan Scott, *When the Waves Ruled Britannia*, who casts the expansion of geographic space within political discourse.

41 I refer here to important studies from a growing body of scholarship that explores the association between romance as a form and pre-modern European expansion and cross-cultural contact, especially Barbara Fuchs's *Mimesis and Empire* (2001), Joan Pong Linton's *The Romance of the New World* (1998), Geraldine Heng's *Empire of Magic* (2003), Brian Lockey's *Law and Empire in English Renaissance Literature* (2006), and Benedict Robinson's *Islam and Early Modern English Literature* (2007).

42 Many genealogies of romance continue to emphasize its roots in the non-classical. Geraldine Heng argues in *Empire of Magic* that medieval romance took the form that we recognize today in the legendary histories of Arthur found in Geoffrey of Monmouth's *History of the Kings of Britain*. This text, she argues, is deeply inscribed by European contact with the East during the First Crusade (6). For further discussion of the Eastern and Arabic roots of romance, see Metlitzki's *The Matter of Araby in Medieval England*, especially her chapter on "History and Romance," 117–210.

43 See especially Patricia Clare Ingham, *Sovereign Fantasies,* Geraldine Heng, *Empire of Magic,* and Michelle Warren, *History on the Edge.*

44 References to Greene's *Orlando Furioso* are taken from Collins's edition of the play.

45 Greene's *Orlando Furioso* exists in two different texts: the printed editions of 1594 and 1599, and a manuscript at Dulwich College, containing only the parts of Orlando, that is believed to be the copy of the actor Edward Alleyn. Both texts are included in the Collins edition.

46 The manuscript has the signature of one "Morganus Evans" at the end of the play, evidence that, along with the manuscript's provenance, points to a likely performance of the play at the Inns of Court in the first decade of the seventeenth century. For further discussion, see Proudfoot.

47 The earliest extant edition of Johnson's narrative was published in 1631, but, according to the editors of the play manuscript, there are entries in the Stationers' Register that suggest earlier publication dates of 1599 and 1607 (xx n. 13). A modern edition of Johnson's *Tom a Lincoln* has been edited by S. M. Hirsch. The popularity of the text is suggested by its multiple editions through the seventeenth and eighteenth centuries, as well as the number of printings the 1631 and 1632 editions went through: 6 and 12, respectively.

48 Proudfoot's evidence of Shakespearean borrowing is less than convincing. He cites, for instance, "for tis in me to yeld or not to yeld" (83) from *Tom a Lincoln* as a parallel to Hamlet's "To be or not to be . . . ," a line that Peter Stallybrass has demonstrated comes from a long tradition of early modern commonplaces (1581).

49 David Wallace, in *Premodern Places*, calls for this kind of transculturally informed historicism. On the question of periodization, and its attendant critical blind spots, see Margreta de Grazia, "The Modern Divide."
50 W. W. Greg notes that the word "Maundev'" in the entry is "uncertain." I have inspected the catalogue pages in the British Library's Add. 27632, and agree that the word is difficult to read, possibly obscured by the writer's haste. The corresponding entry on fol. 30r, however, provides corroboration that the catalogue notations refer to a copy of some form of Mandeville that Harington held in his collection.

1 Romancing Shakespeare

1 These lines from *The Winter's Tale* are taken from *The Norton Shakespeare*, ed. Stephen Greenblatt, et al. (New York: W. W. Norton, 1997). Unless otherwise noted, references to Shakespeare are from the Norton version of the Oxford text.
2 In setting up this "diachronic construct," Jameson allows that it could be subject to "withering contemporary Althusserian or Nietzschean denunciations . . . " My interest is in the axiomatic formulation of Shakespeare's romances, rather than the theoretical point of their invocation here.
3 The use of the word "career" to mean "a person's course or progress through life" or "a course of professional life or employment" arose only in the nineteenth century. The lateness of the critical paradigm described here thus matches the lexical history of that word ("Career" Def. 5 a. and b.).
4 For a discussion of the creation of a Shakespearean chronology in the late eighteenth century, see de Grazia, *Shakespeare Verbatim*, especially 141–51.
5 In the Folio, as in the quarto editions of the play, the title of *Pericles, Prince of Tyre* promises the "true relation of the Whole Historie, aduentures, and fortunes of the said Prince," the closest the play comes to receiving a generic label. The Third Folio did not include any of the seven newly added plays in its Catalogue, and thus retains the same list of plays as the Second Folio. Both the Second and Third Folios correct the omission of *Troilus and Cressida* from the Catalogue of the First Folio.
6 All quotations are from the third edition of the text. Dowden's study has been one of the most widely read and extensively printed works of Shakespearean criticism of the past 150 years. It went through three separate editions in Dowden's lifetime and the most recent printing, in 1967, marked its 26th impression.
7 For his various taxonomies, see Coleridge, 1:208–12 and 2:67–8.
8 For further discussion of Coleridge and the emergence of "psychology" as a term in Shakespearean criticism, see de Grazia, Hamlet *without Hamlet* 15–16.
9 Coleridge, *Shakespearean Criticism* 1:118.
10 In his manuscripts and in his *Literary Remains*, Coleridge sketched out two different attempts at organizing the plays of Shakespeare: one into "epochs" that culminated, as in Dowden, with *The Tempest*, *The Winter's Tale*, and *Cymbeline*, but also a second progression in which the histories mark the end of the canon (1: 212). See Coleridge, 1: 209–13.

210 Notes

11 As Barbara Fuchs notes, it is ironic that Coleridge should assess *The Tempest* with these terms, given that it is "a text that has recently been contextualized by reference to the discourse of colonialism in the Americas, in Ireland and in the Mediterranean," see Fuchs, *Romance* 94.
12 Dowden's formulation of Shakespeare's plays as superior to their sources is part of a long history described recently by Lori Humphrey Newcomb, *Reading Popular Romance in Early Modern England* (New York: Columbia University Press, 2002). Newcomb "reconstructs" the popularity of *Pandosto*, Shakespeare's source for *The Winter's Tale*, as she seeks to "undo critical axiologies that raise Shakespeare's plays above their sources," 13. For a discussion of Shakespeare's relationship to print culture, particularly romances, see also Henderson and Siemon.
13 For his discussion of Shakespeare and the influences of Elizabethan history, see Dowden, *Shakspere; a Critical Study of His Mind and Art* 7.
14 A useful summary of the responses and adaptations of Dowden can be found in Edwards. Edwards identifies earlier objections to Dowden's formulation of the Shakespearean generic chronology, yet these don't disagree with the validity of Dowden's periods, only with Dowden's characterization of the Shakespearean mind. Felperin, too, offers a "Bibliographic Appendix" with a summary of critical responses to these plays from the time of Shakespeare on, though in doing so, he further demonstrates the universality of the category.
15 I am skeptical of the use of the linguistic strings or "language action types" (LATs) employed by Docuscope (the language analysis tool deployed by Witmore and Hope in their study) for generic analysis. The tool tracks "rhetorical effects" by the presence or absence of words relating to psychological interiority, interpersonal relations, and subjective references to objects. Such a linguistic framework seems biased toward the kind of psychological conclusions about literature and genre espoused by Dowden.
16 For a discussion of nineteenth- and early twentieth-century critics who adapted Dowden's procedures early on, see Edwards and Felperin.
17 See also Howard's *Theater of a City: The Places of London Comedy, 1598–1642*.
18 Ralph Cohen provides an excellent analysis of "history and genre" in his essay of the same title. My historical approach to genre study is also indebted to Jameson, particularly as outlined in *The Political Unconscious*.
19 See also Valerie Wayne's essay on *Cardenio* (*Don Quixote*), which contextualizes the play within the publication history of *Don Quijote* in England. I am grateful to her for sharing this unpublished work with me.
20 Barbara Fuchs offers a useful survey of the various critical and historical approaches to the term in *Romance*, 1–11.
21 For further discussion of the Eastern and Arabic roots of romance, see Metlitzki's *The Matter of Araby in Medieval England*, especially her chapter on "History and Romance," 117–210.
22 See Jameson's chapter in *The Political Unconscious*, "Magical Narratives," discussed above and Cooper's "Introduction: Enter, pursued with a Bear" in *The English Romance in Time*.
23 See Dowden, "Elizabethan Romance," 351, 352. That Shakespeare's romances remake and refine an earlier romance tradition is an argument that finds repetition in recent criticism. See, for instance, Christopher J. Cobb, *The Staging*

of Romance in Late Shakespeare, who sees in Shakespeare's late plays "efforts to reform the staging of romance" (62).
24 Dowden named the preceding periods, first, "In the workshop;" second, anticipating Stephen Greenblatt's biography, "In the world" and the third, "out of the depths."
25 For a valuable discussion of Hegel's historical teleology and the notion of the modern, see de Grazia, "The Modern Divide" 453–67.

2 "Asia of the one side, and Afric of the other": Sidney's Unities and the Staging of Romance

1 For a detailed account of the publication history and popularity of *Valentine and Orson*, see Dickson Appendix II and Cooper "The Strange History."
2 There is evidence that Sidney's treatise was known even in its own time. John Florio's 1591 collection of proverbs and popular phrases, *Florios Second Frutes*, contains a clear reference to the *Defense* in this dialogue

> HENRY: The plaies that they plaie in England, are not right comedies.
> THOMAS: Yet they doo nothing else but plaie euery daye.
> HENRY: Yea but they are neither right comedies, nor right tragedies.
> GIOVANNI: How would you name them then?
> HENRY: Representations of histories, without any decorum. (23)

Henry's claim that English plays are "neither right comedies, nor right tragedies" is nearly a direct quotation from the *Defense*. Though not published until 1595 (under its alternative title, *An Apology for Poetry*), Sidney's treatise circulated in manuscripts as early as 1580, in which form Florio may well have seen it. The *Defense* is now often a part of collections on theatrical history. See, for example, Pollard.
3 Eliot also called the *Defense* one of the "striking examples of the futility of corrective criticism" (37). Critics have only rarely engaged in a fruitful and consistent analysis of the *Defense* on drama. Eliot's essay, "An Apology for the Countess of Pembroke" in *The Use of Poetry and the Use of Criticism* remains one of the few examples. More recently, Sidney figures in discussions of dramatic genre in Howard "Shakespeare and Genre" and Orgel "Shakespeare and the Kinds of Drama."
4 "Tragicomedy" is a term often used in modern criticism for the group of plays Dowden described as romances, further adding to the confusion about Shakespearean genres. My project is to identify a separate tradition of romance that can be distinguished from tragicomedy. For a discussion of the terms "tragicomedy" and "romance," see Mowat.
5 Henry Turner argues that we should view the publications of the "Apologie" and *Defense* as containing different modes of argumentation. For further discussion, and for a supplementary view of Sidney's Aristotelianism, see especially 82–113.
6 For an early twentieth-century study of stage romances played at court, see Ellison.

7   See Feullierat, 303, 306–8. Astington uses these details from the court records to give a speculative description of the staging of this play (102–3).
8   In "Ode to Himself," Jonson also famously denounced audiences for favoring the "mouldy" and "stale" *Pericles* (1938).
9   Of the two, only *Common Conditions* was actually printed during this period from 1570–1585. *Clyomon and Clamydes* was printed in 1599.
10 This would set the earliest date of the play at 1583, the year of the founding of the Queen's company. Editors and theater historians, however, have typically dated the play to the 1570s. See Littleton for a complete discussion of the dating of the play, though she says "the whole matter is admittedly conjectural" (30).
11 Since he was familiar with the court drama *Gorboduc*, Sidney may have seen *Clyomon and Clamydes*, a play also performed by the Queen's Men.
12 Parenthetical citations for *Common Conditions* refer to line numbers in the Elizabethan Club edition of the play.
13 Other critics have noted the correlation between Sidney's comments on drama and obscure plays such as *Clyomon and Clamydes*. See Ellison 132–3, Wells 52–3 and O'Connell 218, though O'Connell dismissively calls these early romances a "brief vogue" (n. 6).
14 Sidney also proffers two other loosely-connected objections to English drama: it is indecorous in its mixing of kings and clowns (tragedy and comedy), and its comedies confuse delight with laughter.
15 Although Sidney credits Aristotle with the formulation of the "precept" of unity of time, most scholars agree that Aristotelian prescriptions on unity begin and end with the unity of action, discussed above. In the *Poetics*, Aristotle does point out that tragedy "attempts to keep within a single revolution of the sun," but he does not tie this observation to any requirement that the action represented on the stage take place over such a period of time. For further discussion, see Spingarn 89–101.
16 For a discussion of Sidney's indebtedness to the Italian critics of the sixteenth century, see Myrick and Spingarn.
17 Martyr's text was widely circulated and translated into several languages—Sidney almost surely would have been familiar with it.
18 Pacolet's horse is one of many such devices in romance. Ariosto's Hippogryph in the *Orlando Furioso* is another flying horse. Fortunatus's "wishing cap" (discussed below) also allows its wearer to quickly travel across vast spaces.
19 The latter tradition of strangers on the early modern stage has motivated much recent scholarship, see especially Loomba, who uses the category of "romance" to open questions of gender and imperialism in *Antony and Cleopatra* (*Shakespeare, Race and Colonialism* 112–34) and John Fletcher's *Island Princess* ("'Break her will'"). But the *Foure Prentises*, and plays of its "fashion," constitute a dramatic tradition on the early modern stage that has been largely overlooked. For readings that explore economic principles at work in *Old Fortunatus*, see Sherman, who focuses on early modern gold exchange, and Vitkus, who is interested in the meaning of labor in the play. On *The Foure Prentises*, see Macfarlane and Lisa Cooper.
20 The sixteenth-century German playwright Hans Sachs also adapted the *Fortunatus* story into a play in 1553. It is unclear to me whether there was any relationship between the play of Sachs and Dekker's later adaptation.

21 We know that Thomas Dekker revised an older play for this performance: Henslowe's diary records earlier performances of a two-part play called *Fortunatus* in 1596. In late 1599, Henslowe paid Dekker a total of six pounds (the going price for an entire new play) to prepare *Old Fortunatus* for performance at court during Christmas. For specific entries, see Foakes, 126–8.
22 See Orgel, who states, "In most European languages in the Renaissance the generic term for drama was comedy" ("Shakespeare and the Kinds of Drama" 157).
23 Cited in Osborn; Sidney was Hakluyt's classmate at Christ Church, Oxford. For further discussion, see Osborn, 508.

3 Imagined Empires: The Cultural Geography of Stage Romance

1 See, for example, Douglas Bruster, *Drama and the Market in the Age of Shakespeare*; Aaron Kitch, *Political Economy and the State of Literature in Early Modern England: From Spenser to Jonson*, and Sebek and Deng, *Global Traffic: Discourses and Practices of Trade in English Literature and Culture from 1550 to 1700*.
2 Henry Turner has argued that the formal parameters of stage representation were indebted more to the work of craftsmen, early scientists, and other artisans whose work impelled geometric and spatial theorizing. See also Kristen Poole and Martin Brückner who historicize the idea of "plot" within early mapmaking discourse. As this work shows, there has been a recent tendency toward scientific discourses in the discussion of geography that needs to be supplemented with further investigations of the more fantastical elements of maps.
3 The past twenty years has produced a well-established body of scholarship on early modern mapmaking, cartographic representation, and its impact on the cultural production of literature and theater. Richard Helgerson's *Forms of Nationhood* is arguably the seminal work in this field, as it positioned the mapping of England within the broader "generational project" of Elizabethan nation formation. Successive studies have picked up this foundational idea and viewed the representational form of the map as variously implicated in other early modern "projects": technological development, commerce, colonialism, and even the formulation of a nascent racial discourse.
4 In addition to the work of Sanders, see also Mullaney, Chedgzoy, McCrae, Zucker, and Howard (discussed below).
5 For Howard, this question leads to an investigation of tragedy and its proximate geographies in Shakespeare and his contemporaries. See also her extended work on city comedy in *Theater of a City*.
6 For an exception see Benedict Robinson, *Islam and Early Modern English Literature*. See also Patricia Ingram and Melissa Warren, *Postcolonial Moves* for further examination of romance and the "postcolonial" Middle Ages, and Sylvia Huot, *Postcolonial Fictions in the* Roman de Perceforest.
7 Henry Turner has argued convincingly for the impact of technical skill and craft on the early modern theater and poetics, see *The English Renaissance Stage*. My argument augments his by seeking the imaginative imperatives in both romance and geography.

8   These books included Robert Tanner's 1592 *Briefe Treatise for the Ready vse of the Sphere*, John Blagrave's *Mathematical Iewel* (1585), Thomas Hood's 1592 *The Use of Both the Globes, Celestiall and Terrestriall*, Robert Hues's 1593 *Tractatus de Globis et eorum Usu*. The last two of these, Hood's and Rues's text, are bound together in the British Library, Shelfmark C114 a 12. 1.
9   Herbert Grabes calls the spherical shape of Merlin's mirror "quite original" among other examples of mirrors in Spenser (477). Editors point to Chaucer's "Squire's Tale" as Spenser's source for the mirror, see the Variorum edition of *The Faerie Queene* (216). A. C. Hamilton, in his Longman Edition, also suggests that the globe may be a reference to a crystal ball like the one John Dee used for his prognostications (305).
10 The earliest extant edition of Johnson's narrative was published in 1631, but, according to the editors of the play manuscript, there are entries in the Stationers' Register that suggest earlier publication dates of 1599 and 1607 (xx n. 13). A modern edition of Johnson's *Tom a Lincoln* has been edited by S. M. Hirsch. The popularity of the text is suggested by its multiple editions through the seventeenth- and eighteenth-centuries, as well as the number of printings the 1631 and 1632 editions went through: 6 and 12, respectively.
11 One of the most significant changes the play makes to Johnson's narrative is to have Tom leading a battle against the French, a change that perhaps indicates the play was written during improved relations with the unified Spanish-Portuguese Empire that followed the end of Anglo-Spanish hostilities in 1604.
12 Johnson's portrayal of Prester John's kingdom is idiosyncratic, incorporating elements from other narrative traditions. For further discussion of the tradition of Prester John's kingdom, see Delumeau.
13 *The Tragedy . . . of Guy, Earl of Warwick* was published in 1661, but was performed, according to the title page, "very frequently and with great applause by his late Majesties servants," the King's men. Helen Moore has recently prepared an edition of the play for the Malone Society.
14 The description offered by the chorus is remarkably similar to the entry under "Mauritania" in Thomas Cooper's 1578 Latin dictionary and thesaurus (see especially Sig. Lllllll6v), but it could have been taken from any number of sources that quote Martianus as the authority on this region's geography. See also, for instance, Stephen Batman's 1582 translation of Anglicus Bartholomaeus's *De proprietatibus rerum*, sig. Rr6r.
15 Marshall, one of the few critics to respond to *Tom a Lincoln*, discusses the play in terms of its expansionist ideology, identifying it with the "accretion of imperial notions of expansionism and martialism" that followed the ascension of James I and the unification of Scotland and England (87).
16 See William H. Sherman, "Putting the British Seas on the Map," for further discussion of Dee's cartography, as well as his discussion of the same in *John Dee*.
17 Spelled "Rodes" in the Second Folio, and "Rhodes" in editions thereafter.
18 Nicholas Rowe also used "Rhodes" in his two editions of Shakespeare's works (1709, 1714). It is hard, if not impossible, to determine whether "Rhodes" was Shakespeare's original intention for the line. Matthew Black and Matthias Shaaber, in their catalogue of seventeenth-century Folio emendations, categorize this instance as a "mistaken" alteration, one in which "the reviser's unfamiliarity with a word, or the sense in which it is used, has caused him to

fancy the text corrupt" (217). But this explanation is unpersuasive given the continued use of "road" meaning "harbor," even into the twentieth century. The editors of subsequent Folios chose not to emend other instances of the word used in this sense, indicating an understanding of this meaning. It is also possible that Antonio's echoing of Portia's line "richly come to harbor" with "safely come to road" struck the Second Folio editor as awkward.

19 For a helpful description of the medieval trade routes between Venice and the Levant, see Lane, 68–73.

20 M. M. Mahood discusses the apparent inconsistencies in these geographic allusions in his introduction to the New Cambridge Shakespeare edition of the play (13).

21 An exception is to be found in Elizabeth Spiller, "From Imagination to Miscegenation: Race and Romance in Shakespeare's *The Merchant of Venice*," where she argues that the play's engagement with romance is reflected in its treatment of racial difference.

22 This body of criticism is well represented in the work of Bailey, "Shylock and the Slaves"; Engle, "Thrift Is Blessing"; Lawrence, "To Give and to Receive"; MacInnes, "Ill Luck, Ill Luck?"; Mentz, "The Fiend Gives Friendly Counsel"; Stevens, "Heterogenizing Imagination: Globalization, The Merchant of Venice, and the Work of Literary Criticism"; and Woodbridge, "Payback Time."

23 Cohen, "The Merchant of Venice and the Possibilities of Historical Criticism"; see also Cohen's essay on geography and mercantilism, "The Undiscovered Country: Shakespeare and Mercantile Geography."

24 Kitch is interested, ultimately, in how the play reflects upon "political stability" within the community represented in the play, focusing in particular on the trial scene and Shylock's punishment at the hands of Antonio. See especially 121–8. This reading of Shylock revises New Historicist accounts, like that of John Gillies, which view Shylock as purely oppositional to the mercantile position of Antonio (*Shakespeare and the Geography of Difference* 124–37). Stephen Greenblatt similarly calls Shylock "the antithesis . . . of the Christian mercantilism in Venice" ("Marlowe" 295). For a discussion of the history of Jewish culture in establishing trading networks throughout Europe, see the foundational work of historian Phillip Curtin.

25 John Gillies reads the references to the Golden Fleece myth as evidence of "anxieties about trade, intermixture and miscegenation" (136) within the play. There is, indeed, an unease about these foreign spaces (as there often is in romance), but I read this as a generic problem that romance seeks to resolve, at least temporarily.

26 See Charry, "[T]he Beauteous Scarf" and Wilson, "Veiling an Indian Beauty."

27 For an extended discussion of the syntax and meaning of these lines, see Furness, *Merchant*, 146–8. The commentary there reflects a racialized discourse that I also believe is present in Bassanio's lines. Take, for instance, this commentary from a nineteenth-century critic: "'Indian' is used adjectively, in the sense of *wild, savage, hideous*,—just as we, at the present day, might say a 'Hottentot beauty'" (146).

28 For a different reading of the play's genre, see Valerie Forman's analysis of *The Merchant of Venice* for further discussion of the Shylock/Antonio plot as tragedy, especially 28–30.

29 Cohen also brings the question of genre to bear in his reading of the economics of *The Merchant of Venice*, as he situates the play as romantic comedy, though a problematic one: "*The Merchant of Venice* . . . reveals the formal and ideological limits of Renaissance romantic comedy" ("Merchant" 782).

4 Chronicle History, Cosmopolitan Romance: *Henry V* and the Generic Boundaries of the Second Tetralogy

1 Wright, *Metrical Chronicle*, lines 9986–87. Robert is referring here to the history of Richard Coeur de Lion, and the story to which he refers is likely the surviving fourteenth-century romance. My thanks to Daniel Kempton for consulting with me on this translation.
2 Strohm offers an excellent overview of the terminology associated with medieval romance. For a thorough discussion of the complicated generic vocabulary of romance, see also Fuchs, *Romance*, especially 57–65, and Liu.
3 This is one of the guiding theses of D. R. Woolf's *The Idea of History in Early Stewart England*—that "history in the seventeenth century was conceived of as a form of literature . . . not as a 'discipline' or, still less, a 'science'; it did not really become a discipline before the late eighteenth century . . . " (xv). For further discussion of the intersections of romance and history, also see Woolf's *The Social Circulation of the Past* (300–51), and *Reading History in Early Modern England* (22–36).
4 For further discussion of genre and the First Folio, see Orgel, "Shakespeare and the Kinds of Drama."
5 I use the year in which it was first printed for the dating of *Old Fortunatus*, though there is evidence of earlier performance as I discuss in Chapter 2. The first quarto of *Henry V* was published in 1600, but without the Chorus speeches. Here, I follow Harbage, Craik, and Taylor in using the citation of the Earl of Essex's campaign by the Chorus in act five to assign a performance date of 1599. See Craik's Arden edition for a discussion of the performance history and the Essex allusion (1–6), as well as Taylor's Oxford Edition (4–8). See below (pages 48–50) for a further discussion of the textual history of the Chorus. Brian Walsh has argued that historical representation in *Henry V* was inspired by Dekker's use of the Chorus in *Old Fortunatus*, making the play "a species of the fantastic, and seemingly locates the imaginative work of history within the walls of the playhouse where incredible things are allowed" (180).
6 For an edition of the 1509 German edition of *Fortunatus*, see Roloff.
7 Norman Rabkin's essay on the ethical ambiguity of *Henry V* remains influential, and I would argue that the problematizing of the play's genre ultimately follows his reading. Joanne Altieri calls the play "in the first place a generic puzzle," a metaphor that typifies the mystified critical response to the play's genre. In addition to Altieri, Barton, Frye, and Hedrick, see also Dean and McEachern.
8 Patricia Clare Ingham argues for the influence of "imaginative history" in the Arthurian tradition and the formulation of British identity in *Sovereign Fantasies*. In addition to Heng (discussed below) see also Michelle Warren, *History on the Edge*, and N. J. Higham, *King Arthur, Myth-making and History*.

9 Discussions of the queen and Cloten's view of British identity and politics can be found in Escobedo and Bennett, as well as in Martin Butler's introduction to the *New Cambridge* edition of the play, especially 42 ff.
10 My use of this phrase and subsequent discussion is indebted to Margreta de Grazia's consideration of *Hamlet* and its association with historical empires, see Hamlet *without Hamlet*, 45–80.
11 Schwyzer provocatively shows that Crispin and Crispanus were also world conquerors (*Literature, Nationalism, and Memory* 142).
12 Craik identifies various sources for the idea of the society of bees in addition to Virgil: Elyot's *Governor*, Pliny's *Natural History*, and Lyly's *Euphues* (143). Gary Taylor, the editor of the Oxford edition of the play, is skeptical of the latter three, see especially 110. No editor to my knowledge has identified the parallels with Hakluyt's epistle.
13 Hakluyt loosely adapts Elyot's discussion in the *Governor*, wherein the bees "hauynge theyr capitayne among them, and enuironynge hym, to preserue hym frome harme, issue for the, sekinge a newe habitation: which they ffinde in some tree . . . " (8r). Elyot, however, does not cast this as a model for colonialism or empire.
14 For an excellent reading of these references to Alexander, see Quint, "Alexander the Pig".
15 This reading of Dee's politics runs against the grain of Sherman's skepticism about Dee's commitment to a cosmographic politics, see especially 143–7. If we accept Dee's writing as more speculative, then it better aligns with the romance world view in which I am placing him here.
16 Hakluyt also prints stories about King Arthur and the legendary Welsh prince Madoc's voyage "to the West Indies. Anno. 1170," as well as from Mandeville's Travels (the last appears only in the 1589 edition). For further discussion of Hakluyt and the *Principal Navigations*, see Peter C. Mancall's authoritative treatment in *Hakluyt's Promise: An Elizabethan's Obsession for an English America*.
17 For further discussion of the idea of the "cosmopolitan" in early modern culture, also see essays by Games, Jean Howard, and Alan Farmer for the special issue of *Shakespeare Studies* (Vol. 35, 2007). Also see Margaret Jacob, who extends the history of cosmopolitanism into the eighteenth century in *Strangers Nowhere in the World*.
18 I thus follow the recent work of Jeffrey Knapp and Benedict Robinson, both of whom seek the uneven ways in which *Henry V* attempts to extend its definition of nationhood beyond an insular Britishness. While they point to the play's sometimes problematic engagements with the idea of a transnational Christian community, I emphasize the ways in which empire and transnational geography emerge from the generic formulations within the play. See Knapp, *Shakespeare's Tribe* and Robinson's "Harry and Amurath."
19 For a discussion of the recumbent rhetoric of travel narratives and maps, see Andrew Hadfield, "The Benefits of a Warm Study," in *A Companion to the Global Renaissance*, 101–13. Hadfield's point about the dangers and disincentives of travel underlines my contrast of the work the stage does in encouraging its viewers to action.
20 An excellent summary of this tradition can be found in Baker, *Between Nations*, 20.

21 See especially Schwyzer *Literature, Nationalism and Memory*, 126–50; Baker 17–65; Maley 45–62; and McEachern 83–137.
22 Ricard Helgerson's foundational *Forms of Nationhood* argues for the formulation of English nationhood through Elizabethan literature. Further discussions of the idea of "nation" in *Henry V*, focus upon the political ramifications of the play in Baldo and the situation of *Henry V* within a broader archipelagic literary and cultural history in Kerrigan.
23 Jean Howard and Phyllis Rackin read the marriage between Henry and Catherine as an extension of Henry's conquest on the battlefield and thus a kind of "sexual violence" or rape (196–200). They also argue that Harry and Kate's speech is "inscribed within a distinctively modern erotic discourse," one that eschews the chivalric values of romance (193). While I argue below that the scene is indebted to a romance tradition, I do not think this precludes the feminist reading advanced by Rackin and Howard. Violence has a long tradition within romance, and it may be that the erotic discourse of this moment is changing along with the form of the play.
24 Benedict Robinson offers a compelling reading of the references to the Turk in *Henry V* and the other plays of the tetralogy in light of European religious and political debates. See "Harry and Amurath."
25 See, for instance, Schwyzer's insightful commentary on Henry's strategic use of Welsh identity in *Literature, Nationalism and Memory*, 126–50.
26 Tiffany Stern has argued persuasively that prologues, epilogues, and other "interim texts" were often impermanent pieces of playtexts. While I take her point that we should "profitably reconsider" the idea that these speeches were a permanent fixture of the Shakespearean text, I think that seeing the texts as part of a *generic* tradition (rather than as an expression of character, for instance) helps to show the place of Shakespeare in the wider theatrical context.
27 The centrality of the Chorus to *Henry V* has prompted a number of critical responses. In his introduction to the recently revised Cambridge edition, Andrew Gurr sees it as dictating the terms of the audience's engagement with the King, "providing a means of coercing the audience into an emotionally undivided response to what the Chorus calls 'this star of England'" (7). This sentiment echoes Lawrence Danson: "The Chorus tells us how to respond as an audience, watching a play watching a king. And he does this by linking the two circumstances, the theatrical and the historical, allowing us in both a coherent response" (29). I see these readings reflecting an ethical approach to the play that has become current in *Henry V* criticism. Norman Rabkin argues that the central, irresolvable contradiction of the play's drama lies in the character of the King, and whether the audience is to respond to him (and his campaign) as triumphantly heroic or as reprehensibly cruel. Enlisting the Chorus in this debate does something interesting to what is, essentially, a theatrical device: it turns it into a character that can be assessed and understood outside of dramatic practice.
28 For a discussion of the medieval and classical conventions of Prologues and Choruses, see Butler; and Palmer.
29 The textual history of conveniently underlines the problems with the genre of history I am exploring here. Unlisted in the catalogue of the First Folio, it was later added during the process of printing to the end of the histories, but

is called "The Tragedie of Troilus and Cressida" on the running page titles, suggesting it belongs at the front of the tragedies.
30 Based on its attribution to the "Children of her Maiesties Chappell" on the title page, the modern editors, Farrant and Brawner, put the likely date of performance sometime in the 1580s.
31 This text is taken from Farrant and Brawner's edition of *The Wars of Cyrus*. They move this speech to the beginning of the play, turning it into a prologue. In the original 1594 printing, the lines appear as quoted here, after line 600.
32 Other plays that use the Chorus in this way include *The Travels of the Three English Brothers* and *The true chronicle historie of the whole life and death of Thomas Lord Cromwell* (1602).
33 It is worth noting that Gorboduc was not just any king. He and his sons were the final descendents of Brutus, the Roman who, according to Geoffrey's legend, founded Britain. The deaths of Ferrex and Porrex are epochal in scale because they represent the genealogical break with the Roman past.
34 For further discussion of the significance of "chronicle history" in the printing of the quartos of *Henry V*, see Mulready, "Making History in Q *Henry V*."
35 Gary Taylor gives an alternative explanation for the difference between quarto and folio. In his preface to the Oxford Edition of *Henry V*, he argues that the quarto version of the play represented a performance designed for a smaller cast of characters—perhaps for a traveling troupe that did not have the resources available to stage all of the parts that it could in a performance at the company theater. For Taylor's extensive discussion of this theory, see Wells and Taylor, 72–112. Editors and critics also point to the Chorus's favorable reference to the Earl of Essex and his anticipated return from his Ireland campaign in 1599 as evidence of an earlier composition for the speeches of the Chorus. On the influence of the Essex affair on the printing history of the play, see Patterson.
36 For Wallace's discussion of *Henry V* and Calais, see *Premodern Places*, 71–3.
37 This is a view echoed by Jeffrey Knapp, who argues that in the conclusion of *Henry V* Shakespeare critiques the eastward, crusade-like press of the play, favoring instead a Protestant Christian world community that sees England "is not the end of the world" (*Shakespeare's Tribe* 112).

5 Containing Romance and Plotting Empire in *The Tempest* and *Pericles*

1 These "numerous sites" include the Haitian playwright Aimé Césaire's postcolonial dramatic adaptation, *Une tempête*, George Lamming's *Water with Berries* and *The Pleasures of Exile*, and a host of other adaptations. Peter Hulme analyzes the importance of *The Tempest* in *The Pleasure of Exile* in "The Seeds of Revolt." See also Peichen for an illustration of *The Tempest's* place in Taiwanese colonial history. For a further discussion of the various appropriations, both cultural and critical, see Hulme and Sherman's excellent collection, *The Tempest and its Travels*.
2 There are numerous readings that extend the influence of *The Tempest* beyond its immediate circumstance of performance: See Barbara Fuchs,

220 *Notes*

"Conquering Islands," for a discussion of the Irish context of the play, Eric Cheyfitz on the play's relation to early American linguistic imperialism, David Scott Kastan on the political implications of the play's Mediterranean setting, and Benedict Robinson on the play's relationship to religious cross-cultural exchange (*Islam*), discussed below.

3 There is an enormous body of scholarship on *The Tempest* and its relation to the early colonial context, from early interventions (especially Greenblatt, *Shakespearean Negotiations;* Barker and Hulme; and Paul Brown) to more recent work ranging from ecocritical and oceanic discourse (see Brayton and Mentz) to material cultural analysis of banquets and sugar production (Kim Hall) and cod fisheries (Test). While I acknowledge the wide ranging possibilities for viewing *The Tempest* through these various historical lenses, I aim here to view the structure of the play itself as a part of its response to these historical materials.

4 I thus follow Robinson in searching for a historicized reading of the play's genre, though by turning to the questions of space and dramatic tradition, rather than religion and cross-cultural contacts between East and West. For Robinson's discussion of *The Tempest*, see especially *Islam*, 57–86.

5 For an extended discussion of *The Tempest* and surveying literature, see Poole, *Supernatural Environments*.

6 In the Oxford edition's reconstruction of the play, Wilkins's text has been integrated into certain passages of the play, further establishing the link between narrative and dramatic versions of the story.

7 Daniel Vitkus ("Labor and Travel") casts *Pericles*, alongside *Old Fortunatus*, as an example of travel plays, paying particular attention to how these dramas coalesce around ideas of labor in long-distance trade.

8 Following the Oxford, the Norton edition of the play here modernizes the Folio's "ich" to the more familiar "eke," as it does in *The Merchant of Venice*, where Portia tells Bassanio to wait before choosing the casket, "I speak too long, but tis to piece the time, / To eke [Folio eech] it, and to draw it out in length / To stay you from election" (3.2.22–4). Both the Oxford and the Norton do not follow similar practice with Pericles, and leave it in the unmodernized form, probably to heighten awareness of Gower's characteristic archaism.

9 For further discussion, and for a comprehensive list of examples of Prospero's arresting magic, see de Grazia "*The Tempest*" 250–1. She also notes that his power over the elements "consists of controlling the movements of the elements: stirring air, agitating water, activating fire, and shaking earth—the calling forth of 'mutinous winds,' the pitting of sea against sky, the setting thunder afire, and the shaking of 'the strong-based promontory' that he will eventually abjure" (254).

10 References to *The Faerie Queene* are from the Longman Edition, ed. A. C. Hamilton.

11 See, for instance, the fourteenth-century "Catalan Atlas," in Quinn.

12 The various versions of the St. Brendan story are to be found in Barron and Burgess's excellent edition of the texts.

13 In Book 12 of Homer's *Odyssey*, Odysseus hears of the "Planctae," called "Rovers" in Chapman's translation (Nicoll 12.100). For further examples from the classical tradition, see note to stanzas 10–13 in Greenlaw (356).

14 For such a discussion, see Wall, who seeks to connect the descriptions of the Bower of Bliss to sixteenth-century discourse on the lost Roanoke colony.
15 "Imaginative geography" is the term Edward Said uses to describe the West's geographic (and ideological) construction of the Orient in *Orientalism*. Imaginative geography is the tool with which Western scholarship, literature, and popular culture came to create, and recreate, social and cultural distinctions that were "handed down through the Renaissance" (72). For Said's discussion, see especially 49–73. Part of my concern in this chapter is mapping how romance in the early modern period both complicates and advances such geographic conceptions.
16 Dan Brayton discusses geographical knowledge and the critical tradition of attempting to locate the island depicted in *The Tempest*, see especially 166–95. See Greene for a discussion of the imaginative importance of the island in sixteenth-century Europe.
17 Chivalry and its cognate chevalier both come from the Latin root *caballus*, "horse."
18 For discussions of these stories, see Szkilnik and Luttrell.
19 Newcomb levels a compelling feminist critique against source study by identifying the patriarchal models traditionally employed in the analysis of Shakespeare and his sources ("Sources of Romance").
20 Kermode, in his New Arden edition of the play, famously wrote that "an understanding of this passage will modify our image of the whole play" (46-7 n. 74). Numerous critics have taken up this challenge, including, notably, Brotton ("Carthage"), and Wilson-Okamura.
21 Goldberg discusses the imagined rape of Miranda as well as the possibility of an incestuous relationship between Prospero and Miranda that has been raised in both the criticism and adaptations of *The Tempest* (20–3). See also Robinson (*Islam*), who highlights the "forgotten" plot of Alonso's daughter Claribel and its relevance to the discourse of Islam.
22 See Feerick for a further examination of how *The Tempest* seeks to contain the dangerous elements of foreign geography, an idea that she links to historical concern for "how transplantation would affect the physical and social identity of Englishmen . . . " (114).
23 For Hulme's reading, see the "Prospero and Caliban" chapter in *Colonial Encounters*, 89–134.
24 In "Stormy Weather," his essay on the many misappropriations of his seminal essay "Nymphs and Reapers," Hulme comments that, contrary to what his critics argue, his readings have "been deeply formalist in their approach to the play, basing themselves, for example, on arguments about the relationship of the main plot to the sub-plot or on what might constitute the articulatory principle of different elements of the play's language. The political and the formalist seem to me inextricable . . . " (para. 50). I thus follow Hulme in his insistence on the efficacy of formal readings of the play in colonial interpretations.
25 Quoted from the 1611 King James Bible.
26 Greenblatt discusses the relationship between *The Tempest* and Strachey's letter in *Shakespearean Negotiations* 147–63. Greenblatt reads the relationship between the two texts not on formal grounds, but based on the Bermuda pamphlet's status as "currency" that can pass between two corporate

institutions: the Virginia Company and Shakespeare's joint stock company. The changes that the play makes to the Bermuda materials offer "signs of the process whereby the Bermuda narrative is made negotiable, turned into a currency that may be transferred from one institutional context to another" (155).

27 For "So rare a wondered father and a wise," the Folio has "So rare a wondered father and a wife," a reading endorsed by Orgel in his Oxford edition of the play. For a discussion of the debates on this variant, Orgel's treatment of it, and the critical significance of the line to questions of gender, see Goldberg 55–62.

6 Milton's Imperial *Maske*: Staging Romance on the Border of Wales

1 See "The Case for Comus" in my discussion below.
2 Heather Dubrow has recently assessed *Comus* in the tradition of romance, though for her the genre provides a means of re-evaluating David Norbrook's influential thesis that Milton is engaging in a tradition of the "reformed masque."
3 All quotations from *Comus*, unless otherwise noted, come from the second edition of John Carey's *Milton: Complete Shorter Poems*.
4 Forrest offers a discussion of the matachin and its relationship to the Morris tradition.
5 For further discussion of the many "verbal echoes" of Milton's sources in *Comus*, see Guillory.
6 Cedric Brown offers an informative account of the Egerton family's itinerary during the years leading up to the performance of the *Maske* in "Presidential Travel."
7 See, for example, Mortimer, who discusses the masque in light of the readings prescribed by the Book of Common Prayer for Michaelmas celebrations.
8 Creaser concludes that this document provides evidence that "*Comus* was a civic as well as a family occasion" (131 n. 15).
9 Jean Howard and Phyllis Rackin argue that "Shakespeare's Wales is inscribed in the same register that defined the dangerous power of women" (168). See *Engendering a Nation*, 168–73 for further discussion.
10 For further discussion of *1 Henry IV* and the discourse of Wales in the sixteenth century, see Terence Hawkes's chapter "Bryn Glas" in *Shakespeare in the Present* 23–45, in which he argues that "The unappeased spectre of a subverting, transforming and unmanning Wales haunts the rest of the tetralogy" (36).
11 This brief summary is taken from Williams's discussion. For a broader discussion of the development of the Council of Marches under the English Crown in the fifteenth century, see *Recovery, Reorientation, and Reformation* 52.
12 Gwyn Williams offers a useful exploration of the Tudor use of Welsh history in *When was Wales?* (121–31); see also McEachern 189–90 and Baker 44–54. Schwyzer, in his chapter "'Awake, lovely Wales'" from *Literature, Nationalism, and Memory* 76–96, tells the story of Tudor mythologizing of Wales from the perspective of Welsh scholars and historiographers.

13 See Gwyn Williams, especially 88–98.
14 This passage is also quoted in Wilding 36.
15 For a discussion of the history of Ludlow Castle, see Lloyd.
16 *The Sea Voyage* was first acted in 1622 and printed for the first time in the Beaumont and Fletcher folio of 1647. The play opens with "A Tempest, Thunder, and Lightning," one of the many apparent allusions and correspondences to *The Tempest*. The text is quoted here from Anthony Parr's Revels edition of the play in *Three Renaissance Travel Plays*.
17 Schwyzer offers an extended and useful discussion of the various genealogies for Sabrina in "Purity and Danger," highlighting her foreignness.
18 Smyth's orders are found in a manuscript in the Essex County Records Office and quoted here from the Office's electronic database. An excerpt is also quoted in Canny 37.
19 For Quint's discussion of the "boat of romance," see *Epic and Empire* 248–67.

Coda: Global Romance after Shakespeare

1 Ringrose's narrative was first published in 1685, the edition from which these passages are taken.
2 The story of *Valentine and Orson* was extraordinarily popular through the early modern period and beyond. Even through the nineteenth century there were numerous printed editions and later dramatic adaptations of the play in London and America. For a complete list, see Dickson, Appendix II.

Bibliography

Ainsworth, Edward G. "Reminiscences of the *Orlando Furioso* in *Comus*." *Modern Language Notes* 46.2 (1931): 91–2.
Altieri, J. "Romance in *Henry V*." *Studies in English Literature, 1500–1900* (1981): 223–40.
Andrews, Kenneth R. *Trade, Plunder, and Settlement: Maritime Enterprise and the Genesis of the British Empire, 1480–1630*. Cambridge: Cambridge UP, 1984.
Anghiera, Pietro Martire. *The Decades of the Newe Worlde Or West India Conteynyng the Nauigations and Conquestes of the Spanyardes, with the Particular Description of the Moste Ryche and Large Landes and Ilandes Lately Founde in the West Ocean Perteynyng to the Inheritaunce of the Kinges of Spayne. . . . Wrytten in the Latine Tounge by Peter Martyr of Angleria, and Translated into Englysshe by Rycharde Eden. 1555. The First Three English Books on America*. Ed. Edward Arber. New York: Klaus Reprint, 1971.
Archer, John Michael. *Old Worlds: Egypt, Southwest Asia, India, and Russia in Early Modern English Writing*. Palo Alto: Stanford UP, 2001.
Ariosto, Lodovico. *Orlando Furioso*. Trans. John Harington. Oxford: Clarendon P, 1972.
Armitage, David. *The Ideological Origins of the British Empire*. Cambridge: Cambridge UP, 2000. Ideas in Context 59.
"Arras." *The Oxford English Dictionary Online*. 2nd edn. Web.
Artese, Charlotte. "King Arthur in America: Making Space in History for *The Faerie Queene* and John Dee's *Brytanici Imperii Limites*." *Journal of Medieval and Early Modern Studies* 33.1 (2003): 125–41.
Ascham, Roger. *The scholemaster or plaine and perfite way of teachyng children, to vnderstand, write, and speake, the Latin tong but specially purposed for the priuate brynging vp of youth in ientlemen and noble mens houses, and commodious also for all such, as haue forgot the Latin tonge*. London, 1570.
Astington, John. *English Court Theatre 1558–1642*. Cambridge: Cambridge UP, 1999.
Bailey, Amanda. "Shylock and the Slaves: Owing and Owning in *The Merchant of Venice*." *Shakespeare Quarterly* 62.1 (2011): 1–24.
Baker, David J. "'The Allegory of a China Shop': Jonson's *Entertainment at Britain's Burse*." *English Literary History* 72.1 (2005): 159–80.
———. *Between Nations: Shakespeare, Spenser, Marvell, and the Question of Britain*. Stanford: Stanford UP, 1997.
Baldo, Jonathan. "'Into a thousand parts': Representing the Nation in *Henry V*." *English Literary Renaissance* 38.1 (2004): 55–82. Web. 3 Aug. 2011.
Bale, Anthony. "Where Are the 'Isles of Wonder?'" *OUPBlog* 10 Aug. 2012. Web. 31 Aug. 2012.
Barbour, Richmond. *Before Orientalism: London's Theatre of the East, 1576–1626*. Cambridge: Cambridge UP, 2003.
Barker, Francis and Peter Hulme. "'Nymphs and Reapers Heavily Vanish': The Discursive Con-texts of *The Tempest*." *Alternative Shakespeares*. 2nd edn. Ed. John Drakakis. London: Routledge, 2002. 195–209. New Accents.

Barlow, William. *The nauigators supply. Conteining many things of principall importance belonging to nauigation, with the description and vse of diuerse instruments framed chiefly for that purpose; but seruing also for sundry other of cosmography in generall: the particular instruments are specified on the next page.* London, 1597.

Bartolovich, Crystal. "'Baseless Fabric': London as World City." *The Tempest and Its Travels*. Ed. Peter Hulme & William H. Sherman. Philadelphia: U of Pennsylvania P, 2000. 13–26.

Barton, Anne. "The King Disguised: Shakespeare's *Henry V* and the Comical History." *The Triple Bond: Plays, Mainly Shakespearean, in Performance*. Ed. Joseph G. Price and Helen D. Willard. University Park: Pennsylvania State UP, 1975. 92–117.

Bate, Jonathan. "The Politics of Romantic Shakespearean Criticism: Germany, England, France." *European Romantic Review* 1.1 (1990): 1–26.

Batman, Stephen. *Batman vppon Bartholome his booke De proprietatibus rerum, newly corrected, enlarged and amended: with such additions as are requisite, vnto euery seuerall booke: taken foorth of the most approued authors, the like heretofore not translated in English. Profitable for all estates, as well for the benefite of the mind as the bodie.* London, 1582.

Bauer, Ralph. *The Cultural Geography of Colonial American Literatures: Empire, Travel, Modernity*. Cambridge: Cambridge UP, 2003.

Beaumont, Francis. *The Knight of the Burning Pestle*. Ed. Michael Hattaway. New Mermaids. London: Black, 2000.

Bennett, Josephine Waters. "Britain among the Fortunate Isles." *Studies in Philology* 53 (1956): 114–40.

Black, Matthew W. and Mathias A. Shaaber. *Shakespeare's Seventeenth-Century Editors, 1632–1685*. New York: Modern Language Association, 1937.

Blundeville, Thomas. M. *Blundevile his exercises, containing sixe treatises, the titles wherof are set down in the next printed page: which treatises are verie necessarie to be read and learned of all yoong gentlemen that haue not bene exercised in such disciplines, and yet are desirous to hau knowledge as well in cosmographie, astronomie, and geographie, as also in the arte of navigation, in which arte it is impossible to profite without the helpe of these, or such like instructions. To the furtherance of which arte of navigation, the said M. Blundevile speciallie wrote the said treatises and of meere good will doth dedicate the same to all the young gentlemen of this realme.* London, 1594.

Boehmer, Elleke. *Colonial and Postcolonial Literature: Migrant Metaphors*. Oxford: Oxford UP, 1995.

Boyle, Danny. "Isles of Wonder." *Media Guide: London 2012 Olympic Games Opening Ceremony*. London: n.p., 2012. 11. Web.

Brayton, Dan. *Shakespeare's Ocean: An Ecocritical Exploration*. Charlottesville, VA: U of Virginia P, 2012. Under the Sign of Nature: Explorations in Ecocriticism.

"Broad Cloth." *The Oxford English Dictionary Online*. 2nd edn. Web.

Brotton, Jerry. "Carthage and Tunis, *The Tempest* and Tapestries." *The Tempest and Its Travels*. Ed. Peter Hulme & William H. Sherman. Philadelphia: U of Pennsylvania P, 2000. 132–7.

———. *The Renaissance Bazaar: From the Silk Road to Michelangelo*. Oxford: Oxford UP, 2002.

———. *Trading Territories: Mapping the Early Modern World*. Ithaca, NY: Cornell UP, 1998.

Brown, Carleton Fairchild, ed. *The Stonyhurst Pageants*. Baltimore: Johns Hopkins UP, 1920.
Brown, Cedric C. "Presidential Travels and Instructive Augury in Milton's Ludlow Masque." *Milton Quarterly* 21.4 (1987): 1–12.
Brown, Paul. "'This Thing of Darkness I Acknowledge Mine': *The Tempest* and the Discourse of Colonialism." *Political Shakespeare: New Essays in Cultural Materialism*. Ed. Jonathan Dollimore and Alan Sinfield. Manchester: Manchester UP, 1985. 48–71.
Brückner, Martin, and Kristen Poole. "The Plot Thickens: Surveying Manuals, Drama, and the Materiality of Narrative Form in Early Modern England." *English Literary History* 69.3 (2002): 617–48.
Bruster, Douglas. *Drama and the Market in the Age of Shakespeare*. Cambridge: Cambridge UP, 1992.
———. "The Materiality of Shakespearean Form." *Shakespeare and Historical Formalism*. Ed. Stephen Cohen. Burlington, VT: Ashgate, 2007. 31–48.
Burton, Jonathan. *Traffic and Turning: Islam and English Drama, 1579–1624*. Cranbury, NJ: Associated U Presses, 2005.
Butler, Michelle M. "Baleus Prolocutor and the Establishment of the Prologue in Sixteenth-Century Drama." *Tudor Drama before Shakespeare, 1485–1590: New Directions for Research, Criticism, and Pedagogy*. Ed. Lloyd Kermode, Jason Scott-Warren, and Martine Van Elk. New York: Palgrave Macmillan, 2004. 93–109.
Canny, Nicholas. "The Permissive Frontier: The Problem of Social Control in English Settlements in Ireland and Virginia." *The Westward Enterprise: English Activities in Ireland, the Atlantic, and America 1480–1650*. Ed. K. R. Andrews, N. P. Canny and P. E. H. Hair. Detroit: Wayne State UP, 1979. 17–44.
Certeau, Michel de. *The Practice of Everyday Life*. Trans. Steven F. Rendall. U of California P, 1984.
Charry, Brinda. "'[T]he Beauteous Scarf': Shakespeare and the 'Veil Question'." *Shakespeare* 4.2 (2008): 112–26. Web. 9 Dec. 2012.
Chedgzoy, Kate. "The Cultural Geographies of Early Modern Women's Writings: Journeys Across Spaces and Times." *Literature Compass* 3.4 (2006): 884–95.
Cheyfitz, Eric. *The Poetics of Imperialism: Translation and Colonization from* The Tempest *to Tarzan*. Philadelphia, PA: U of Pennsylvania P, 1997.
Cobb, Christopher J. *The Staging of Romance in Late Shakespeare: Text and Theatrical Technique*. Newark, DE: U of Delaware P, 2007.
Cohen, Stephen. *Shakespeare and Historical Formalism*. Burlington, VT: Ashgate, 2007.
Cohen, Walter. "The Literature of Empire in the Renaissance." *Modern Philology: A Journal Devoted to Research in Medieval and Modern Literature* 102.1 (2004): 1–34. Web. 23 June 2010.
———. "*The Merchant of Venice* and the Possibilities of Historical Criticism." *ELH* 49.4 (1982): 765–89.
———. "The Undiscovered Country: Shakespeare and Mercantile Geography." *Marxist Shakespeares*. Ed. Jean E. Howard. London: Routledge, 2001. 128–58. Accents on Shakespeare.
Coleridge, Samuel Taylor. *Shakespearean Criticism*. 2nd edn. Ed. Thomas Middleton Raysor. 2 vols. London: Dent, 1964. Everyman's Library.
Colie, Rosalie Littell. *The Resources of Kind: Genre-theory in the Renaissance*. Berkeley: U of California P, 1973.

Collins, John Churton, ed. *The Plays & Poems of Robert Greene*. Vol. 1. 2 vols. Freeport, NY: Books for Libraries P, 1905.
Collinson, Sir Richard. *The Three Voyages of Martin Frobisher: In Search of a Passage to Cathaia and India by the North-west, A.D. 1576–8*. London: Hakluyt Society, 1867.
Common Conditions. Ed. Tucker Brooke. Elizabethan Club Reprints No. 1. New Haven: Yale UP, 1915.
Cooper, Helen. *The English Romance in Time: Transforming Motifs from Geoffrey of Monmouth to the Death of Shakespeare*. Oxford: Oxford UP, 2004.
———. "Location and Meaning in Masque, Morality, and Royal Entertainment." *The Court Masque*. Ed. David Lindley. Manchester: Manchester UP, 1984. 135–48.
———. *Shakespeare and the Medieval World*. London: Methuen, 2010. Arden Critical Companions.
———. "The Strange History of Valentine and Orson." In *Tradition and Transformation in Medieval Romance*, ed. Rosalind Field. Woodbridge: Boydell & Brewer, 1999. 153–68.
Cooper, Lisa H. "Chivalry, Commerce, and Conquest: Heywood's *The Four Prentices of London*." *Material Culture and Cultural Materialisms in the Middle Ages and Renaissance*. Turnhout, Belgium: Brepols, 2001. 159–75.
Cooper, Thomas. *Thesaurus linguae Romanae & Britannicae tam accurate congestus, vt nihil penè in eo desyderari possit, quod vel Latinè complectatur amplissimus Stephani Thesaurus, vel Anglicè, toties aucta Eliotae Bibliotheca: opera & industria Thomae Cooperi Magdalenensis. . . . Accessit dictionarium historicum et poëticum propria vocabula virorum, mulierum, sectarum, populorum, vrbium, montium, & caeterorum locorum complectens, & in his iucundissimas & omnium cognitione dignissimas historias*. London, 1578.
Corneille, Pierre. *The Cid a Tragicomedy, out of French Made English: And Acted before Their Majesties at Court, and on the Cock-Pit Stage in Drury-Lane by the Servants to Both Their Majesties*. Trans. John Rutter. London, 1637.
Cornwallis, William. *Essayes*. London, 1600.
Craik, T. W. "Introduction and Notes." *King Henry V*. London: Routledge, 1995. The Arden Shakespeare.
Creaser, John. "'The Present Aid of this Occasion': The Setting of *Comus*." *The Court Masque*. Ed. David Lindley. Manchester: Manchester UP, 1984. 111–34.
Cressy, David. *Bonfires and Bells: National Memory and the Protestant Calendar in Elizabethan and Stuart England*. Berkeley: U of California P, 1989.
"Curiosity." *The Oxford English Dictionary Online*. 2nd edn. Web.
Curtin, Philip D. *Cross-Cultural Trade in World History*. Cambridge: Cambridge UP, 1984.
Danson, Lawrence. "*Henry V*: King, Chorus, and Critics." *Shakespeare Quarterly* 34.1 (1983): 27–43. Web. 23 June 2010.
Davis, John. *The seamans secrets deuided into 2. partes, wherein is taught the three kindes of sayling, horizontall, peradoxall [sic], and sayling vpon a great circle: also an horizontall tyde table for the easie finding of the ebbing and flowing of the tydes, with a regiment newly calculated for the finding of the declination of the sunne, and many other most necessary rules and instruments, not heeretofore set foorth by any*. London, 1595.
de Grazia, Margreta. *Hamlet without Hamlet*. New York: Cambridge UP, 2007.
———. "The Modern Divide: From Either Side." *Journal of Medieval and Early Modern Studies* 37.3 (2007): 453–68.

———. *Shakespeare Verbatim: The Reproduction of Authenticity and the 1790 Apparatus.* Oxford: Clarendon P, 1991.

———. "*The Tempest*: Gratuitous Movement Or Action without Kibes and Pinches." *Shakespeare Studies* 14 (1981): 249–65.

Dean, Paul. "Chronicle and Romance Modes in *Henry V.*" *Shakespeare Quarterly* 32.1 (1981): 18–27.

Dee, John. *General and rare memorials pertayning to the perfect arte of nauigation annexed to the paradoxal cumpas, in playne: now first published: 24. yeres, after the first inuention thereof.* London, 1577.

Degenhardt, Jane Hwang. *Islamic Conversion and Christian Resistance on the Early Modern Stage.* Edinburgh: Edinburgh UP, 2010.

Dekker, Elly. "Globes in Renaissance Europe." *Cartography in the European Renaissance.* Ed. David Woodward. Chicago: U of Chicago P, 2007. 135–59. The History of Cartography v. 3, pt. 1.

Dekker, Thomas. *Old Fortunatus.* 1600. *The Dramatic Works of Thomas Dekker.* Ed. Fredson Bowers. Vol. 1. Cambridge: Cambridge UP, 1953.

Delumeau, Jean. *History of Paradise.* New York: Continuum, 1995.

Dessen, Alan C., and Leslie Thomson. *A Dictionary of Stage Directions in English Drama, 1580–1642.* Cambridge: Cambridge UP, 1999.

Dickson, Arthur. *Valentine and Orson: A Study in Late Medieval Romance.* New York: Columbia UP, 1929.

Dimmock, Matthew. *New Turkes: Dramatizing Islam and the Ottomans In Early Modern England.* Burlington, VT: Ashgate, 2005.

Dimock, Wai Chee. "Introduction: Genres as Fields of Knowledge." *PMLA* 122.5 (2007): 1377–88.

Doddridge, John. *The history of the ancient and moderne estate of the principality of Wales, dutchy of Cornewall, and earldome of Chester Collected out of the records of the Tower of London, and diuers ancient authours. By Sir Iohn Dodridge Knight, one of his Maiesties iudges in the Kings Bench. And by himselfe dedicated to King Iames of euer blessed memory.* London, 1630.

Dowden, Edward. *Essays Modern and Elizabethan.* London: Dent, 1910.

———. *Introduction to Shakespeare.* London: Blackie, 1893.

———. *Shakspere.* London: Macmillan, 1931. Literature Primers.

———. *Shakspere; a Critical Study of his Mind and Art.* London: Routledge, 1967.

Driver, Felix. *Geography Militant: Cultures of Exploration and Empire.* Oxford: Blackwell, 2001.

Dubrow, Heather. "The Masquing of Genre in *Comus.*" *Milton Studies* 44 (2005): 62–83.

Duncan-Jones, Katherine. "Introduction and Notes." *Sir Philip Sidney: The Major Works.* Ed. Katherine Duncan-Jones. Oxford: Oxford UP, 2002. Oxford World's Classics.

Duncan, Ian. *Modern Romance and Transformations of the Novel: The Gothic, Scott, Dickens.* Cambridge: Cambridge UP, 1992.

Eden, Richard. *A Treatise of the New India.* 1553. *The First Three English Books on America.* Ed. Edward Arber. New York: Kraus Reprint, 1971. 3–43.

Edwards, Philip. "Shakespeare's Romances: 1900–1957." *Shakespeare Survey* 11 (1958): 1–18.

Eliot, T. S. "An Apology for the Countess of Pembroke." *The Use of Poetry and the Use of Criticism: Studies in the Relation of Criticism to Poetry in England.* Cambridge, MA: Harvard UP, 1986. 29–44.

Elliott, J. H. *The Old World and the New: 1492–1650*. Cambridge: Cambridge UP, 1992.
Ellison, Lee Monroe. *The Early Romantic Drama at the English Court*. Menasha, WI: Banta-Collegiate, 1917.
Elyot, Thomas. *The Boke Named the Gouernour, Deuysed by Syr Thomas Elyot Knight*. London, 1537.
Engle, Lars. "'Thrift Is Blessing': Exchange and Explanation in *The Merchant of Venice*." *Shakespeare Quarterly* 37.1 (1986): 20–37.
Escobedo, Andrew. "From Britannia to England: *Cymbeline* and the Beginning of Nations." *Shakespeare Quarterly* 59.1 (2008): 60–87. Project Muse. Web. 3 Aug. 2011.
Fale, Thomas. *Horologiographia The art of dialling: teaching an easie and perfect way to make all kinds of dials vpon any plaine plat howsoeuer placed: vvith the drawing of the twelue signes, and houres vnequall in them all. Whereunto is annexed the making and vse of other dials and instruments, whereby the houre of the day and night is knowne. Of speciall vse and delight not onely for students of the arts mathematicall, but also for diuers artificers, architects, surueyours of buildings, free-Masons and others*. London, 1593.
The Famous Victories of Henry the Fifth: Containing the Honourable Battell of Agin-Court: As It Was Plaide by Thc [sic] Queenes Maiesties Players. London, 1598.
Feerick, Jean E. *Strangers in Blood: Relocating Race in the Renaissance*. Toronto: U of Toronto P, 2010.
Felperin, Howard. *Shakespearean Romance*. Princeton: Princeton UP, 1972.
Feuillerat, Albert. *Office of the Revels. Documents Relating to the Office of the Revels in the Time of Queen Elizabeth*. Materials for the Study of the Old English Drama 21. Vaduz: Kraus Reprint, 1963.
Fleay, Frederick Gard. *A Chronicle History of the London Stage, 1559–1642*. Burt Franklin Bibliography and Reference Series 51. New York: Franklin, 1964.
Florio, John. *Second Frutes. 1591*. Gainesville, FL: Scholars', 1953.
Floyd-Wilson, Mary. *English Ethnicity and Race in Early Modern Drama*. Cambridge: Cambridge UP, 2003.
Foakes, R. A., ed. *Henslowe's Diary*. 2nd edn. Cambridge: Cambridge UP, 2002.
Forman, Valerie. *Tragicomic Redemptions: Global Economics and the Early Modern English Stage*. Philadelphia: U of Pennsylvania P, 2008.
Forrest, John. *The History of Morris Dancing, 1458–1750*. Toronto: U of Toronto P, 1999.
Frye, Northrop. *Anatomy of Criticism: Four Essays*. Princeton: Princeton UP, 1971.
Fuchs, Barbara. "Conquering Islands: Contextualizing *The Tempest*." *Shakespeare Quarterly* 48 (1997): 45–62.
——. "Imperium Studies: Theorizing Early Modern Expansion." *Postcolonial Moves: Medieval Through Modern*. Ed. Patricia Clare Ingham and Michelle R. Warren. New York: Palgrave Macmillan, 2003. 71–90.
——. *Mimesis and Empire: The New World, Islam, and European Identities*. Cambridge: Cambridge UP, 2001.
——. *Romance*. New York: Routledge, 2004. New Critical Idiom.
Fuchs, Barbara, and David J. Baker. "The Postcolonial Past." *Modern Language Quarterly* 65.3 (2004): 329–40.
Fuller, Mary C. "Ralegh's Fugitive Gold: Reference and Deferral in *The Discoverie of Guiana*." *Representations* 33 (1991): 42–64.

Furness, Horace Howard, ed. *The Merchant of Venice*. Vol. 7. Philadelphia: Lippincott, 1888. A New Variorum Edition of Shakespeare.
——. *The Tempest*. Vol. 9. Philadelphia: Lippincott, 1892. A New Variorum Edition of Shakespeare.
Games, Alison. *The Web of Empire: English Cosmopolitans in an Age of Expansion, 1560–1660*. Oxford: Oxford UP, 2008.
Geoffrey of Monmouth. *The History of the Kings of Britain*. Trans. Lewis G. M Thorpe. London: Penguin, 1966. Penguin Classics.
Gilbert, Allan H. *Literary Criticism: Plato to Dryden*. Detroit: Wayne State UP, 1962.
Gillies, John. "Introduction: Elizabethan Drama and the Cartographizations of Space." *Playing the Globe: Genre and Geography in English Renaissance Drama*. Ed. John Gillies and Virginia Mason Vaughan. Madison, NJ: Fairleigh Dickinson UP, 1998. 19–45.
——. *Shakespeare and the Geography of Difference*. Cambridge: Cambridge UP, 1994.
Goldberg, Jonathan. *Tempest in the Caribbean*. Minneapolis: U of Minnesota P, 2004.
Gossett, Suzanne. "Introduction." *Pericles*. Ed. Suzanne Gossett. London: Methuen, 2004. The Arden Shakespeare Third Series.
Gosson, Stephen. *Plays Confuted in Fiue Actions Prouing That They Are Not to Be Suffred in a Christian Common Weale, by the Waye Both the Cauils of Thomas Lodge, and the Play of Playes, Written in Their Defence, and Other Obiections of Players Frendes, Are Truely Set Downe and Directlye Aunsweared*. London, 1582.
Grabes, Herbert. "Mirrors." *The Spenser Encyclopedia*. Ed. Albert C. Hamilton. Toronto: U of Toronto P, 1990. 477–8.
Greenblatt, Stephen J. "Marlowe, Marx, and Anti-Semitism." *Critical Inquiry* 5.2 (1978): 291–307. *JSTOR*. Web. 12 Dec. 2012.
——. *Marvelous Possessions: The Wonder of the New World*. Chicago: U of Chicago P, 1991.
——. *Shakespearean Negotiations: The Circulation of Social Energy in Renaissance England*. Berkeley: U of California P, 1988. The New Historicism: Studies in Cultural Poetics 4.
Greene, Robert. "Orlando Fvrioso." The Plays & Poems of Robert Greene. Ed. John Churton Collins. Vol. 1. 2 vols. Freeport, NY: Books for Libraries P, 1970. 220–65.
Greene, Roland Arthur. *Unrequited Conquests: Love and Empire in the Colonial Americas*. Chicago: U of Chicago Press, 1999.
Greenlaw, Edwin et al., eds. *The Works of Edmund Spenser: A Variorum Edition*. Vol. 2. Baltimore: The Johns Hopkins P, 1966.
Greg, W. W. *A Bibliography of the English Printed Drama to the Restoration*. Vol. 4. 4 vols. London: Bibliographical Society, 1970. Bibliographical Society. Illustrated Monographs, No. 24.
Gregory, Derek. *The Colonial Present: Afghanistan. Palestine. Iraq*. Malden, MA: Blackwell, 2004.
——. *Geographical Imaginations*. Cambridge, MA: Blackwell, 1994.
——. "Imaginative Geographies." *Progress in Human Geography* 19.4 (1995): 447–85.
Gregory, Derek et al. *The Dictionary of Human Geography*. 5th edn. Malden, MA: Blackwell, 2009.

Guillory, John. *Poetic Authority: Spenser, Milton, and Literary History*. New York: Columbia UP, 1983.
Gumbrecht, Hans Ulrich. *Making Sense in Life and Literature*. Minneapolis: U of Minnesota P, 1992.
Hadfield, Andrew. "The Benefits of a Warm Study: The Resistance to Travel before Empire." *A Companion to the Global Renaissance: English Literature and Culture in the Era of Expansion*. Ed. Jyotsna G. Singh. Malden, MA: Wiley-Blackwell, 2009. 101–13.
——. *Literature, Politics, and National Identity: Reformation to Renaissance*. Cambridge: Cambridge UP, 1994.
——. *Literature, Travel, and Colonial Writing in the English Renaissance, 1545–1625*. Oxford: Clarendon P, 1998.
Hakluyt, Richard. *Diuers voyages touching the discouerie of America, and the ilands adiacent vnto the same made first of all by our Englishmen, and afterward by the Frenchmen and Britons: and certaine notes of aduertisements for obseruations, necessarie for such as shall heereafter make the like attempt, with two mappes annexed heereunto for the plainer vnderstanding of the whole matter*. London, 1582.
——. *The Principal Navigations, Voyages, Traffiques and Discoveries of the English Nation: Made by Sea Or Ouer-Land, to the Remote and Farthest Distant Quarters of the Earth, at any Time within the Compasse of these 1600 Yeres: Divided into Three Seuuerall Volumes, According to the Positions of the Regions, Whereunto they were Directed: The First Volume Containeth the Worthy Discoveries, &c. of the English Toward the North and Northeast by Sea . . . : The Second Volume Comprehendeth the Principall Navigations, Voyages, Traffiques, and Discoveries of the English Nation made by Sea Or Ouer-Land, to the South and South-East Parts of the World, as Well within as without the Streight of Gibralter, at any Time within the Compasse of these 1600 Yeres: Diuided into Two Seueral Parts, &c*. London, 1599.
Halio, Jay L., ed. *The Merchant of Venice*. New York: Oxford UP, 1998. Oxford World's Classics.
Hall, Edward. *The Actes Done in Bothe the Tymes of the Princes, Bothe of the One Linage and of the Other, Beginnyng at the Tyme of Kyng Henry the Fowerth, the First Aucthor of This Deuision, and so Successiuely Proceadyng to the Reigne of the High and Prudent Prince Kyng Henry the Eight, the Vndubitate Flower and Very Heire of Both the Sayd Linages*. London, 1548.
Hall, Kim F. "Sugar and Status in Shakespeare." *Shakespeare Jahrbuch* 145 (2009): 49–61.
Hamilton, A. C. *Sir Philip Sidney: A Study of His Life and Works*. Cambridge: Cambridge UP, 1977.
Harbage, Alfred, S. Schoenbaum, and Sylvia Stoler Wagonheim. *Annals of English Drama, 975–1700: An Analytical Record of All Plays, Extant or Lost, Chronologically Arranged and Indexed by Authors, Titles, Dramatic Companies & C*. 3rd edn. London: Routledge, 1989.
Harley, J. B. "Deconstructing the Map." *The New Nature of Maps: Essays in the History of Cartography*. Baltimore: Johns Hopkins UP, 2002. 150–68.
——. "Maps, Knowledge, and Power." *The New Nature of Maps: Essays in the History of Cartography*. Baltimore: Johns Hopkins UP, 2002. 52–81.
Harris, Jonathan Gil. *Sick Economies: Drama, Mercantilism, and Disease in Shakespeare's England*. Philadelphia: U of Pennsylvania P, 2004.

Hawkes, Terence. *Shakespeare in the Present*. London: Routledge, 2002.
Hays, Michael. "A Bibliography of Dramatic Adaptations of Medieval Romances and Renaissance Chivalric Romances First Available in English through 1616." *Research Opportunities in Renaissance Drama* 28 (1985): 87–109.
Hedrick, Donald. "Advantage, Affect, History, *Henry V*." *PMLA: Publications of the Modern Language Association of America* 118.3 (2003): 470–87.
Hegel, Georg Wilhelm Friedrich. *On Art, Religion, Philosophy; Introductory Lectures to the Realm of Absolute Spirit*. 1st edn. New York: Harper, 1970. Harper torchbooks, 1463.
Helgerson, Richard. *Forms of Nationhood: The Elizabethan Writing of England*. Chicago: U of Chicago P, 1992.
Henderson, Diana E. and James Siemon. "Reading Vernacular Literature." *A Companion to Shakespeare*. Ed. David Scott Kastan. Malden, MA: Blackwell, 1999. 206–22.
Heng, Geraldine. *Empire of Magic: Medieval Romance and the Politics of Cultural Fantasy*. New York: Columbia UP, 2003.
Herrick, Marvin T. *Italian Tragedy in the Renaissance*. Urbana: U of Illinois P, 1965.
Herzman, Robert B., Graham Drake, and Eve Salisbury, eds. Introduction. *Four Romances of England*. Kalamazoo: Medieval Institute Publications, 1999.
Heywood, Thomas. *The Foure Prentises of London; with, the Conquest of Ierusalem*. London, 1615.
Higham, N. J. *King Arthur: Myth-Making and History*. London: Routledge, 2002.
Householder, Michael. *Inventing Americans in the Age of Discovery: Narratives of Encounter*. Burlington, VT: Ashgate, 2011.
Howard, Jean E. "Shakespeare and Genre." *A Companion to Shakespeare*. Ed. David Scott Kastan. Malden, MA: Wiley-Blackwell, 1999. 297–310.
——. "Shakespeare, Geography, and the Work of Genre on the Early Modern Stage." *Modern Language Quarterly* 64.3 (2003): 299–322.
——. *Theater of a City: The Places of London Comedy, 1598–1642*. Philadelphia: U of Pennsylvania P, 2007.
Howard, Jean E., and Phyllis Rackin. *Engendering a Nation: A Feminist Account of Shakespeare's English Histories*. New York: Routledge, 1997.
Hoxby, Blair. "The Wisdom of Their Feet: Meaningful Dance in Milton and the Stuart Masque." *English Literary Renaissance* 37.1 (2007): 74–99.
Hulme, Peter. *Colonial Encounters: Europe and the Native Caribbean, 1492–1797*. London: Methuen, 1986.
——. "The Seeds of Revolt: George Lamming and *The Tempest*." *The Locations of George Lamming*. Ed. Bill Schwarz. Oxford: Macmillan, 2007. 112–31. Warwick University Caribbean Studies.
——. "Stormy Weather: Misreading the Postcolonial Tempest." *Early Modern Culture* 3 (2003): 1–53. 3 Web. July 2006.
Hulme, Peter, and William H. Sherman. *"The Tempest" and Its Travels*. Philadelphia: U of Pennsylvania P, 2000.
Huot, Sylvia Jean. *Postcolonial Fictions in* The Roman de Perceforest: *Cultural Identities And Hybridities*. Woodbridge: Boydell & Brewer, 2007.
The Hystory of the two Valyaunte Brethren Valentyne and Orson Sonnes unto the Emperor of Grece. London, n.d. [1565?].
Ingham, Patricia Clare. *Sovereign Fantasies: Arthurian Romance and the Making of Britain*. Philadelphia: U of Pennsylvania P, 2001. The Middle Ages series.

Ingham, Patricia Clare and Michelle R. Warren, eds. *Postcolonial Moves: Medieval Through Modern*. New York: Palgrave Macmillan, 2003.
Jacob, Margaret C. *Strangers Nowhere in the World: The Rise of Cosmopolitanism in Early Modern Europe*. Philadelphia: U of Pennsylvania P, 2006.
Jameson, Fredric. *The Political Unconscious: Narrative as a Socially Symbolic Act*. Ithaca, NY: Cornell UP, 1981.
Jauss, Hans Robert. *Toward an Aesthetic of Reception*. Trans. Timothy Bahti. Minneapolis: U of Minnesota P, 1982.
Johnson, Richard. *The most pleasant history of Tom a Lincolne*. Ed. Richard S. M. Hirsch. Columbia, SC: Published for the Newberry Library by the U of South Carolina P, 1978. Renaissance English Text Society.
Jonson, Ben. *Every Man Out of His Humour*. Ed. Helen Ostovich. Manchester: Manchester UP, 2001. Revels Plays.
——. *The Magnetic Lady*. Ed. Peter Happé. The Revels Plays. Manchester: Manchester UP, 2000.
——. "Ode to Himself." *Ben Jonson*. Ed. C. H. Herford and Percy Simpson. Vol. 6. Oxford: Clarendon P, 1938. 492.
Kamps, Ivo. *Historiography and Ideology in Stuart Drama*. New York: Cambridge UP, 1996.
Kastan, David Scott. "'The Duke of Milan / And His Brave Son': Dynastic Politics in *The Tempest*." *Critical Essays on Shakespeare's The Tempest*. Ed. Virginia Mason Vaughan & Alden T. Vaughan. London: G.K. Hall, 1998. 91–103.
Kermode, Frank, ed. *The Tempest*. By William Shakespeare. 6th edn. Cambridge, MA: Harvard UP, 1958. The New Shakespeare.
Kerrigan, John. *Archipelagic English: Literature, History, and Politics, 1603–1707*. Oxford: Oxford UP, 2008.
Kirke, John. *The Seven Champions of Christendome Acted at the Cocke-pit, and at the Red-Bull in St. Iohns streete, with a generall liking. And never printed till this yeare 1638. Written by I.K.* London, 1638.
Kirkman, Francis, tran. *The Honour of chivalry, or, The famous and delectable history of Don Bellianis of Greece continuing as well the valiant exploits of that magnanimous and heroick Prince, son to the Emperor Don Bellaneo of Greece: as also the wars between him and the Souldan of Persia: wherein is likewise described the strange and dangerous adventures that befel him in the prosecution of his love towards the Princess Florisbella, daughter to the Souldan of Babylon, his releasing of her father the Souldan from a strange enchantment, and vanquishing the Emperor of Trebizond / now newly written in English by F.K.* London, 1671.
Kirkman, Francis. *The Unlucky Citizen experimentally described in the various misfortunes of an unlucky Londoner calculated for the meridian of this city but may serve by way of advice to all the cominalty of England, but more perticularly to parents and children, masters and servants, husbands and wives: intermixed with severall choice novels: stored with variety of examples and advice, president and precept: illustrated with pictures fitted to the severall stories*. London, 1673.
Kitch, Aaron. *Political Economy and the States of Literature in Early Modern England*. Burlington, VT: Ashgate, 2009.
Knapp, Jeffrey. *An Empire Nowhere: England, America, and Literature from* Utopia *to* The Tempest. Berkeley: U of California P, 1992.
——. *Shakespeare's Tribe: Church, Nation, and Theater in Renaissance England*. Chicago: U of Chicago P, 2002.

Lamming, George. *The Pleasures of Exile*. Ann Arbor: U of Michigan P, 1992.
——. *Water with Berries*. New York: Holt, 1972.
Lane, Frederic Chapin. *Venice, A Maritime Republic*. Johns Hopkins UP, 1973.
Langbaine, Gerard. *An account of the English dramatick poets, or, Some observations and remarks on the lives and writings of all those that have publish'd either comedies, tragedies, tragi-comedies, pastorals, masques, interludes, farces or opera's in the English tongue*. Oxford, 1691.
Lawrence, Sean. "'To Give and to Receive': Performing Exchanges in *The Merchant of Venice*." *Shakespeare and the Cultures of Performance*. Ed. Paul Yachnin and Patricia Badir. Aldershot: Ashgate, 2008. 41–51. Studies in Performance & Early Modern Drama (SPEMD).
Levinson, Marjorie. "What Is New Formalism?" *PMLA* 122.2 (2007): 558–69.
Linton, Joan Pong. *The Romance of the New World: Gender and the Literary Formations of English Colonialism*. Cambridge: Cambridge UP, 1998.
Littleton, Betty J., ed. *Clyomon and Clamydes: A Critical Edition*. The Hague: Mouton, 1968.
Liu, Yin. "Middle English Romance as Prototype Genre." *Chaucer Review: A Journal of Medieval Studies and Literary Criticism* 40.4 (2006): 335–53.
Lloyd, David. "Ludlow Castle." *Milton Quarterly* 21.4 (1987): 52–8.
Lockey, Brian. *Law and Empire in English Renaissance Literature*. Cambridge: Cambridge UP, 2006.
Lodge, Thomas. *A Margarite of America*. By T. Lodge. London, 1596.
——. *Rosalynde. Euphues Golden Legacie Found After His Death in His Cell at Silexedra. Bequeathed to Philautus Sonnes, Noursed Vp with Their Father in England. Fetcht from the Canaries by T.L. Gent*. London, 1592.
Loomba, Ania. "'Break her will, and bruise no bone sir': Colonial and Sexual Mastery in Fletcher's *The Island Princess*." *Journal for Early Modern Cultural Studies* 2.1 (2002): 68–108.
——. *Shakespeare, Race, and Colonialism*. Oxford: Oxford UP, 2002.
Luttrell, Claude. "Arthurian Geography: The Islands of the Sea." *Neophilologus* 83.2 (1999): 187–96.
Macfarlane, Fenella. "To 'Try What London Prentices Can Do': Merchant Chivalry as Representational Strategy in Thomas Heywood's *The Four Prentices of London*." Ed. John Pitcher. *Medieval and Renaissance Drama in England* 14 (2001): 136–64.
MacInnes, Ian. "'Ill Luck, Ill Luck?': Risk and Hazard in *The Merchant of Venice*." *Global Traffic: Discourses and Practices of Trade in English Literature and Culture from 1550 to 1700*. Ed. Barbara Sebek & Stephen Deng. New York: Palgrave Macmillan, 2008. 39–55. Early Modern Cultural Studies 1500–1700.
MacLean, Gerald M. *Looking East: English Writing and the Ottoman Empire Before 1800*. Basingstoke: Palgrave Macmillan, 2007.
——. *Re-Orienting the Renaissance: Cultural Exchanges with the East*. Basingstoke: Palgrave Macmillan, 2005.
MacMillan, Ken. *Sovereignty and Possession in the English New World: The Legal Foundations of Empire, 1576–1640*. Cambridge: Cambridge UP, 2006.
MacMillan, Ken and Jennifer Abeles, eds. *John Dee: The Limits of the British Empire. Studies in Military History and International Affairs*. Westport, CT: Praeger, 2004.

Mahood, M. M. "Introduction." *The Merchant of Venice*. Ed. M. M. Mahood. Cambridge: Cambridge UP, 2003. New Cambridge Shakespeare.
Maley, Willy. *Nation, State, and Empire in English Renaissance Literature: Shakespeare to Milton*. New York: Palgrave Macmillan, 2003.
Mancall, Peter C. *Hakluyt's Promise: An Elizabethan's Obsession for an English America*. New Haven: Yale UP, 2007.
Markley, Robert. *The Far East and the English Imagination, 1600–1730*. Cambridge: Cambridge UP, 2006.
Marlowe, Christopher. *Doctor Faustus* A- and B- Texts (1604, 1616). Ed. David M. Bevington and Eric Rasmussen. Manchester UP, 1993.
Marshall, Tristan. *Theatre and Empire: Great Britain on the London Stages Under James VI and I*. Manchester: Manchester UP, 2000.
Martyr, Peter. *The Decades of the Newe Worlde or West India Conteynyng the Nauigations and Conquestes of the Spanyardes, with the Particular Description of the Moste Ryche and Large Landes and Ilandes Lately Founde in the West Ocean Perteynyng to the Inheritaunce of the Kinges of Spayne* . . . Trans. Richard Eden. London, 1555.
Matar, Nabil. *Turks, Moors and Englishmen in the Age of Discovery*. New York: Columbia UP, 1999.
McDonald, Russ. *Shakespeare's Late Style*. Cambridge: Cambridge UP, 2006.
McEachern, Claire Elizabeth. *The Poetics of English Nationhood, 1590–1612*. Cambridge: Cambridge UP, 1996.
McKeon, Michael. *The Origins of the English Novel, 1600–1740*. Baltimore: Johns Hopkins UP, 1987.
McMullan, Gordon. "Stage-mandevilles: The Far East and the Limits of Representation in the Theatre, 1621–2002." *A Knight's Legacy: Mandeville and Mandevillian Lore in Early Modern England*. Ed. Ladan Niayesh. Manchester: Manchester UP, 2011. 173–94.
——. *Shakespeare and the Idea of Late Writing: Authorship in the Proximity of Death*. Cambridge: Cambridge UP, 2007.
——. "What Is a 'Late Play'?" *The Cambridge Companion to Shakespeare's Last Plays*. Ed. Catherine M. S. Alexander. Cambridge: Cambridge UP, 2009. 5–28.
McMullan, Gordon, and Jonathan Hope, eds. *The Politics of Tragicomedy: Shakespeare and After*. London: Routledge, 1992.
McRae, Andrew. *Literature and Domestic Travel in Early Modern England*. Cambridge: Cambridge UP, 2009.
Media Guide: London 2012 Olympic Games Opening Ceremony. London: n.p., 2012. Web.
Mentz, Steve. *At the Bottom of Shakespeare's Ocean*. London: Continuum, 2009. Shakespeare Now.
——."The Fiend Gives Friendly Counsel: Launcelot Gobbo and Polyglot Economics in *The Merchant of Venice*." *Money and the Age of Shakespeare: Essays in New Economic Criticism*. Ed. Linda Woodbridge. New York: Palgrave Macmillan, 2003. 177–87. Early Modern Cultural Studies 1500–1700.
Mercator, Gerard, et al. *Historia Mundi: Or Mercator's Atlas Containing His Cosmographicall Description of the Fabricke and Figure of the World. Lately Rectified in Divers Places, as also Beautified and Enlarged with New Mappes and Tables; by*

the Studious Industry of Iudocus Hondy. Englished by W.S. Generosus, & Coll. Regin. Oxoniæ. London, 1635.

Meres, Francis. *Palladis Tamia* (1598). Ed. Don Cameron Allen. New York: Scholars' Facsimiles & Reprints, 1938.

Metlitzki, Dorothee. *The Matter of Araby in Medieval England*. New Haven: Yale UP, 1977.

Middleton, Christopher. *The famous historie of Chinon of England, with his strange aduentures for the loue of Celestina daughter to Lewis King of Fraunce. VVith the worthy atchiuement of Sir Lancelot du Lake, and Sir Tristram du Lions for fair Laura, daughter to Cador Earle of Cornewall, beeing all knights of King Arthurs round table*. London, 1597.

Milton, John. *A Brief History of Moscovia*. 1682. Complete Prose Works. Ed. Don M. Wolfe, et al. Vol. 8. New Haven: Yale UP, 1982. 454–538.

——. *Complete Shorter Poems*. Ed. John Carey. London: Longman, 1971.

——. *A Maske Presented at Ludlow Castle, 1634 on Michaelmasse Night, before the Right Honorable, Iohn Earle of Bridgewater, Vicount Brackly, Lord Præsident of Wales, and One of His Maiesties most Honorable Privie Counsell*. London, 1637.

——. *Selected Prose*. Ed. C. A. Patrides. Columbia: U of Missouri P, 1985.

Mortimer, Anthony. "*Comus* and Michaelmas." *English Studies: A Journal of English Language and Literature* 65.2 (1984): 111–19.

Moseley, C. W. R. D. "'Whet-stone leasings of old Maundeuile': Reading the Travels in Early Modern England." *A Knight's Legacy: Mandeville and Mandevillian Lore in Early Modern England*. Ed. Ladan Niayesh. Manchester: Manchester UP, 2011. 28–50.

Mowat, Barbara A. "'What's in a Name?' Tragicomedy, Romance, or Late Comedy." *A Companion to Shakespeare's Works*. Ed. Richard Dutton and Jean E. Howard. Vol. 4. 4 vols. Oxford: Blackwell. 129–49.

Mullaney, Steven. *The Place of the Stage: License, Play, and Power in Renaissance England*. New edn. U of Michigan P, 1995.

Mulready, Cyrus. "Making History in Q *Henry V*." *English Literary Renaissance* 43.3 (2013): n. pag.

Münster, Sebastian. *A Treatyse of the Newe India, with Other New Founde Landes and Islandes, Aswell Eastwarde as Westwarde, as They Are Knowen and Found in These Oure Dayes, After the Description of Sebastian Munster in His Boke of Universall Cosmographie: Wherin the Diligent Reader May See the Good Successe and Rewarde of Noble and Honeste Enterpryses, by the Which Not Only Worldly Ryches Are Obtayned, but Also God Is Glorified, [and] the Christian Faythe Enlarged. Translated Out of Latin into Englishe. By Rycharde Eden*. London, 1553.

Myrick, Kenneth. *Sir Phillip Sidney as a Literary Craftsman*. Cambridge, MA: Harvard UP, 1935; Lincoln, NE: U of Nebraska P, 1965.

Netzloff, Mark. *England's Internal Colonies: Class, Capital, and the Literature of Early Modern English Colonialism*. New York: Palgrave Macmillan, 2003.

——. "The Lead Casket: Capital, Mercantilism, and *The Merchant of Venice*." *Money and the Age of Shakespeare: Essays in New Economic Criticism*. Ed. Linda Woodbridge. New York: Palgrave Macmillan, 2003. 159–76. Early Modern Cultural Studies 1500–1700.

Newcomb, Lori Humphrey. *Reading Popular Romance in Early Modern England*. New York: Columbia UP, 2002.

———. "The Sources of Romance, the Generation of Story, and the Patterns of the *Pericles* Tales." *Staging Early Modern Romance: Prose Fiction, Dramatic Romance, and Shakespeare*. Ed. Mary Ellen Lamb and Valerie Wayne. New York: Routledge, 2009. 21–46. Routledge studies in Renaissance literature and culture 11.
Nicoll, Allardyce, ed. *Chapman's Homer: The Odyssey*. Bollingen Series XLI. Princeton, Princeton UP, 2000.
Nixon, Anthony. *A true Relation of the Trauels of M. Bush. a Gentleman: who with his owne handes without any other mans helpe made a Pynace, in which hee past by Ayre, Land, and Water: From Lamborne, a place in Barkshire, to the Custome house Key in London*. London, 1607.
Norbrook, David. "The Reformation of the Masque." *The Court Masque*. Ed. David Lindley. Manchester: Manchester UP, 1984. 94–110.
Norton, Thomas, and Thomas Sackville. *Gorboduc, or, Ferrex and Porrex*. Ed. Irby B. Cauthen. London: Arnold, 1970.
Oakeshott, Walter. "Sir Walter Ralegh's Library." *The Library* 5th ser. 33.4 (1968): 285–327. Web. 13 Jan. 2013.
O'Connell, Michael. "The Experiment of Romance." *The Cambridge Companion to Shakespearean Comedy*, ed. Alexander Leggatt. Cambridge: Cambridge UP, 2001. 215–29.
Orgel, Stephen. *The Authentic Shakespeare and Other Problems of the Early Modern Stage*. New York: Routledge, 2002.
———. "The Case for *Comus*." *Representations* 81.1 (2003): 31–45.
———. "Introduction." *The Tempest*. Oxford: Oxford UP, 1987.
———. "Shakespeare and the Kinds of Drama." *The Authentic Shakespeare and Other Problems of the Early Modern Stage*. New York: Routledge, 2002. 143–58.
Osborn, James Marshall. *Young Philip Sidney, 1572–1577*. New Haven: Yale UP, 1972. The Elizabethan Club Series 5.
Palfrey, Simon. *Late Shakespeare: A New World of Words*. Oxford: Clarendon P, 1997.
Palmer, D. J. "'We shall know by this fellow': Prologue and Chorus in Shakespeare." *Bulletin of the John Rylands University Library of Manchester* 64.2 (1982): 501–21.
Parker, Patricia. *Inescapable Romance: Studies in the Poetics of a Mode*. Princeton: Princeton UP, 1979.
———. "Romance and Empire: Anachronistic *Cymbeline*." *Unfolded Tales: Essays on Renaissance Romance*. Ed. George M. Logan and Gordon Teskey. Ithaca: Cornell UP, 1989. 189–207.
Parr, Anthony, ed. *Three Renaissance Travel Plays: The Travels of the Three English Brothers, the Sea Voyage, the Antipodes*. Manchester: Manchester UP, 1995.
Parry, Glyn. "John Dee and the Elizabethan British Empire in Its European Context." *The Historical Journal* 49.03 (2006): 643–75. Web. 31 Jan. 2011.
Patterson, Annabel. "Back by Popular Demand: The Two Versions of *Henry V*." *Renaissance Drama* 19 (1988): 29–62.
Peele, George. *Farewell Entituled to the famous and fortunate generalls of our English forces: Sir Iohn Norris & Syr Frauncis Drake Knights, and all theyr braue and resolute followers. Whereunto is annexed: a tale of Troy*. Oxford, 1589.
Pettet, E. C. *Shakespeare and the Romance Tradition*. London: Staples, 1949.
Pigafetta, Antonio. *The Voyage of Magellan*. Trans. Paula Spurlin Paige. Englewood Cliffs, NJ: Prentice-Hall. 1969.

Pollard, Tanya, ed. *Shakespeare's Theater: A Sourcebook*. Malden, MA: Blackwell, 2004.
Poole, Kristen. *Supernatural Environments in Shakespeare's England: Spaces of Demonism, Divinity, and Drama*. Cambridge: Cambridge UP, 2011.
Proudfoot, G. R., ed. *Tom a Lincoln*. Oxford: Published for the Malone Society by Oxford UP, 1992. Malone Society Reprints.
Puttenham, George. *The Art of English Poesy by George Puttenham: A Critical Edition*. Ed. Frank Whigham and Wayne A. Rebhorn. Ithaca, NY: Cornell UP, 2007.
Quinn, David Beers. "Atlantic Islands." *Atlantic Visions*. Ed. John de Courcy Ireland and David C. Sheehy. Dublin: Boole, 1989. 77–94.
Quint, David. "'Alexander the Pig': Shakespeare on History and Poetry." *Boundary 2: A Journal of Postmodern Literature and Culture* 10.3 (1982): 49–68.
———. *Epic and Empire: Politics and Generic form from Virgil to Milton*. Princeton: Princeton UP, 1993. Literature in History.
Rabkin, Norman. "Rabbits, Ducks, and *Henry V*." *Shakespeare Quarterly* 28.3 (1977): 279–96.
Ralegh, Sir Walter. *The Discovery of Guiana: With Related Documents*. Ed. Benjamin Schmidt. Boston: Bedford-St. Martin's, 2007.
Raman, Shankar. *Framing "India": The Colonial Imaginary in Early Modern Culture*. Stanford, CA: Stanford UP, 2001.
Rasmussen, Mark David, ed. *Renaissance Literature and Its Formal Engagements*. New York: Palgrave Macmillan, 2002.
Reichl, Karl. "Orality and Performance." *A Companion to Medieval Popular Romance*. Ed. Raluca Radulescu and Cory Rushton. Woodbridge: Boydell & Brewer, 2009. 132–49.
Ringrose, Basil. *Bucaniers of America. The second volume: Containing the dangerous voyage and bold attempts of Captain Bartholomew Sharp, and others, performed upon the coasts of the South Sea, for the space of two years, &c.: from the original journal of the said voyage*. London, 1685.
Robinson, Benedict S. "Harry and Amurath." *Shakespeare Quarterly* 60.4 (2009): 399–424.
———. *Islam and Early Modern English Literature: The Politics of Romance from Spenser to Milton*. New York: Palgrave Macmillan, 2007. Early modern cultural studies.
Roloff, Hans-Gert. *Fortunatus: Studienausgabe nach der Editio princeps von 1509*. Stuttgart: Reclam, 1996.
Sabin, Joseph, ed. *A Dictionary of Books Relating to America, From its Discovery to the Present Time*. Vol. IV. New York: Bibliographic Society of America, 1873.
Said, Edward W. *Orientalism*. New York: Vintage Books, 1994.
Sanders, Julie. *The Cultural Geography of Early Modern Drama, 1620–1650*. Cambridge UP, 2011.
Sanford, Rhonda Lemke. *Maps and Memory in Early Modern England: A Sense of Place*. New York: Palgrave Macmillan, 2002.
Schwyzer, Philip. *Literature, Nationalism, and Memory in Early Modern England and Wales*. Cambridge: Cambridge UP, 2004.
———. "Purity and Danger on the West Bank of the Severn: The Cultural Geography of A Masque Presented at Ludlow Castle, 1634." *Representations* 60 (1997): 22–48.

Scott, Jonathan. *When the Waves Ruled Britannia: Geography and Political Identities, 1500–1800*. Cambridge: Cambridge UP, 2011.
Sebek, Barbara. "Global Traffic: An Introduction." *Global Traffic: Discourses and Practices of Trade in English Literature and Culture from 1550 to 1700*. Ed. Barbara Sebek and Stephen Deng. New York: Palgrave Macmillan, 2008. 1–18.
Sebek, Barbara, and Stephen Deng. *Global Traffic: Discourses and Practices of Trade in English Literature and Culture from 1550 to 1700*. New York: Palgrave Macmillan, 2008.
Shakespeare, William. *Cymbeline*. Ed. Martin Butler. Cambridge: Cambridge UP, 2005. The New Cambridge Shakespeare.
———. *Henry V*. Ed. Gary Taylor. Oxford UP, 1982. The Oxford Shakespeare.
———. *King Henry V*. Ed. Andrew Gurr. Cambridge: Cambridge UP, 2005. New Cambridge Shakespeare.
———. *The Tempest*: A New Variorum Edition of Shakespeare. Ed. Horace Howard Furness. Philadelphia: Lippincott, 1871.
———. *The Winter's Tale*. Ed. John Pitcher. London: Arden Shakespeare, 2010. Arden Shakespeare. Third Series.
Sherman, William H. "'Gold is the Strength, the Sinnewes of the World': Thomas Dekker's *Old Fortunatus* and England's Golden Age." *Medieval and Renaissance Drama in England* 6 (1993): 85–102.
———. *John Dee: The Politics of Reading and Writing in the English Renaissance*. Amherst: U of Massachusetts P, 1995. Massachusetts Studies in Early Modern Culture.
———. "Putting the British Seas on the Map: John Dee's Imperial Cartography." *Cartographica: The International Journal for Geographic Information and Geovisualization* 35.3 (1998): 1–10. Web. 11 Jan. 2013.
Sidney, Philip. "The Defence of Poesy." *Sir Philip Sidney: The Major Works*. Ed. Katherine Duncan-Jones. Oxford: Oxford UP, 2002. 212–50. Oxford World's Classics.
Singh, Jyotsna. "Introduction: The Global Renaissance." *A Companion to the Global Renaissance: English Literature and Culture in the Era of Expansion*. Ed. Jyotsna Singh. Malden, MA: Wiley-Blackwell, 2009. 1–27.
Smith, Alan Gordon Rae. *The Emergence of a Nation State: The Commonwealth of England 1529–1660*. 2nd edn. London: Longman, 1997.
Smith, Donald Kimball. *The Cartographic Imagination in Early Modern England: Re-Writing the World in Marlowe, Spenser, Raleigh and Marvell*. Burlington, VT: Ashgate, 2008.
Smyth, Thomas. "Offices necessarie in the Colony of Ardes and orders agreed vppon." 1573. Ms. D/DSh/O1/7. Essex County Records Office, Chelmsford, UK. Essex Archives Online. Web. 1 June 2006.
Spenser, Edmund. *The Faerie Queene*. Ed. A. C. Hamilton, Hiroshi Yamashita, and Toshiyuki Suzuki. Harlow: Pearson, 2001.
Spiller, Elizabeth A. "From Imagination to Miscegenation: Race and Romance in Shakespeare's *The Merchant of Venice*." *Renaissance Drama* 29 (1998): 137–64.
Spingarn, J. E. *A History of Literary Criticism in the Renaissance*. 2nd edn. New York: Columbia UP, 1924.
Sprott, Samuel Ernest, ed. A Maske: *The Earlier Versions*. Toronto: U of Toronto P, 1973.

Stallybrass, Peter. "Against Thinking." *PMLA* 122.5 (2007): 1580–6. Web. 26 May 2009.

Stern, Tiffany. *Documents of Performance in Early Modern England*. Cambridge: Cambridge UP, 2009.

Stevens, Paul. "Heterogenizing Imagination: Globalization, *The Merchant of Venice*, and the Work of Literary Criticism." *New Literary History* 36.3 (2005): 425–37.

Strohm, Paul. "The Origin and Meaning of Middle English Romaunce." *Genre* 10 (1977): 1–28.

"Supposition." *The Oxford English Dictionary Online*. 2nd edn. Web.

Szkilnik, Michelle. "Seas, Islands and Continent in *L'Estoire Del Saint Graal*." *RLA: Romance Languages Annual* 1 (1989): 322–7.

Taylor, E. G. R. "A Letter Dated 1577 from Mercator to John Dee." *Imago Mundi* 13 (1956): 56–68.

Test, Edward M. "*The Tempest* and the Newfoundland Cod Fishery." *Global Traffic: Discourses and Practices of Trade in English Literature and Culture from 1550 to 1700*. Ed. Barbara Sebek and Stephen Deng. New York: Palgrave Macmillan, 2008. 201–20. Early Modern Cultural Studies 1500–1700.

Thorne, Alison, ed. *Shakespeare's Romances*. Basingstoke: Palgrave Macmillan, 2003. New Casebooks.

Tillyard, Eustace Mandeville Wetenhall. *Shakespeare's History Plays*. New York: Penguin, 1991.

Turner, Henry. *The English Renaissance Stage: Geometry, Poetics, and the Practical Spatial Arts 1580–1630*. New York: Oxford UP, 2006.

Valentine and Orson. 1503. Trans. Henry Watson. Ed. Arthur Dickson. Early English Text Society Original Ser. No. 204. London: Oxford UP, 1937.

Valentine and Orson. The Two Sonnes of the Emperour of Greece. Newly corrected and amended, with new pictures lively expressing the historie. Printed at London: By Thomas Pnrfoot [sic]. London, 1637.

Vitkus, Daniel. "'The Common Market of All the World': English Theater, the Global System, and the Ottoman Empire in the Early Modern Period." *Global Traffic: Discourses and Practices of Trade in English Literature and Culture from 1550 to 1700*. Ed. Barbara Sebek and Stephen Deng. New York: Palgrave Macmillan, 2008. 19–38.

——. "Labor and Travel on the Early Modern Stage: Representing the Travail of Travel in Dekker's *Old Fortunatus* and Shakespeare's *Pericles*." *Working Subjects in Early Modern English Drama*. Ed. Michelle M. Dowd and Natasha Korda. Burlington, VT: Ashgate, 2011. 225–42.

——. *Turning Turk: English Theater and the Multicultural Mediterranean*. New York: Palgrave Macmillan, 2003.

The Voyage of Saint Brendan: Representative Versions of the Legend in English Translation with Indexes of Themes and Motifs from the Stories. Ed. Glyn S. Burgess and W. R. J. Barron. Exeter: U of Exeter P, 2005.

Wall, John N., Jr. "'Fruitfullest Virginia': Edmund Spenser, Roanoke Island, and the Bower of Bliss." *Renaissance Papers* (1984): 1–17.

Wallace, David. *Premodern Places: Calais to Surinam, Chaucer to Aphra Behn*. Malden, MA: Blackwell, 2004.

Walsh, Brian. *Shakespeare, the Queen's Men, and the Elizabethan Performance of History*. Cambridge: Cambridge UP, 2010.

Warren, Michelle R. *History on the Edge: Excalibur and the Borders of Britain, 1100–1300.* U of Minnesota P, 2000.
Warren, Roger. "Introduction." *A Reconstructed Text of Pericles, Prince of Tyre.* Ed. Roger Warren. Oxford: Oxford UP, 2003. The Oxford Shakespeare.
Wayne, Valerie. "*Don Quixote* and Shakespeare's Collaborative Turn to Romance." *The Quest for* Cardenio*: Shakespeare, Fletcher, Cervantes, and the Lost Play.* Ed. David Carnegie & Gary Taylor. Oxford: Oxford UP, 2012. 217–38.
——. "Romancing the Wager: *Cymbeline's* Intertexts." *Staging Early Modern Romance: Prose Fiction, Dramatic Romance, and Shakespeare.* Ed. Mary Ellen Lamb and Valerie Wayne. New York: Routledge, 2009. 163–87. Routledge studies in Renaissance literature and culture 11.
Weimann, Robert. *Author's Pen and Actor's Voice: Playing and Writing in Shakespeare's Theatre.* Ed. Helen Higbee and William West. Cambridge: Cambridge UP, 2000. Cambridge Studies in Renaissance Literature and Culture 39.
——. *Shakespeare and the Popular Tradition in the Theater: Studies in the Social Dimension of Dramatic Form and Function.* Ed. Robert Schwartz. Baltimore: Johns Hopkins UP, 1978.
Wells, Stanley. "Shakespeare and Romance." *Later Shakespeare.* Ed. John R. Brown and Bernard Harris. London: Arnold, 1966. 49–80. Stratford-upon-Avon Studies: 8.
Wells, Stanley W., and Gary Taylor. *William Shakespeare, a Textual Companion.* New York: Norton, 1997.
Whetstone, George. *The Right Excellent and Famous Historye, of Promos and Cassandra: Deuided into Two Commicall Discourses. Old English Drama.* Students' Facsimile Edition. Amersham: Farmer, 1913.
Wilding, Michael. "Milton's 'A Masque Presented at Ludlow Castle, 1634': Theatre and Politics on the Border." *Milton Quarterly* 21.4 (1987): 35–51.
Wilkinson, L. P. *The Georgics of Virgil: A Critical Survey.* Cambridge: Cambridge UP, 1978.
Williams, Glanmor. *Recovery, Reorientation and Reformation: Wales c. 1415–1642.* Oxford: Clarendon–U of Wales P, 1987.
Williams, Gwyn A. *When was Wales?: A History of the Welsh.* London: Black Raven, 1985.
Wilson-Okamura, David Scott. "Virgilian Models of Colonization in Shakespeare's Tempest." *ELH* 70.3 (2003): 709–37.
Wilson, Richard. "Veiling an Indian Beauty: Shakespeare and the Hijab." *Shakespeare* 4.4 (2008): 379–96. Web. 9 Dec. 2012.
Witmore, Michael, and Jonathan Hope. "Shakespeare by the Numbers: On the Linguistic Texture of the Late Plays." *Early Modern Tragicomedy.* Ed. Subha Mukherji and Raphael Lyne. Woodbridge: Boydell & Brewer, 2007. 133–53.
Woodbridge, Linda. "Payback Time: On the Economic Rhetoric of Revenge in *The Merchant of Venice.*" *Shakespeare and the Cultures of Performance.* Ed. Paul Yachnin and Patricia Badir. xiii, 210 pp. Aldershot: Ashgate, 2008. 29–40. Studies in Performance & Early Modern Drama (SPEMD).
Woolf, D. R. *The Idea of History in Early Stuart England: Erudition, Ideology, and the "Light of Truth" from the Accession of James I to the Civil War.* Toronto: U of Toronto P, 1990.
——. *Reading History in Early Modern England.* Cambridge: Cambridge UP, 2000.

―――. *The Social Circulation of the Past: English Historical Culture, 1500–1730*. Oxford: Oxford UP, 2003.

Wright, William Aldis, ed. *The Metrical Chronicle of Robert of Gloucester*. Vol. 2. 2 vols. London, 1887.

Yates, Frances Amelia. *Shakespeare's Last Plays: A New Approach*. London: Routledge, 1975.

Zucker, Adam. *The Places of Wit in Early Modern English Comedy*. Cambridge UP, 2011.

Index

A Margarite of America (Thomas Lodge), 85, 234
Abeles, Jennifer, 5–6, 10, 204, 234
Aeneid, 121, 162–4
Ainsworth, E. G., 176, 224
Albion's England (Warner), 139
Alleyn, Edward, 24, 208
Altieri, Joanne, 111, 216, 224
Amadis of Gaul, 20, 57, 60, 149
"An Apology for Smectymnuus" (Milton), 186
Angelica (Greene; *Orlando Furioso*), 102–3
Anghiera, Pietro Martire, 23, 26, 103, 224
Antipodes, the, 9, 84–5, 112, 237
Apology for Actors, An (Heywood), 135
Appollonius of Tyre, 161
Arcadia (Sidney), 46, 50, 53, 161, 202
Areopagitica (Milton), 182
Argonauts, the, 25–6, 103
Ariosto, Ludovico, 22, 25, 47, 68, 102, 131, 157, 175–6, 190–1, 200–1, 212, 224
Aristotle, 21, 23, 39, 47, 52, 60, 61–3, 66, 68, 111, 137, 138, 163, 212
Ascham, Roger, 20, 224
Astington, John, 212, 224

Bachelard, Gaston, 79
Baker, David, 13, 122, 205–6, 217–18, 222, 224, 229
Bale, Anthony, 193, 224
Barlow, William, 83, 90–1, 99–101, 104, 225
Barton, Anne, 110, 216, 225
Bate, Jonathan, 39, 225
Bauer, Ralph, 143, 171, 225
Beaumont, Francis, 58, 71, 203, 223, 225
Blundeville, Thomas, 9, 88–91, 104, 225

Boehmer, Elleke, 194, 225
Boiardo, Matteo Maria, 68
Boyle, Danny (Director), 193–4, 198–9, 225
Branagh, Kenneth, 193, 198–9
Brendan, the Voyage of St., 6, 156–7, 220, 240
Bridgewater Manuscript, the 172–3, 176
Bridgewater, John, Earl of, 173, 177, 182, 184
Britain, 7, 48, 113–14, 120, 122, 125–6, 138, 159, 181, 205, 208, 219, 224–5, 229–30, 232, 235, 241
British Empire, 5–7, 12, 29–31, 80–1, 89, 91–3, 96–7, 99, 118–20, 181, 194, 204–6, 208–9, 224, 234, 237
Brome, Richard, 84
Brotton, Jerry, 3, 79, 162–3, 205, 221, 225
Brückner, Martin, 146, 148, 213, 226
Bush, William, 90, 106
Butler, Michelle, 129, 218, 226
Butter, Nathanial, 90

Cabot, John, 156
cartography
 and the fantastical in romance, 3, 10, 29, 32, 81
 and "speculative geography," 83, 87, 91–2, 96
Castelvetro, Lodovico, 22, 63–5, 67–9
Cavendish, Thomas, 85, 87, 89–90
Certeau, Michel de, 11, 226
Césaire, Aimé, 219
Charlemagne, 106, 139, 207
Chaucer, Geoffrey, 201, 214, 234, 241

Index

Chorus
 choric, 96, 127, 129, 133
 directing action over/eliding disparities in space and time, 117, 120–1, 124, 126–35, 140–1, 151–2, 154, 173
 Helen Cooper on, 134
 in *Henry V*, 109, 115–17, 120, 121, 126, 128–9, 130, 132–5, 151–2, 173
 as later addition to *Henry V*, 140
 in *Magnetic Lady*, 58
 in *Old Fortunatus*, 75, 121, 130, 132–3, 152
 as paradoxical theatrical device, 133
 in *Pericles*, 151
 in *Richard III*, 130
 soliciting audiences' imaginations, 71–3, 96, 109–10, 113–14, 121, 127, 132, 140
 in the "Stonyhurst Pageants," 134
 as strategy associated with romance, 140
 as targeted to readers rather than audiences, 140–1
 in *The Tempest*, 127, 131, 154, 173
 theatrical device of, 29, 110
 as Time, 48–9, 95
 in *Tom a Lincoln*, 94–6
 in *Troilus and Cressida*, 131
 as undermining historical authenticity, 141
 in *Warres of Cyrus*, 132
Cicero, 7, 205
Cid, Le (Corneille), 46–7, 227
Cohen, Walter, 13–14, 20, 99, 205–7, 210, 215–16, 226
Coleridge, Samuel Taylor, 28, 34, 36–9, 43, 45, 137, 170–1, 209–10, 226
Colie, Rosalie, 18, 207, 226
Collins, John Churton, 24, 208, 227, 230
Collinson, Sir Richard, 1, 204, 227
colonialism, 14, 27, 32, 146, 171, 190, 194, 210, 212, 217, 226, 234, 236
Columbus, Christopher, 148, 156–7, 204

commerce and trade
 in global Renaissance scholarship, 13, 205–6
 and *The Merchant of Venice*, 97–8, 106–7
 in Sidney's *Defense*, 66–7, 73–4, 76
 and stage romance, 22, 96, 100
Comus (Milton), 30, 172–7, 183–9, 191–2, 222, 224, 227–8, 236–7
Confessio Amantis (Gower), 152
Cooper, Helen, 16, 20, 33, 48, 134–5, 149, 158, 173, 200, 207, 210–12, 214, 227
Corneille, Pierre, 46–7, 227
cosmopolitanism, 123, 217, 232
Creaser, John, 177–8, 222, 227
Cressy, David, 178, 227
Crusades, 15, 19, 27, 48, 69, 113, 195, 208, 219
Cyropaedia (Xenophon), 133

Davis, John, 83, 227
Day, John, 113, 156, 202–3, 238
de Grazia, Margreta, 40, 153, 209, 211, 217, 220, 227
Dee, John, 9, 29, 81, 83–4, 95–7, 104, 114, 118–21, 126, 181, 204–5, 214, 217, 224, 228, 234, 237, 239–40
 and the idea of "Cosmopoliticall gouernment", 119
 "Limits of the British Empire," 5–7, 92, 96–7, 119, 234
Defense of Poesy (Sidney), 21, 28, 52–5, 60, 65, 70, 77–8, 133, 208, 211
Dekker, Elly, 87
Dekker, Thomas, 29, 31, 54, 67, 69, 71–6, 109–10, 121, 130, 202–3, 212–13, 216, 228, 239–40
"Delos, th'Isle of" (Ovid), 157
Dessen, Alan, 59, 228
Dickson, Arthur, 55, 211, 223, 228, 240
Dimmock, Matthew, 205, 228
Dimock, Wai Chee, 22, 228
Doctor Faustus (Marlowe), 18, 73–4, 81–2, 103, 235
Doddridge, John, 181–2, 228
Don Bellanis of Greece (Kirkman), 18

Dowden, Edward, 17–18, 27–8, 34–45, 48–51, 111, 144–5, 193–4, 207, 209–11, 228
Drake, Francis, 84, 87, 89–90, 196, 232, 237–8
Driver, Felix, 10, 228

Eccles, Ambrose, 98
Eden, Richard, 66, 84, 196, 224, 228, 235–6
Edgar, King, 92–3, 119–20
Eliot, Thomas Stearns (T. S.), 54, 211, 228
Elizabeth I, 5, 56, 92, 97, 189, 215, 229, 235, 239
Ellison, Lee Monroe, 200, 211–12, 229
empire
  and dramatic unity, 148–55
  in *Henry V*, 113–27, 141–3
  and romance, 2–3, 5–7, 12–15, 80–2, 91–3
  and Wales, 180–2
epic, 22, 63, 65, 67–8, 77, 131, 137, 149, 162–4, 223, 238
epilogues, 109, 127, 141, 152, 154, 169, 205, 218
Erne, Lukas, 140–1

Faerie Queene, The (Spenser), 91–2, 149, 155, 157–8, 164–5, 169, 185, 214, 220, 224, 239
Fale, Thomas, 88, 229
Felperin, Howard, 41, 210, 229
Ferrex (*Gorboduc*) *see also* Porrex, 138, 219, 237
Feuillerat, Albert, 56, 212, 229
Fleay, Frederic Guard, 200, 229
Fletcher, John, 186, 212, 223, 234, 241
Floyd-Wilson, Mary, 123–4, 229
Forrest, John, 59, 222, 229
Fortune, 73–4, 76, 160, 201
Foxe, John, 136
Frobisher, Martin, 1–3, 5, 193, 204, 227
Frye, Northrop, 12, 20, 110, 216, 229
Fuchs, Barbara, 15, 17, 43, 206–8, 210, 216, 219, 229

Gates, Sir Thomas, 168
genre
  defined in Renaissance criticism, 18–21, 63–8
  historical formalism, 13, 19–20, 44, 170, 209, 215, 230
  history as genre, 107–12, 136–40
  and space/geography, 10–11, 27–9, 204–6, 213–17
  as strategy, 16–18
Geoffrey of Monmouth, 6, 15, 48, 108–9, 111, 138, 208, 219, 227, 230
geographic places mentioned or discussed
  Africa, 6, 24, 28, 52, 61–2, 65–6, 75, 82, 89, 94–5, 103, 133, 144, 162–3, 211
  Amazon, 25, 94, 157
  America, 5, 9, 77, 85, 93, 103, 116, 195–7, 217, 223–4, 226, 228, 231–5, 238
  Arabia, 60, 98–9, 133–4, 136, 200
  Arctic, 3, 6, 10, 84, 193
  Atlantic, 5, 118, 156, 163, 168, 172, 226, 238
  Asia, 6, 9, 28, 52, 61–2, 65–6, 75, 117, 133, 205, 211, 224
  Babylon, 73, 75, 201, 233
  Brazil, 85, 156, 196
  Calicut, 28, 52, 54, 66–7, 77–9, 112, 198
  Canary Islands, 85, 156, 234
  Caribbean, 205, 230, 232
  Carthage, 94, 137, 162–4, 167, 221, 225
  Cathay (China), China, 1, 23, 148, 191, 205
  Cyprus, 24, 73, 75
  Egypt, 102, 134, 205, 224
  France, 24, 57, 69, 93, 96, 109, 114–15, 117, 123–7, 130–1, 135, 139–41, 144, 159, 225, 236
  Greece, 18, 26, 59, 103, 233, 240
  Guiana, 1, 11, 31–2, 204, 229, 238
  India, 2, 23, 25, 66, 73, 75, 83, 96, 98, 204–6, 224, 227–8, 235–6, 238
  Indies, 1, 83, 88–9, 98, 102, 105, 136, 196, 202, 217

246 *Index*

geographic places mentioned or discussed – *continued*
Ireland, 14, 19, 69, 93, 112, 122, 125, 127, 181, 189, 210, 219, 226, 238
Jerusalem, 2, 19, 57–8, 69, 70, 89, 113, 201–3, 232
The Levant, 48, 98–9, 215
Mauritania, 94–5, 214
Mediterranean, 19, 49, 60, 95, 98, 144, 161–3, 210, 220, 240
Mexico, 24–5, 98, 102, 105
Orient, 3, 42–3, 189, 221
Persia, 95, 99, 233
Peru, 28, 52, 54, 66–7, 77–9, 112, 157, 195, 198
Rhodes, 97–8, 107, 214
Russia (Muscovy), 23, 49, 183–4, 191
Spain, 23, 47, 82, 94, 101, 184
Tunis, 162–3, 225
Tyre, 59, 144, 151, 161, 209, 241
Wales, 14, 30, 113–15, 135, 149–50, 172–5, 177–85, 187–91, 196–7, 222, 228, 236, 238, 241
geography
and dramatic representation, 71, 75–7, 130–1
and romance, 3–6, 9–11, 25–7, 80–9, 118–21, 144–9, 155–7, 165–7
speculative geography, 81–91
Georgics (Virgil), 115–16, 241
Gesta Romanorum, 102
Gestis Arthuri Britanni, Lost Account of Arthurian Knights as explorers, 5–6
Gilbert, Alan H., 23, 47, 61–5, 68, 136–7, 230
Gillies, John, 10–11, 76, 79, 121, 204–5, 215, 230
Giraldi (Giovambattista Giraldi Cinthio), 22, 68–9
globes, 1, 3, 5, 7, 9, 11–13, 15, 17, 19, 21, 23, 25–7, 29–31, 40, 48, 76, 81–2, 84–5, 87–94, 97, 99–101, 103, 140, 143, 146, 148, 169, 191, 196, 204, 214, 228, 230
Godfrey of Bulloigne, 17, 58, 72, 201–3

Goldberg, Jonathan, 143, 221–2, 230
Goodwyn, John, 100–1
Gorboduc (Sackville and Norton), 61–2, 138, 212, 219, 237
Gossett, Suzanne, 161, 230
Gosson, Stephen, 55, 57–8, 60, 230
Gower, John, 129, 149, 151–2, 154, 169–70, 220
Greenblatt, Stephen, 3, 42, 205, 209, 211, 215, 220–1, 230
Greene, Robert, 17, 23–7, 40, 48, 102–3, 106, 136, 201, 206–8, 221, 227, 230
Greenlaw, Edwin, 156, 220, 230
Gregory, Derek, 79, 205, 230

Hadfield, Andrew, 12, 122, 181, 206, 217, 231
Hakluyt, Richard, 6–7, 29, 77, 81, 88, 92–3, 97, 116, 119–20, 146, 183, 204, 213, 217, 227, 231, 235
Hall, Edward, 110, 179, 182, 220, 231, 233, 237
Hamilton, Albert C., 165, 214, 220, 230–1, 239
Hancock, Raffe, 55
Harington, Sir John, 24, 31–2, 209, 224
translation of *Orlando Furioso* 157, 175–6, 190–1
Hariot, Thomas, 84
Harley, J. B., 10–11, 81, 231
Hathawaye, Richard, 55
Hawkins, John, voyage of, 156
Hedrick, Donald, 110, 216, 232
Hegel, Georg Wilhelm Friedrich, 49–50, 211, 232
Heng, Geraldine, 48, 80, 111, 208, 216, 232
Henslowe, Philip, 1–2, 55, 58, 74, 201–2, 204, 213, 229
Heylyn, Peter, 196
Heywood, Thomas, 19, 54, 57–8, 67, 69, 71, 106, 131, 135, 201, 203, 227, 232, 234
Historia Regum Britanniae (Geoffrey of Monmouth), 15, 108, 111, 138

Index 247

history
  and geography, 6–9, 79, 121–2
  and romance, 32, 108–9, 115–23, 170–1
  as a term for romance, 16, 21–2, 35, 47–8, 72, 136–7
Holinshed, Raphael, 110, 136
Homer, 26, 68, 139, 220, 236
Hope, Jonathan, 41–2, 89, 206, 210, 235, 241
Horace, 23, 47, 61–62, 138, 229, 239
Howard, Jean, 19, 41, 45, 80, 206–7, 210–11, 213, 217–18, 222, 226, 229, 232, 236, 239
Hoxby, Blair, 192, 232
Hulme, Peter, 143, 168, 204–5, 219–21, 224–25, 232

imagination
  in dramatic representation, 22, 25–6, 70, 75–6, 109, 112–14, 125–31, 134–5, 140, 150–4, 169–70
  and empire, 12, 119–21, 140–2, 198
  in geographic representation, 3, 7, 10–15, 29–31, 79–92, 190–1
  and romance, 91–2, 157–8, 190–1
imperialism, 13–14, 31, 117, 212, 220, 226
Inns of Court, 93, 208
Islam, 22, 27, 145, 208, 213, 220–1, 226, 228–9, 238
island(s), 5, 9, 30, 84–5, 114, 124, 127, 144–6, 148–9, 152–9, 160–3, 165–71, 175–6, 186, 188, 190–1, 195–7, 212, 221, 234, 238, 240

Jameson, Frederic, 17, 22, 33, 48, 146, 171, 194, 198, 207, 209–10, 232
Jason (Greek myth), 25, 103–4, 121, 226
Jauss, Hans Robert, 16, 233
Johnson, Richard, 16–17, 26, 86, 93–6, 136, 203, 206, 208, 214, 233
Jonson, Ben, 37, 45, 58, 151–2, 205, 212–13, 224, 233

Kamps, Ivo, 136, 233
Kirke, John, 16, 203, 233
Kirkman, Francis, 18–19, 25, 82, 233

Kitch, Aaron, 101–2, 205, 213, 215, 233
Knapp, Jeffrey, 13–14, 141, 217, 219, 233

Langbaine, Gerard, 35, 46, 233
"laws of poesy" (Sidney), 21, 62, 73, 138
Lockey, Brian, 93, 208, 234
Lodge, Thomas, 17, 40, 50, 85–6, 90, 230, 234
Logistilla (*Orlando Furioso*), 175, 190
Loomba, Ania, 101, 212, 234
Ludlow castle, 30–1, 172–4, 177–9, 182–3, 187–90, 192, 223, 226, 234, 236, 238, 241
Lyly, John, 65–6, 77, 217

MacMillan, Ken, 5–6, 10, 92–3, 234
Madoc, 6, 217
Magellan, Ferdinand, 25, 85, 103, 195–6, 237
magical horses
  Griffeth Horse (*Orlando Furioso*), 175, 190–1
  Hippogryph, 131, 157, 212
  Pacolet's Horse (Sidney), 28, 52–3, 55, 66–7, 73, 77, 82, 86, 131, 198, 212
magical mirrors, 82–3, 91–2, 214
Magnetic Lady (Jonson), 58, 233
Maley, Willy, 122, 218, 234
Malone, Edmond, 27, 37, 204
Malory, Sir Thomas, 91, 202
Mandeville, Sir John, 1–3, 6, 10–11, 17, 22, 24–5, 31–2, 84, 139, 156, 193–4, 201, 204–5, 209, 214, 217, 235–6, 240
maps, 1, 3–7, 9–11, 22, 29, 34, 66, 72, 79, 81, 83, 85, 87–9, 91–2, 95, 101, 107–8, 113, 118, 121–2, 139, 143, 146–9, 156–7, 198, 204, 213–14, 217, 231, 235, 238–9
  atlases, 7–9, 11, 84, 142, 220, 235
Marlowe, Christopher, 73–4, 81–2, 103, 164, 215, 230, 235, 239
Martyr, Peter, 66, 84, 136, 196, 212, 224, 235

248 *Index*

masque, 30–1, 74, 87–8, 167–9, 172–8, 181–2, 185, 187–92, 222, 226–7, 232, 234, 237–8, 241
McDonald, Russ, 41, 235
McEachern, Claire, 122, 216, 218, 222, 235
mercantilism, 99, 215, 231, 236
Mercator, Gerard, 1, 3–10, 29, 84–5, 87, 104, 121, 142, 204–5, 235, 240
  Historia Mundi, 7–8
Meres, Francis, 44–5, 235
Merlin, 82–3, 91–2, 203, 214
Middleton, Christopher, 83, 202, 226, 236
Milton, John, 30, 172–8, 181–7, 189–92, 194, 222, 226, 228, 230, 232, 234, 236, 238, 241
Minturno, Antonio, 22–3, 47, 67–9, 116
Molyneux, Emery, 83–4, 87–90, 92
Monmouth, Geoffrey of, 6, 15, 48, 108, 111, 138, 208, 227, 230
Moscovia, Brief History of (Milton), 183–4
Mowat, Barbara, 35–36, 42, 206, 211, 236
Munday, Anthony, 55
Münster, Sebastian, 83, 236

narrative romance and transition to drama, 17–22, 25–8, 32, 46–9, 63–8, 72–7, 108–10, 127–33, 134–5
Nash, Thomas, 164, 198
nationalism, 114–15, 122, 125, 217–18, 222, 238
neoclassical, 28, 47, 52, 54, 57, 64, 69, 73, 76, 170
Netzloff, Mark, 99, 104, 107, 206, 236
Newcomb, Lori Humphrey, 46, 160–1, 207, 210, 221, 236
Nixon, Anthony, 90, 106, 237
Normans/Norman invasion, 6, 124, 181–2, 216, 218, 238
Norton, Thomas, 61, 138
Nuntius, *see also* Chorus, Narrator, 64, 134

Odyssey, The, 26, 220, 236
Orgel, Stephen, 45, 168, 173–4, 177, 184, 187–8, 206, 211, 213, 216, 222, 237
Orientalism (Edward Said), 79, 205, 221, 224, 238
Orlando Furioso (Ariosto), 21, 23–7, 56, 68, 102, 106, 136, 157, 175, 190, 200–1, 208, 212, 224
Orson (*Valentine and Orson*), 18, 28, 31, 52–3, 55–6, 86, 131, 195–9, 202, 211, 223, 227–8, 240
Ortelius, Abraham, 121, 146–8, 205
  "Aevi Veteris, Typus Geographicus," *146*
  Theatrum Orbis Terrarum, 121, 146–7

Palfrey, Simon, 43, 237
Palladis Tamia: Wit's Treasury (Meres), 44, 235
Palmer, D. J., 129, 237
Pandosto (Greene), 48, 207, 210
Parker, Patricia, 114, 164–5, 237
Perceforest, 58, 201, 213, 232
Pettet, E. C., 41, 237
Pigafetta, Antonio, 196, 237
Pitcher, John, 48–9, 234, 239
Plato, 187, 230
Plautus, 44, 129
Poetica, L'Arte (Minturno), 67
Poetics (Aristotle), 52, 61, 63, 137, 163, 212
Pollard, Tanya, 211, 237
Poole, Kristen, 146, 148, 205, 213, 220, 226, 237
postcolonial, 13, 15, 23, 102, 145, 213, 219
Prester John, 49, 75, 93–6, 214
  Kingdom of, 2, 144
  Mandeville in the Court of, 17
  Tom a Lincoln and 25, 94
Prologues (*see also* Chorus), 69–70, 70, 72, 76, 129, 131, 171, 218, 226, 237
Promos and Cassandra (Whetstone), 57, 241
Proudfoot, G. R., 26–7, 208, 237
Ptolemy, 91
Purchas, Samuel, 105, 183, 196

Purfoot, Thomas, 86
Puttenham, Thomas, 21, 207, 238

Quiller-Couch, Arthur, 98
Quinn, David Beers, 156, 220, 238
Quint, David, 14, 118, 162–4, 166, 190, 217, 223, 238
Quixote, Don (Cervantes), 46, 210, 241

Ralegh, Sir Walter, 1–2, 11, 84, 97, 204, 229, 237–9
Ringrose, Basil, 195–8, 223, 238
Robinson, Benedict, 27, 145, 208, 213, 217–18, 220, 238
Romance
  Authurian, 5, 25, 48, 56, 81–2, 86, 91, 95–6, 108, 143, 159, 200–3, 207, 216, 232, 234
  defined, 16–18, 22, 49, 54, 58, 61, 69, 106
  early modern romance, 3, 39, 41, 48, 93
  list of lost and extant plays, 200–3
  medieval romance, 1, 23, 25, 48, 58, 81, 96, 111, 151, 159, 201
  Romance drama, 27, 30, 42
  plays discussed:
  Bordeaux, Huon of, 56
  Chinon of England, Famous Historie of, 82–3, 202, 23
  Cloridon and Radiamanta, 56, 200
  Clyomon and Clamydes, 21, 58–60, 136, 201, 203, 212, 234
  Common Conditions, 58, 60–1, 133–4, 136, 200, 212, 227
  Foure Prentises of London, 19, 54, 57–8, 61, 69, 71, 76, 79, 106, 203, 212, 232
  Four Sons of Aymon, The, 18, 202
  Historie of the Solitarie Knight, The, 56
  Huon of Bordeaux, 56
  Irisshe Knight, The, 56
  Knight of the Burning Pestle, 58, 71, 203, 225
  Knight of the Burning Rock, The, 56, 58, 71, 200, 203, 225
  Mucedorus, 161, 202
  Old Fortunatus, 18, 21, 29, 31, 54, 69–76, 79, 82, 109–10, 122, 127, 130–4, 152, 202, 212–13, 216, 220, 228, 238–40
  Palmerin of England, 71
  Seven Champions of Christendom, 10, 16, 18
  Sir Giles Goosecap, Knight, 31, 203
  Tom a Lincoln, 23, 25–7, 29, 32, 49, 80–1, 86, 91, 93–6, 106, 123, 143, 203, 208, 214, 236–7
  Uther Pendragon, 56
  Valentine and Orson, 18, 28, 31, 52–3, 55–6, 86, 131, 195–8, 202, 211, 223, 227–8, 240
  Romance fiction, 12, 25, 93
  Romance geography, 9, 79, 149, 166
  Romance motifs, 16–17, 41–2, 59, 158, 165, 194, 198, 206–7
  Shakespearean Romance, 15, 17, 23, 26, 28, 30, 40–4, 51, 193, 207
  stage romance, 2, 3, 9–10, 12, 16–18, 22, 28–31, 49, 53–4, 57–8, 61, 65, 69–71, 76, 78, 80–1, 94, 98, 106, 108, 110–11, 122–3, 127, 129, 133, 141, 145, 149–52, 161, 173–4, 191, 200
  see also narrative romance and transition to drama
Rosalynde (Lodge), 50, 85–6, 234
Rowley, William, 203
Rutter, Joseph, 46–7, 227

Sabin, Joseph, 197, 238
Sackville, Thomas, 61, 138, 237
Said, Edward, 79, 205, 221, 238
Sanders, Julie, 80, 213, 238
Scaliger, J. C., 64
Schwyzer, Philip, 115, 122, 181, 217–18, 222–3, 238
Seneca, 44, 61, 129, 138
Shakespeare, William, 2–3, 8, 15, 17–18, 26–41, 43–51, 54, 60, 70, 80–1, 85, 88, 98, 100–7, 109–13, 115–17, 120–2, 125–31, 135–6, 139–41, 143–5, 149–51, 153, 157, 160–1, 166, 170–1, 173–4, 178–9, 181–2, 188, 193–9, 203–7, 209–19, 221–42
  chronologies of the composition of plays, 34, 36, 40, 45, 170, 209–10

250 Index

Shakespeare, William – *continued*
  characters in:
  Alonso (*The Tempest*), 155, 159, 163, 166, 221
  Antonio (*Merchant of Venice*), 47, 67, 97–8, 100, 102, 105–7, 162, 166, 196, 215, 237
  Bassanio (*Merchant of Venice*), 102–4, 107, 215, 220
  Caliban (*The Tempest*), 40, 153–4, 166–71, 188, 193, 196, 198–9, 221
  Dido (*The Tempest*), 162–4, 167
  Ferdinand (*The Tempest*), 153, 159, 166–7, 169
  Hermione (*The Winter's Tale*), 33, 48–9
  Innogen (*Cymbeline*), 113–14, 149–50, 196–7
  Katherine (*Henry V*), 114, 127, 218, 226
  Leontes (*The Winter's Tale*), 33, 49
  Miranda (*The Tempest*), 40, 154–5, 166–7, 170, 186, 190, 193, 196, 198, 221
  Portia (*The Merchant of Venice*), 97–8, 102–4, 106–7, 215, 220
  Prospero (*The Tempest*), 40, 70, 87–8, 127, 129, 144, 149, 152–5, 160–3, 166–71, 188, 190, 193, 196–7, 220–1
  Sebastian (*The Tempest*), 83, 162, 166, 186, 236
  Setebos (*The Tempest*), 196
  Shylock (*The Merchant of Venice*), 102, 104–7, 215, 224
  plays discussed:
  The Comedy of Errors, 34, 44
  Cymbeline, 15, 17, 27–30, 35, 37–8, 46, 113–15, 141, 144, 146, 149–50, 188, 196–7, 209, 229, 237, 239, 241
  Hamlet, 40, 129, 140, 199, 208–9, 217, 227
  1 Henry IV, 129, 178, 181, 222
  Henry IV, 44, 113, 124, 129–31, 178–9, 181, 202, 204, 222, 238
  Henry V, 29, 70, 108–11, 113–16, 117–18, 120–36, 139, 140–3, 150, 151–2

  Henry VIII, 37, 180, 182
  The Merchant of Venice, 44, 81, 91, 97–101, 104, 106–7, 215–16, 220, 224, 226, 229
  A Midsummer Night's Dream, 36, 44
  Pericles, 15, 17, 28, 30, 35, 37, 46, 60, 129, 131, 133, 143–6, 149, 151–2, 159–61, 166, 169–70, 209, 212, 219–20, 230, 236, 240–1
  Richard II, 44, 56, 97, 112–13, 115, 155, 157–8, 211, 223
  Richard III, 44, 130, 149
  The Tempest, 15, 17, 27–8, 30, 34–8, 64, 87, 106, 111, 127, 131, 142–6, 148–9, 152–4, 156, 159–63, 166–8, 170–1, 173, 186, 193–4, 196, 205, 209–10, 219–21, 223–6, 228–30, 232–3, 237, 239–41
  Troilus and Cressida, 37, 131, 209, 219
  The Winter's Tale, 15, 17, 27–8, 30, 33–5, 37, 48–9, 94, 111, 144, 207, 209–10, 239
Sharp, Captain Bartholomew, 195, 238
Sherman, William H., 96, 118, 143, 205, 212, 214, 217, 219, 225, 232, 239
Sidney, Philip, 16, 21, 28–9, 40, 46, 50, 52–67, 69–73, 75–8, 86, 98, 108, 111–12, 116, 133–4, 137–9, 161, 171, 181, 195, 198, 202, 207, 211–13, 228, 231, 236–7, 239
Singh, Jyotsna, 14, 206, 231, 239
Smith, Alan Gordon Rae, 180–1, 190, 198, 202–4, 239
Smyth, Sir Thomas, 189, 223, 239
Sparke, John, 156
Spenser, Edmund, 91–2, 97, 156–8, 164–6, 174, 175, 181, 183, 185, 213–14, 224, 230, 238–40
  Faerie Queene, 91–2, 149, 155, 157–8, 164–5, 169, 185, 214, 220, 224, 239: Bower of Blisse, 155, 158, 165, 183, 190, 221, 240; Guyon, 17, 20–1, 39, 49, 56, 60, 94, 111, 129, 132, 155, 158, 165, 183–5, 190, 203, 207, 214, 218, 231–2, 239

Spingarn, J. E., 64, 212, 239
Sprott, Samuel Ernest, 172, 176, 239
"Stonyhurst Pageants", the, 134, 226
Strachey, William, 168, 221
Strohm, Paul, 109, 207, 216, 240

Taylor, Gary, 6–7, 35–6, 44, 160, 170, 204–5, 216–17, 219, 226, 239–41
Terence, 52, 129
Thompson, Leslie, 59, 228
Thorne, Alison, 41, 240
Tillyard, E. M. W., 136, 240
tragedy, 16, 21, 35, 37, 44–5, 62–5, 74, 77, 110, 115, 133, 137–8, 212–15, 219, 232
tragicomedy, 16, 35, 42, 47, 54, 205–6, 211, 227, 229, 234–6, 241
Transilvanius, Maximilianus, 25, 103
translatio imperii, see also *Maske at Ludlow Castle* (Milton), 189

unities
　in Italian criticism, 63–9
　Pericles and the violation of unity, 160–1
　Shakespeare and, 38–9, 170
　Sidney's definition, 53–4, 61–5, 138
　in *The Tempest*, 144–5, 169

Venetus, Marcus Paulus, 148
Virgil, 68, 115–16, 162, 217, 238, 241

voyages, 7, 10, 12, 25, 77, 84–7, 89–90, 101, 116, 119, 156, 158–9, 165, 195, 204, 227, 231
Vulgate Cycle (of Authurian Romance), 159

Wallace, David, 141, 209, 219, 241
Wallerstein, Immanuel, 13
Warner, William, 139–40
Warren, Roger, 80, 144–5, 208, 213, 216, 226, 229, 232, 241
Warres of Cyrus (Anonymous), 132
Watson, Thomas, 52
Wayne, Valerie, 45–6, 210, 226, 230, 236, 238, 241
Weimann, Robert, 128, 241
Wells, Stanley, 35, 44, 206, 212, 219, 241
Whetstone, George, 57–8, 204, 241
White, William, 55
Wilkins, George, 151, 160–1, 220
Wilkinson, L. P., 116, 241
Williams, Gwyn, 180–1, 222–3, 241
Wilson, John Dover, 98, 123–4, 215, 221, 229, 241
Witmore, Michael, 41–2, 210, 241
Woolf, D. R., 109, 205, 216, 242

Xenephon, 132

Yates, Frances, 42–3, 242

Zeni, Katherino, 148

Printed and bound by CPI Group (UK) Ltd, Croydon, CR0 4YY